I0791835

SILENT NO MORE

REBECCA WAITES

BALBOA PRESS

A DIVISION OF HAY HOUSE

Balboa Press books may be ordered through booksellers or by contacting:

Balboa Press
A Division of Hay House
1663 Liberty Drive
Bloomington, IN 47403
www.balboapress.co.uk
1 (877) 407-4847

Because of the dynamic nature of the Internet, any web addresses or links contained in this book may have changed since publication and may no longer be valid. The views expressed in this work are solely those of the author and do not necessarily reflect the views of the publisher, and the publisher hereby disclaims any responsibility for them.

The author of this book does not dispense medical advice or prescribe the use of any technique as a form of treatment for physical, emotional, or medical problems without the advice of a physician, either directly or indirectly. The intent of the author is only to offer information of a general nature to help you in your quest for emotional and spiritual well-being. In the event you use any of the information in this book for yourself, which is your constitutional right, the author and the publisher assume no responsibility for your actions.

Any people depicted in stock imagery provided by Getty Images are models, and such images are being used for illustrative purposes only. Certain stock imagery © Getty Images.

Print information available on the last page.

ISBN: 978-1-9822-8012-3 (sc)
ISBN: 978-1-9822-8010-9 (e)

Balboa Press rev. date: 01/10/2019

Contents

Author's Note

This is a true story about my life, family and friends whom I love and have lost. All of the names and locations have been changed (except Belfast) to protect their identities.

To my siblings who have gone before me.

I would like to dedicate this book to my siblings, Alvin, Frederick and Robyn. In loving memory of you all. Gone too soon but never ever forgotten.

Your loving sister,
Rebecca Waites

Back Where It All Began

I was the middle child in a family of seven; I had two older brothers, Alvin the eldest and Frederick. Below me are my sisters Robyn and Amber. My father was Frank Waites and my mother was Rebecca, whom I was named after.

As a child, growing up at 109 Glenmore Gardens was never easy. Frederick and I suffered the most physical form of abuse from my father for reasons unknown to us both. I also received beatings from my mother, but she was better at inflicting emotional abuse, whereas my father's way to punish us was mostly physical.

I don't have any memories of my early childhood. More about this later.

My father was a chronic alcoholic but had been dry for sixteen years beginning in the late 1980s. Things were different when he drank. There were never any hugs or kisses, drunk or sober. Neither one of my parents showed us any love. None of us were ever told that we were good, loved, wanted or special.

I never did well at primary school. I wasn't encouraged by my teachers or my parents. My primary school teacher's name was Miss Dance. All I remember from her class were the slaps she gave me on both my hands with a cane whenever the notion took her, which was on a regular basis. I could not escape abuse at home or at school.

I did much better at secondary school. I enjoyed art and music. My teachers were a lot better. My English teacher, Mrs Walker, was wonderful. She, like me, loved music. I trusted her and we got on really well. She would invite me down to her mother's house where we listened to John Lennon records. We talked for hours about everything. I told her how unhappy I was living at home. She was always there to listen and help me in any way she could.

After a beating I got one Sunday afternoon from my father, I think I was about ten years old at the time, I ran from the house down the Jamestown Road. I knew of a man called Mr Hill who lived not far from Glenmore. He worked with abused children; he was a social worker I guess. I knocked on the front door of his house and when he opened the door I began telling him what had happened to me. I showed him the bruises on my arms and legs and pleaded with him to put me into care. He said he would help me and that I could go on home. I never heard from him again. I felt trapped and utterly helpless.

I left school at thirteen, mainly because my mother needed my help. It was at the height of the troubles. In Belfast you could leave school at whatever age you liked; no one was going to stop you. My mother went into hospital to have a hysterectomy. I was left in charge to cook and clean and look after my dad, brothers and sisters. When my mother came home from hospital I had the house spotless for her. I wanted her to be proud of me. I wanted my dad to quit drinking. I wished that we could all be happy, but of course that didn't happen. I was disappointed, hurt and so very tired of the way my dad was treating us all. I had this entire responsibility heaped upon me. I was like a surrogate mother. All I wanted was to be free and to live life as a normal teenager.

I remember one day my father coming home drunk and demanding his dinner. He opened the oven door, took his dinner from the oven and threw it against the kitchen wall. He had done this so many times before. He was an angry, violent drunk. He was screaming and shouting insults at my mother and threatening to hit her. I was afraid he was going to really hurt her as she was still weak from her operation. I lifted four milk bottles, three in one hand and one in the other, from the sink and threw them at him. He went crazy. I ran out of the house and jumped over a wall to a neighbour's house. I banged hard on their back door, screaming for someone to let me in. Our next door neighbour opened the door and I began to explain to her what had happened. She took me in and after she calmed me down (I was shaking with fear) my neighbour took me back home. My parents told her I would not be punished.

Another time I had taken a radio from the house without my father's permission. I wanted to listen to music with my friends. While we were standing at the Farm shops a man who knew one of my friends came over and noticed that I had his radio. He asked, "What are you doing with it?" I told him who my father was. He took the radio from me and said that he would be seeing my father about it.

I knew I was in big trouble and I hoped my father would not get angry with me. But when I arrived home he was waiting for me. His eyes were red with fury. He grabbed me by the hair, shouting in my face, "What have you done with my radio?"

I tried to tell him what had happened. I was really scared, but he just kept hitting me and screaming at me. He opened the front door and pushed me out. He came after me, still hitting and slapping me. I was crying and begging him to stop but that just made him more enraged. He kept pushing me to hurry up the whole way to the Farm shops. He then started kicking me and, because of the fear I felt, I wet myself.

As we approached the shops, the man who had taken the radio from me was standing with his friends. As soon as my father saw him he knew the radio belonged to him. The man explained to my father what had happened. He could see I was crying and upset. He told my father it was alright. Thankfully, after my father had spoken with the man, he calmed down.

I felt so embarrassed by my father's behaviour towards me. I think the man felt sorry for me. He could clearly see the emotional state I was in. I was shamed in public, and that's something that stays with you.

My oldest brother, Alvin, went to live in Southeast when he was sixteen. I felt very sad when he left. He used to look out for me. He was my protector, saving me from beatings at home and on the street. When he left home I felt lonely and scared. Frederick left about a year after Alvin. (He was just sixteen years of age.) I was left with clothes and a tin whistle that Alvin had given me.

Then the news came that a friend of Alvin's had died. He had fallen from a building in Southeast. He was just nineteen. Alvin, Frederick and their other friends came home to Belfast for the funeral. It was a very sad time for them all.

There was such a change in Alvin, and it was more than grief. I could sense there was something else. He was nasty and rude to everyone. I could not understand why he seemed so angry. And his behaviour towards me was so different. We fought a lot and he called me names and picked on me for no reason. He started hitting me. I hated living there. After a while, Alvin and Frederick returned to Southeast.

It wasn't until years later that I learned that both Alvin and Fredrick had become heroin addicts while living in Southeast.

When they came back home again they were dressed like hippies. I loved their clothes and their long hair and beards. Frederick gave me a blue-and-white striped jacket which I wore until a friend of theirs, Cathy Bell, offered to swap her leather jacket for mine. I wasn't sure at first. I liked my new coat, but so did Cathy, and because she was a bit older than me and knew how to get what she wanted, I gave in and handed over my jacket. I regretted it immediately.

The violence continued on a more regular basis. My father would come home from the pub drunk almost every night and a fight would start. Alvin and Frederick would beat him when he got nasty with our mother. He thought he could get away with his violent behaviour like he always had when we were younger, but Alvin and Frederick stood up to him and showed little mercy. A few times our father ended up in hospital.

Frederick began bringing alcohol into the house, and he and his friends would sit and drink. Alvin, seeing that he was getting away with it, started bringing in large carry-outs of beer and cider. It was horrendous. With all the drunkenness and insanity, it was like living in a nightmare.

Violence was all around me in my home and on the streets, but when there was rioting on on the streets it felt frightening and exciting at the same time. I didn't really understand what it was all about until later.

One Sunday evening I was coming home from a disco with two of my friends. We were about twelve or thirteen years old at the time. We decided to stay and have a swing in the park before going home. After a while, when we were about to cross the road into our street, we were suddenly blinded and almost deafened by the sound of automatic gunfire. We hit the ground for cover and crawled along on our hands and knees as quickly as we could until we reached the gardens across the road. We kept crawling along the grass all the way to our houses further up the street. The whistling sounds from the gunfire ringing in my ears and flashes of light above my head frightened me nearly half to death. I thought we were all going to be killed that night.

It's a miracle none of us were. God was watching over us all but we were left shaken by the events of that Sunday evening. At the top of my street was an Army barracks which was nicknamed Silver roof by the locals because it was made from corrugated iron. Years later, I heard about the Army force. They were a covert intelligence-gathering and counter-insurgency unit of the army. The unit was formed during the summer of 1971 and operated until late 1972 or early 1973. A former member described it as a 'Legalised death squad'. I hadn't a clue who was shooting at us. All I knew was that whoever it was tried to kill or maim three innocent teenagers. We most certainly were no threat to anyone.

At the age of fifteen I got a job working as a machinist at a stitching factory, Kelly's on the Bells Road. I hated the job but as I hadn't any qualifications or money I took the job so that I would be able to support myself.

It was 1972. I loved the music. I felt I was different from other girls my age because of the way I liked to dress. I preferred listening to artists like Bob Dylan and Leonard Cohen. I loved Motown artists like Stevie Wonder, Marvin Gaye and Al Green. I have loved music for as long as I can remember, especially a soulful voice, one that when you hear it lets you know that the person has been or is living with pain. It makes the hair on the back of my neck stand up when I hear artists like Marvin Gaye sing; a voice like his touches my soul. I have heard so many brilliant singers whose songs have inspired me and helped me get through many difficult times in my life.

At the stitching factory where I worked, the boss's son used the factory to design clothes. He would then make trousers and shirts for himself to wear. When I was around eight years of age I had wanted to become a dress designer, just like him. I had a scrap book of many drawings of clothes and really believed that when I grew up that's what I would become.

I used to come to work wearing trousers that Alvin and Frederick had brought me back from Southeast; I wore hippie beads around my neck and the most amazing psychedelic bracelets. I used to paint small daisies below my right eye.

I had my own ideas; I painted a pair of cotton shoes that my mother got me as they were a boring white colour. I decided to jazz them up with an array of pastel shades. The boss's son would look at me coming in through the doors of the factory. I could tell he was interested in my clothes; he seemed to get some ideas from the clothes I wore because in a few days he would turn up to work wearing trousers very similar to the ones I had worn.

After one year I quit the job at Kelly's. I'd had enough; it nearly drove me out of my mind.

At sixteen I got a job in the local supermarket at the top of my street. I was put in charge of the fruit and vegetable department. I loved it and I was able to use my artistic flair. I took great pride in arranging the display of fruit and veg. Everyone admired my work, including my boss who told me how pleased he was and offered me a pay rise, but said I shouldn't tell anyone about it.

My art teacher from secondary school came into the shop to buy fruit for her lunch one day. When she saw that it was me working there she smiled and said that I shouldn't waste my talent. She admired my work and urged me to go to art college. I thanked her and said I would think about it but I never did; my self-esteem was so low at that time and I didn't think I was good enough.

I met a guy from Milestown who was staying in digs in Kerry Flats. His name was Harry Montgomery. We met at a club in Belfast; we got on very well and were going out about six months or so when we got engaged. He was a quiet man who was nine years my senior. I didn't want our relationship to continue as I realized I did not want to marry him and called off our engagement. I was only sixteen. Looking back, I think I was looking for a father figure. When I told my mother I no longer wanted to be with Harry she went crazy.

I was still carrying a torch for my first love, a guy named Johnny Watson. He was also nine years older than me. I had met Watson when I was fifteen in a social club in Jamestown.

I was going out with him on and off for about a year. More off than on, to be honest. He was so good looking and he knew it. When my brother Frederick introduced us in the FF club, we got on like a house on fire.

During the evening we were locked in conversation. I lied about my age. I told him I was sixteen and a half. Johnny told me he was separated from his wife and that he had two children. He was twenty-five at the time. I really took a fancy to him. So did every other girl.

He asked if he could walk me home and of course I said yes. I was over the moon.

Even though he was much other than me· he never once took advantage of me in a sexual way. I enjoyed his company and he enjoyed mine; that was it, although we must have seen each other no more than eight times after we first met.

I tried to explain to my mother that I wasn't in love with Harry. She didn't know about Watson. I really did like Harry but not enough to want to spend the rest of my life with him. Mother wanted me to marry Harry and to this day I still don't know why. My assumption is that because Harry was a country man maybe she thought he would make a good husband.

She tried everything in her power to get us back together again but it didn't work. A week or so after that she sold my engagement ring. She gave me five pounds for it.

In June 1974 my mother started work as kitchen manager in the Hutson's Hotel, working nights. I was working in a supermarket in Lower Alan Street. Mother would sometimes ask me to help her out and I did whenever I could. The first night I went to work with her she showed me what I had to do. While she and I were working a very thin pale-faced guy walked over to where mother and I were working. He seemed very friendly and asked my mother to introduce us, which she did. He was laughing and telling jokes. I thought he was a very funny guy with a great personality.

I felt good about helping my mother out. The night flew in and morning came around so quickly. As mother and I were walking out towards the security hut, heading for home, the very charismatic thin white-faced guy came running towards us, smiling broadly. It wasn't until we were outside the building that I realized why. He pulled from his coat some plates that he'd stolen and in a sarcastic tone of voice he started boasting how hard it had been for him to get the plates out past the security men.

A week or two later, when I was walking along Long Street on my way to work, I heard my name being called; I turned around and saw Jeffrey White waving (the palefaced guy I had met at my mother's work place.) As he approached with a friend he asked how I was keeping. He wanted to know where I was going. I told him I was on my way to work. We chatted for a few minutes and I said for a second time that I had to get to work. He commented on my sunburn and joked about the way the sun had only caught one of my arms. He asked me if I had fallen asleep on the right side of my body. I just smiled and said, "I'm off now". He and his friend said goodbye. They had just finished work and were on their way home.

A few days later, when mother came home from work, she handed me a note. She said that Jeffrey had asked her to pass it on to me. I went into the living room and sat down to read it. He wanted to know if I would meet him outside St Mary's Chapel at the bottom of Bells Road on Sunday evening at seven thirty. He asked me to write back and give my response to my mother so she could pass it on to him in work.

After a day or two I decided I would meet him. My mother seemed very keen that I should go out on a date with him; she liked him a lot and said he was a lovely person. When I arrived at St Mary's at half past seven Jeffrey was standing there looking very nervous. He smiled at me and said hello. He was fidgeting with his hair and seemed unable to relax. He then suggested going for a walk up the Bells Road. I nodded my head in agreement and as soon as we started walking we both were able to relax.

Jeffrey made me laugh with his jokes. We found it so easy to talk with each other; the conversation was flowing and we talked about everything under the sun, the things he liked and the things I liked. We spent about two hours walking that first night. He asked if I would see him again and I said I would. He left me home and gave me a quick kiss on the lips. We made arrangements to see each other the following Friday.

I came into the house and went straight up to bed as I had work the next morning. In those days, getting to work on time was becoming increasingly difficult. You could stand an hour waiting for a bus only to discover they were taken off the road because of burning or hijacking.

Fridays at work were great; you only had to work the morning shift which meant an early start to your weekend. My friend and I went shopping after work and called into a bar for some lunch. Sitting in the pub over a pint was a friend of Johnny's, a guy named James Berry. He called us over and invited us to sit with him, which we did. James was great craic, (craic meaning great fun) a hilariously funny man and an extremely nice guy.

We had a drink together and James then offered to buy another round of drinks. I told him I had to go as I had a date and wanted to get home before the mad rush for the bathroom started. All I had was one pint of beer and it had gone to my head. I couldn't drink during the day. James was in stitches at me and said, "I don't believe you'd be able to handle another pint, Rebecca." How right he was. My friend and I left the pub and walked across the street to the bus stop. I arrived home and started to get myself ready. I was looking forward to a night out.

I met Jeffrey outside a bar at the bottom of the Bells Road (now a doctor's surgery and butcher's shop) just across from St Mary's Hospital. We went into the bar and sat down. Jeffrey ordered a drink for us both. We were sitting chatting when out of the blue he asked me to marry him! I was aghast; was he being serious? After the shock wore off I told him that I had just broken off my engagement because I was too young to be settling down. I wanted to travel and see the world. He said he was just joking but I knew he wasn't.

We met a few more times after that and even though he wasn't my type I really enjoyed his company. He seemed to know how to make me laugh and I certainly needed it. Living at home was very depressing. I wanted to move over to Southport with a friend but my mother was emphatically against the idea, just as she was when I asked her to let me move to Diggen.

Later on, when I told her that Jeffrey had asked me to marry him, she never hesitated at all. She immediately said that I should. In retrospect, I suppose she was thinking it was the best thing for her eldest daughter. Mother was from the old school of thought, believing that a woman was unable to support herself and that becoming a wife and mother was what was expected of her.

I was still in love with Johnny. I knew in my heart that we were never going to have a future together. I was desperate to get out of 109 Glenmore Gardens; I was seventeen years old with no confidence and a low sense of self esteem.

Jeffrey and I were still going out together; he introduced me to his parents and his two older sisters, Colette, who lived in Newpart with her husband and seven children, and Margaret, who lived in the country. She had moved away from home at an early age, just like the rest of the White siblings. She lived in a bungalow with a priest whose name was Fr Frank, a lovely, gentle person who was suffering from cancer.

Jeffrey's mother was an abominable woman who spoke in a strident voice most of the time. She had made her feelings crystal clear about her son's relationship with me. She didn't like my parents or me but then that's the kind of person she was. She found fault with everyone. Despite all that, we kept on seeing each other. Jeffrey was as keen to leave home as I was, although I didn't find this out until later.

Jeffrey pointed out to me that we had met on the seventh of May and got engaged on the seventh of October, so why not set a date and marry on the seventh? We set a date to marry on the seventh of November 1974. We had only known each other six months and there we were, making plans for the future.

I had lost my job at the supermarket because on the morning that Pathworth prison burnt down I, like many others, couldn't get to work. I remember it well; it was a Wednesday morning and I must have stood for two hours waiting on a bus or taxi, but none arrived. The roads were completely quiet and there was the smell of smoke still hanging in the air. The atmosphere was spooky. Finally I gave up and returned home. It was half day on Wednesday, not that that mattered. The following day, when I arrived at work, I was called to the office and was told by the manager that I was sacked. When I tried to explain what had happened he shook his head at me and asked me to leave his office. He sacked my friend as well, even though we had rung work on Wednesday and explained why we were unable to get there. My friend and I wanted to take it to a tribunal for unfair dismissal but we never did. She quickly found herself another job and I was making plans for my wedding.

On one occasion when I called for Jeffrey his mother answered the front door and told me Jeffrey wasn't at home. As I walked away, his mother came walking behind me and went into a neighbour's house next door. After that, the front door opened and his father called out my name. I looked back at him. He was waving at me to come back. When I walked into the living room Jeffrey was sitting there looking half asleep. His dad had woken him up. I never said anything to him about the lie his mother told me. He said that he was shattered; he didn't get in from work until ten that morning from eight o'clock the night before.

He showed me a nest of tables he had bought from his mother for fifteen pounds. We were trying to gather up bits and pieces of furniture for our flat that Jeffrey had managed to get for us. A friend he knew was buying a house and Jeffrey asked his friend for the flat, or at least that's what he told me. The keys to the flat were given to Jeffrey on Halloween night. I was ecstatic and could hardly wait until the 7th of November to move into our new home.

Jeffrey was making all the arrangements for our wedding. What I wanted didn't seem to matter. My wishes and suggestions were ignored by him and his mother. I didn't want a big fuss. I had lost my job and didn't have a lot of money to spend on a big wedding. Neither one of us did. I was led to believe that his parents were paying for the reception and that I needn't worry; everything was going to be all right.

I bought my wedding dress from a girl I used to work with. She was to marry a guy she had been with for two years. A week before the set date he called off their wedding. That should have been a warning sign. I thought about it for a while but quickly put the notion out of my head, choosing instead to think of the beautiful dress I had bought that only cost me ten pounds.

Presents were starting to arrive from people we both knew. These included bedspreads, cutlery and lots of booze and dinner sets. My aunt Kathleen had bought us a gun which could be used as a lighter. I loved her gift to us- it was very different, just like she was. My mother had given us a three-piece suite for the living room as well as a lamp, curtains and various other useful gifts for our new home.

I asked Jeffrey to bring over the nest of tables he had bought for the flat. That's where we were storing our wedding gifts until after our big day. I was so eager to get things just right for us both. I had made sure that the flat was spotlessly clean for us moving in after our wedding. He said his mother had sold the tables to their next door neighbour for the same price she had sold them to him. I was not very pleased to say the least. I asked Jeffrey to get the money back from his mother as we needed every penny. He assured me everything would be okay and not to worry about a thing.

I remember the time when Jeffrey and I were over visiting James, his older brother. We were standing waiting on a taxi when along came his mother with Gerard, another brother. They had been drinking in the pub at the top of the Millers Road. Mrs White started shouting abuse at Jeffrey, calling him a ginger-haired bastard. She tried to physically assault him. I grabbed her hands and held them down by her sides. Gerard then tried to attack me because I was trying to stop their mother from hitting Jeffrey. A black taxi drove up. Jeffrey opened the door and pushed me in. He jumped in after me. The taxi driver drove off. Jeffrey's mother and Gerard were screaming that they would get us both. I was upset and angry. I couldn't believe his mother could be so cruel as to publicly embarrass her son and his fiancee in that way. My heart went out to Jeffrey after that night. We never spoke another word about it ever again.

Jeffrey and I had fallen out a few times just before our big day over silly things. We were out one evening and on our way home he hardly spoke a word to me. I asked him why. He said he didn't like the way I was dressed! When I asked him to explain exactly what he meant he complained about my long dress and jewellery and said I looked like a hippy. I was hurt because I tried to look my. best. I liked the way I dressed; it gave me my identity, my own unique self. I didn't like the way he dressed but kept it to myself. He wore tartan trousers and white shirts with tartan stripes on the sleeves; he was a 'Hall Rollers' fan. A pop group in the 70's who I disliked immensely. I went home by myself and a couple of days later Jeffrey called to the house as if nothing had happened.

On the seventh of October 1974 we had a party to celebrate our engagement; it was held in the Casablanca club in Belfast city centre just above where the B&M used to be. (Now where Max and Island are). When we got outside a fight had started. There were about four or five men on top of this one guy, beating the hell out of him. I couldn't stand the thought of these men against one man. Me being me, I tried to get over to help him but Jeffrey prevented me by grabbing hold of me and saying that he deserved all he got. He said the guy had stolen three purses from women who were at the party. The police arrived. They jumped out of their jeeps and just stood there watching. I was totally disgusted with their behaviour too. Jeffrey fell out with me over that incident. I couldn't understand why.

My Big Day Had Arrived.

On the morning of our wedding Margaret, Jeffrey's sister, called up to help me get ready. She was my bridesmaid. All I could think about was making my bed and leaving my bedroom tidy. Margaret was more excited about the day than I was.

The drive in the limousine to the church seemed to be over before it had even started, although I was glad to get out because of the stupid song being played which was "I'll take you home again Rebecca".

I felt so calm walking down the aisle. It was as if I were watching someone else's wedding; I didn't feel excitement or whatever a woman's supposed to be feeling on her big day.

Fr Jack, cc, said jokingly, "Smile, Rebecca; anyone would think you were attending a funeral instead of your wedding".

The wedding reception was held in the old Country club on the Holly Road, not far from the Deer Avenue park. When we arrived, all our guests seemed to be enjoying themselves. Tom Gracey, a friend of my brother Alvin, had said his band would play at our reception for half the money they usually charged. My mother paid for the band. She helped us out enormously. I was extremely grateful to her for all her financial support. My father never put his hand in his pocket to help with anything. Nothing new there. When we, his children, reached eleven he stopped buying birthday cards or presents. Even at Christmas time we received nothing.

I had changed out of my wedding dress too soon. When we had our photographs taken cutting the cake I was wearing my new outfit that I had bought for the occasion.

There was a bit of an upset between my Aunt Kathleen and Anne Weithers, my dad's cousin. My mother wasn't happy. She had asked my father not to invite Kathleen and his cousin as my mother never got on with either of them. As I mentioned earlier, my wedding plans were ignored by my parents, my new husband and his mother. They took over. There was nothing I could do about it. The whole thing from beginning to end was topsy-turvy.

As Jeffrey and I were about to leave, yet another incident was taking place. This time it was between my mother and Jeffrey's Aunt Geraldine. They were arguing over who should get my wedding bouquet. Geraldine said that Jeffrey told her she could keep the flowers. My mother's logic was that as she had bought the flowers she should keep them. I didn't know what to do. Jeffrey sorted it out by sharing the bouquet between the two of them. What a nightmare. It was supposed to be the happiest day of my life.

We managed to get away after thanking everyone, including the band who were fantastic. We stood outside on the pavement waiting for a black taxi to take us to our flat in New Park. No car journey to a hotel, no honeymoon; that wasn't on the agenda. I was a virgin and didn't know what to expect. Our first night together was nothing special. I was nervous and shy. I don't have fond memories of our first night together, or any other night in the fifteen years we spent together as man and wife.

It slowly became clear to me why I had only been kissed a few times throughout my marriage to this man and why I never experienced loving tenderness, caresses and the feeling that I was wanted and loved.

We hadn't a penny to our name. When we got home we had one packet of cigarettes between us and we lived on the top tier of our wedding cake for a week. Jeffrey told me a few things that left me totally flabbergasted. For instance, he never thought to mention that he had been paid off a week before our wedding. The reason he was so broke was because his parents failed to pay the balance for the reception, despite the fact that Jeffrey had paid the deposit.

My mother helped us out by giving us food and inviting us up for dinner the odd time. Jeffrey couldn't get money from the Department of Social Security until after Christmas. What I didn't realize at the time was that he couldn't get any money right away because he had left his job at the Mara Hospital. Never before in my life had I had to go without. At home we were always provided with food if nothing else. I remember as a young child coming downstairs on Christmas morning; there were toys stacked high for all five of us but the joy was short-lived after my father got drunk from his home-made beer and wine. I remember later on that day my mother and father arguing and him becoming violent, as he usually did.

My father had his own business at that time, a shop in Green Street where he and his business partner worked as electrical engineers, repairing and selling televisions.

Things were getting worse financially for me and Jeffrey. We both smoked and I found it very frustrating having to go without a smoke. I would go across the landing to our neighbours' flat and ask could I borrow a cigarette. I called up to my mother's almost every day and while there, I would clean the house for her. She suggested paying me for my help and asked me to come up three days a week and do the jobs that were being neglected because she was at work. I said yes. It would mean I would have some money to live on. As it turned out I would have been better getting a job elsewhere. It only lasted a couple of weeks. She told me she didn't see why she had to pay her own daughter to do some housework for her.

Any time I did do any work for my mother she made sure it was done to perfection. She was extremely house proud and a perfectionist. She never used a mop to wash floors. I had to get down on my hands and knees to wash and polish the floors at home.

Every Friday before I was married my chores involved cleaning the living room from top to bottom. She meant cleaning absolutely everything in the room, and after that was done I had the bedrooms to clean, the bathroom, stairs and then finally the week's ironing. It took me until six o'clock in the evening to get my work finished.

Alvin and Frederick would come in and wash their hair. They would leave the bathroom looking as if it hadn't been cleaned in a week. Towels were thrown on the floor. It didn't matter to them or anyone else that I had worked my fingers to the bone scrubbing the bathroom. My two older brothers were treated like royalty. At dinner time my mother would serve them their dinners on a tray in the living room by the open coal fire while my sisters and I were made to sit in the kitchen. There were times when the boys got frying steak and we girls got the cheaper version, mince steak.

I was the only one in our family made to do things. The boys, like my two younger sisters, were asked to do little or nothing. Amber, who was the youngest, was spoiled rotten by our mother. Robyn was dad's blue eye and she could get away with anything, and did.

Christmas was just around the comer and we still had no money. I was desperate for our situation to change. Jeffrey suggested selling our wedding gifts and the bottles of alcohol we had received from friends of his. He also suggested that I sell my clothes; I had quite a lot of really nice dresses, blouses, skirts and coats. I agreed we needed money to live on. Jeffrey said he would ask his sister Colette if she would sell them for us. He said that she would be able to get us a good price. She had her own stall from where she used to sell all kinds of things, although it was mostly clothes she sold. Jeffrey and I began gathering up all our wedding presents to give to Colette to sell for us. I had left myself two changes of clothes and held on to my afghan coat. I couldn't bear to part with it. It was my favourite item of clothing. Jeffrey called to Colette's with all our belongings that were to be sold.

A few days later I asked Jeffrey to call down to Colette's. We were starving and gasping for a smoke. On his return he handed me three pounds. I looked at him and asked him what is this? He said "It's what Colette got for selling our stuff'.

I found it hard to believe what he had said; I told him no way was I prepared to be taken for a fool. All our presents were brand new and my clothes were in excellent condition. I said that I would go down and see Colette myself. Jeffrey was panicking. He said he would get us money and for me not to worry. I told him it was the principle of the matter; we were penniless and being ripped off by his sister who was always pleading poverty. A woman who had the gift of the gab like the rest of the White clan.

Jeffrey insisted he would take care of things. I didn't understand why he was so reluctant for me or him to confront his sister. In the end I decided just to leave it.

Our finances stayed the same until after Christmas. My mother and Jeffrey's two brothers, James and Peter, invited us to their houses for our Christmas dinner. We ended up going to my mother's.

A week before Christmas Jeffrey came home one day with a puppy dog in his arms. It was about six or seven weeks old. What really got me was that he didn't talk to me about it first; a dog was the last thing we needed.

We seemed to argue and fall out every other day. On Christmas morning I was horrified to find our Christmas tree in tatters on the living room floor and what few presents we had had been ripped open. The dog had relieved itself all over the living room floor. I went into our bedroom and woke Jeffrey up. I was crying and in a state. I explained what the dog had been up to in the night while we were both asleep. He laughed and thought the whole thing was just hilarious. I was furious. He got up and gave me a hand to clean the mess up. I told him I didn't want the dog. Jeffrey said he would train it but he never did. He did however give my afghan coat to the puppy to use as a bed. He never thought to ask me if that was okay.

We were to be up in mother's house for two o'clock. After getting the flat cleaned up we got ready and walked up to my mother's. We had our Christmas dinner and afterwards walked back to New Road. We spent the evening with James and his wife Eileen. That was our first Christmas together. We were depending on other people's generosity with not a penny to our name.

Six weeks into the marriage we were arguing more and more. One evening, I don't remember what over, it turned quite nasty. Jeffrey's face turned red with anger. He was shouting at me and calling me some hurtful names. I threw a small brass candlestick across the living room floor in anger. Jeffrey lunged towards me and grabbed me by the hair. He started hitting me about the head and yelled into my face never to do that ever again. He looked as if he was possessed; I felt very frightened and tried to keep my arms over my head to protect myself. I was agreeing with whatever he was demanding and as soon as I was able I ran straight for the front door and made my escape.

I just kept running until I reached the top of the Bells Road. I jumped into a taxi. I was in tears and didn't care what anyone thought. I asked the taxi driver if I could owe him the fare. He said not to worry about it and drove me into town. As I walked away, he told me to take care of myself.

I began running towards Vicks Street, my eyes blinding me with tears as I was running. A car drove up beside me. I noticed the car window coming down and a man's voice shouted out to me, "Need a lift, love?" I yelled no. I was terrified he would get out of his car and come after me. I ran even quicker up Vicks Street. It was after midnight and anyone could see that I was in a state. I wasn't wearing a coat and it was very cold as it was January.

I was heading for the Hutsons Hotel as I knew my mother was on night duty that night. Finally I arrived. I walked into the foyer of the hotel and took the lift up to the kitchen. I noticed my mother working at the dishwasher machine. I walked towards her, my eyes red and sore with all the crying I had done. She looked at me and asked me what I was doing there. I told her what had happened to me; her response was cold. She said that I had made my bed and that I should lie in it. She let me know that tea and sympathy weren't going to come from her. She said that I should go home and make it up with my husband; I was making a big deal out of nothing and that all marriages go through bad patches.

I felt so rejected and abandoned. I had nowhere else to go to, nor was there anyone I felt I could turn to. I was left with no other choice; I had to return to the flat.

Jeffrey let me in and asked me where I had been. I said I had been to see my mother. He walked on into the bedroom and got into bed. I stayed up for an hour or so, sitting and thinking until exhaustion got the better of me. I couldn't keep my eyes open any longer so I dragged myself off the chair and went to bed.

After Christmas, Jeffrey got a job in the Glen Hospital as a gardener. I would get up with him in the morning and make his breakfast; sometimes I would walk with him to the taxi stand so I could wave him off.

I thought I was happy and took pride in my new role as Jeffrey's wife. I couldn't wait to have a child. In my naivete I thought we could live happily together as man and wife and raise a family. All I wanted was for us to be together forever. I was no longer thinking about Watson; he was long forgotten. I wanted my marriage to work and took my wedding vows very seriously, even at the tender age of seventeen.

I met my old school friend Maggie Monaghan while I was in Jamestown shopping. It was just after Christmas. I invited her up on Sunday for dinner as I was keen to have a friend see me in my new role as a wife. Jeffrey's brother Terence came for dinner as well. He and Maggie got on really well together and they went out on a date. I only saw my friend a few times after that day. Terence never asked her out on another date. I heard that she had got back with her boyfriend Bryan a while later.

In February 1975 I fell pregnant. It had only taken two months. I thought it was never going to happen but when it did I was over the moon, as was Jeffrey. Our baby was due on the sixteenth of October 1975. I remember my first hospital appointment. I felt very nervous, not knowing what to expect. The nurse explained to me that the doctor needed to give me an internal examination to check that everything was alright. I found that first visit very uncomfortable and embarrassing. I was glad when it was over.

After a few months Jeffrey wanted to move. He came home after work one day and told me about the new houses being built in Greenvale. He went on and on about them, saying how good it would be for us to have our own house. I wasn't that keen as I was happy where I was in our flat. Jeffrey suggested going up to see the houses. He said he had been up to see the new housing estate and told me the houses were really lovely. He was very excited about it so I gave in and went up with him to look at the houses for myself. The houses were great. We picked one out for ourselves and went home to pack. Jeffrey had got us a van and before long we had loaded it up with all our belongings, ready for our move to Greenvale. When we arrived at the house we noticed that the curtains we had put up earlier had been taken down.

As we were walking towards the front door of the house a man came out and asked us what we wanted. Jeffrey told him that we had all our stuff ready to unload into the house; the man said it was his home. I could hardly believe my ears; I asked him what he meant.

He explained to us that he and his wife had been allocated the house and had been given a date to move in. He showed us the letter they had received from the Housing Association stating that they had indeed been offered the house. There was nothing left to say on the matter. I was extremely disappointed and unsure what to do next because Jeffrey had given our flat away to a couple he knew earlier that day. So there we were, homeless and with a van load of furniture. I got myself into a terrible state; I couldn't stop crying. Jeffrey suggested going to my mother's house and I agreed. There was nowhere else for us to go. My mother let us move in with her. I hated living back there as I had no privacy. My two sisters, Amber and Robyn, used to rummage through my belongings, helping themselves to whatever they fancied.

My mother was a very nosy woman; she would come into the bedroom whenever she thought I was asleep and lift up the bed clothes. I don't know what she was hoping to find. She would peep through the gap in the serving door from the kitchen into the dining room. Jeffrey got so fed up with it that he taped the gap with masking tape.

Tensions were high. My mother didn't want us living with her and she would throw subtle hints every chance she got. Jeffrey said that we should move out and go back up to Greenvale, only this time he would leave me in the house while he got our furniture. That's what we did. We gathered what we could and went up in a car. We walked around, looking to see which house we could move into but the only houses that were not occupied were the ones the builders were still working on behind a wire fence. Jeffrey crawled underneath first then lifted the wire up for me to crawl under. We walked over to the houses and let ourselves into one that looked more finished than the others. I stayed in the house until Jeffrey got our furniture. There was no running water or electricity, but that didn't stop us from moving in.

By this stage I was seven months pregnant and was finding it increasingly difficult to get in and out from under the wire fence around the houses. The workmen locked up at around half five which meant being behind the wire until morning. Luckily I knew one of the workmen, a guy called Paul, who would get me water and whatever else I needed. I would have been lost without his help. Even so, I knew I had to get out.

I had no other choice but to ask my mother if it would be alright for Jeffrey and me to move back in with her. Thankfully she said yes. We gathered our things together once more and put them into boxes and bags. Jeffrey asked his mother and his friend's sister if they would look after our bits and pieces for us. They both said they would.

A week later we went up to visit the woman who was supposed to be minding our furniture, only to find that she was using it without asking our permission. I thought my eyes were deceiving me. I found it hard to believe that anyone could take advantage of us in our situation. Jeffrey knew I was angry. He kept nipping my arm, not wanting me to say anything and I didn't until we got outside her house.

I was more annoyed with Jeffrey's silence. When I asked him why he didn't say anything or let me say anything, he said we had no one else to look after our stuff. He went on, "It won't be long until we have our own place". He said it was better to leave it. I disagreed with him but it made no difference what I thought.

A few days after finding out about our furniture being used by Jeffrey's friend's sister in Greenvale, we then discovered his mother was using our things as well.

One Sunday afternoon we walked over to Lodge Road to visit his brother Mike and his wife Jolene. After a while Jolene told me that she had been to visit Mrs White and noticed that she had got new cushion covers on her suite of furniture. When Jolene asked her where she had bought them Mrs White replied, "Jeffrey let me have the use of them".

When Jeffrey and I left Jolene and Mike's flat I asked Jeffrey about it. He told me that he had no idea his mother was using our cushion covers. I wanted to go to Jeffrey's mother's and find out what was going on. Again, Jeffrey said to leave it for him to sort out. He said he didn't want me getting upset.

The Birth of My First Child-Cathy.

On my next visit to the hospital Jeffrey came with me. After my examination the doctor said my blood pressure was dangerously high and that I needed to be admitted right away. I became very upset by the news. I didn't understand what was happening to my baby or my body. The next day I was taken down to the labour ward after being probed by the doctors. They said they would induce me so as to speed up the delivery process. I had never seen so many machines; I was wired up to these machines so they could monitor my baby's heartbeat and, at the same time, get a reading which informed them about the frequency of my contractions.

The midwife informed me every time I had a contraction. I couldn't see the reading on the machine without my glasses. I lay on the bed thinking "This isn't so bad, I don't feel any pain". That was the first stage of labour that lasted right through that first day. The midwife removed the wires so that I could get some sleep.

First thing the next morning I was hooked up again. By early afternoon the doctor broke my waters and said that it wouldn't be long before I gave birth to my baby. I waited and waited but still nothing.

The only change was that the contractions were getting stronger and becoming more frequent. This went on through the night. I was unable to get any sleep and the pain was so intense. I was no longer thinking that childbirth wasn't that bad.

The next morning the doctor came in to see me. I was becoming very anxious, wondering if there was something wrong. Were they keeping something from me? The midwife gave me gas and air to help ease the pain and then finally I gave birth to a beautiful baby girl on the 10th of October 1975.

She weighed in at six pounds and twelve ounces. It was a forceps delivery. I was surprised, considering that the doctors had told me I was going to have a big baby. Nevertheless I was elated at my perfect first born baby daughter. Jeffrey was over the moon; he told everyone she looked just like him and said that her hair was ginger, when in fact it was strawberry blonde.

The long labour, nearly seventy hours, took a lot out of me. I lost a lot of blood and I felt very weak. When Jeffrey's mother came to visit us in the hospital she wanted me to name my baby after her or my mother.

I had decided on a name when I was in the early stages of my pregnancy. I really liked the name Cathy. Jeffrey liked the name too, although he would have done what his mother wanted and expected. After what I had been through to bring her into this world, there was no way I was letting his mother or him dictate to me what I should call my baby.

After five days' stay in hospital Cathy and I were ready to go home. My mother's home, that is. I was very nervous with my new baby; she was so tiny and I was eager to get things right. At bath time my mother would tell me to be very careful and to watch I wouldn't let Cathy slip into the water. Of course, comments like that made me feel even worse. Thankfully, I managed just fine, despite her negative comments.

A week before Cathy's christening we were informed by the police that my brother Frederick had been shot and left for dead at the Dunn Cutts, not far from where we lived. It was rumoured that it was the Official IRA who were responsible. I have no idea who was responsible.

We were very upset by this; Frederick was shot in the stomach and was critically ill. He was admitted to the River Valley Hospital in Linn Town in the early hours of Sunday morning.

The following Sunday Cathy was christened in St Martha's Church. She only had the one godparent- my mother. This arrangement was made between my husband and my mother; I wasn't asked about it, just told. Frederick was to be her godfather but unfortunately he was still in hospital and would remain there for some months to come.

I went to visit Frederick in hospital on his 21st birthday; I bought a pair of Dr Martens black boots for him. He was still very ill and complaining about severe abdominal pain. He was on morphine for the pain. He looked so helpless lying there, having to depend on the hospital staff to minister to his needs. He didn't feel up to having a conversation and I could tell he was in a lot of pain. I said my goodbyes and told him I would call to see him again in a day or two.

Living at my mother's house with my newborn baby was getting me down. Jeffrey and I went to the Housing Association to make enquiries about getting a home of our own. We were informed by an office clerk that because we wanted to be housed in Jamestown we would have to wait two to three years. I knew I couldn't survive two more weeks, let alone two years. At that time there were two new housing developments just built; one was in Henahead, the other was in Whiteroad.

Our New Home Out of Belfast.

The British Government were offering a grant of three to five hundred pounds as an incentive to encourage people to move out of Belfast and into these areas. We were offered a house in either Henahead or Whiteroad and when I asked how long it would be before we could move we were told a week to ten days. Jeffrey and I both agreed to be housed in either area, whichever came first. One week later we were allocated a house in Ramoan, Whiteroad. I was so excited. At last, a place I could call my own. We began packing right away; it didn't take long to gather our belongings. We were given the keys to view the house before we moved into it.

Jeffrey and I set out to explore our new home. I enjoyed the bus journey with Cathy and Jeffrey- it was the beginning of many more to come, or so I thought!

As children, neither I nor any of my siblings ever got away on holiday with our parents, not even a day trip. This was like a day trip for me. I was travelling on a blue bus to somewhere I had never been before- very exciting indeed.

We found our way to Ramoan. I had a friend who lived there with her husband, not far away from our house. We called in on them first to ask them what they thought of living in Whiteroad. They both said that it was a great place to live and told us about their own experience living with relatives and how pleased they were to have their own home.

The house in Ramoan had three bedrooms with plenty of room for the three of us. It needed work done in almost every room, the kitchen being the worst. The walls were scorched and needed to be plastered. There were boards covering all the downstairs windows which made the house look very gloomy. But none of that mattered; the Housing Association said that they would carry out any repairs for us as soon as possible.

The first room we decorated was our bedroom. Jeffrey said he didn't know how to paper. I used to help my father when he papered my mother's house. When Jeffrey told me he couldn't paper I said "Well then, I'll do it myself". When he saw that I was willing to do the papering he decided to lend a hand. We ended up papering the bedroom together.

After a few weeks in the house, when our friends would come to visit, Jeffrey would tell them about the strange happenings that were going on in the house. He would tell our friends that any time he approached the bottom stairs his body would get very cold and that he felt a presence. Of course, our friends were intrigued and believed every word. Jeffrey couldn't understand why these stories didn't frighten me. He would ask me to go out to the stairs to experience what he said he had experienced. I told him that his ghost, or whatever it was, didn't seem that interested in me. I would then start to laugh; Jeffrey would give me a look that let me know he was annoyed with me for not believing him.

Jeffrey made friends very easily. He introduced me to a couple he had met, from where I don't know. The man was a hairdresser and his ex wife Anne was the mother of their two sons. Jeffrey told me their marriage broke up because he was gay; I wasn't that shocked by this revelation. Why should I have been? Jeffrey was telling me stuff about people I didn't know. I went out a few times with my new found friend into Whiteroad town; she was a real party animal and loved attention. One night when we were out in a hotel at a dance she was behaving a bit crazy. She was flirting with all the men and driving me nuts. I had to get out of the place. I asked her to come with me but she was having none of it. It wasn't until years later that I realized why.

Ann craved male attention, and when you've been starved of love and affection in the way that we had been you gain an understanding, an insight, as to the reasons why people behave the way they do.

On my way out the door a guy stopped me and asked me if he could take me home. I told him I was married and wanted to get home. He offered me a lift. He was French and seemed like a nice person. I felt I could trust him so I said yes to his offer. Stupid, I know, but I hadn't enough money for a taxi and I wasn't wearing my glasses and couldn't see very well. I was frightened and just wanted to get home. We didn't have a phone at home so I had taken a chance; thankfully I made it home safely. That was my last night out with Anne.

My mother came to visit us a couple of times, as did Frederick and his friend Frank Murray. One evening when Frederick and Frank called to see us we were sitting having a laugh; Frederick was a lot better and in great form.

I went into the kitchen to make us something to eat when all of a sudden I heard a loud noise coming from the living room. I walked back into the living room and saw Jeffrey standing at the back of the settee. Frederick was trying to help Frank and he asked me to get a spoon. Frank had taken an epileptic fit, his eyes were rolling in the back of his head, he had kicked over the coffee table and his long arms were punching the air. I got the shock of my life. Frank looked so evil to me. He looked like a man possessed. Jeffrey was visibly shaken by what he had seen, too. Frederick stayed calm as he was used to it. Before long, Frank came round. He had no idea what had happened to him.

We had been living in Whiteroad a few months when Jeffrey was offered a house in Larkin Street, Force Road. He was really keen for us to move back to Belfast. I wasn't in a hurry to move back- I liked living in Whiteroad. I had got used to the house and I had friends living there.

I was happy enough. Jeffrey suggested we go and have a look at the house. We were being asked for one hundred pounds key money to move into the house.

My parents thought it was a good idea for us to move back to Belfast where we knew everyone. Jeffrey and I went to view the house. It was in a terrible condition. I had never seen so much filth and dirt in one place in my life. There was an outside toilet in the back yard. It looked horrible to me, all of it. Jeffrey managed to manipulate me and make it sound so much better than it was. His powers of persuasion overtook me. We hadn't got the money to move, but again, he assured me everything would work out just fine and that he could get the money.

He continued, "All we have to do is decorate- we could have it looking like a palace. We'll be so much better off living back in Belfast".

He talked me into it; within a week we had packed up and moved back to Belfast. I scrubbed the house with bleach and disinfectant from top to bottom. Jeffrey and I decided to paper the back bedroom first and have it nice for Cathy. While we were rolling up an old carpet from the bedroom to throw out Jeffrey started yelling, "There's a mouse, there's a mouse!" I jumped on his back to get away from it but he shrugged me off and grabbed a brush and started beating the carpet. When the mouse ran out he hit it with the brush and killed it. I was petrified. That was the first time I had ever seen a mouse in my life and it scared me nearly half to death. Later on that evening, when the fear had gone, we found it hilarious that a tiny creature could cause us to behave like two lunatics.

My brother Alvin called to see me with his friend Jim; it was a lovely summer's day. I was surprised to see him. It wasn't like him to visit but I was very pleased that he had. He was playing with Cathy who was lying on her blanket on the living room floor when he asked, "What are those red marks on her arms and face?" I said I wasn't sure. I told him that she was teething and maybe that was the reason. He picked her up from the floor and had a closer look. He said I should take her to the hospital. He thought the marks were insect bites.

I was horrified and immediately took her to the hospital where she was examined by a doctor. After he examined her he confirmed that the marks on her body were caused by flea bites.

All I could think about was getting as far away as possible from Larkin Street. I rang Jeffrey from the hospital to let him know what had happened. I was crying and in a dreadful state. He said for me to calm down and get back to the house and wait until he got in from work. I said I would go to my mother's house and wait for him there. I couldn't bear the thought of going back into that house and exposing Cathy and me to the vermin in it. I told the doctor all about the state of the house when we moved in and about scrubbing it with disinfectant and bleach to make it clean enough for us to live in. He told me we would have to get it fumigated and said that I needed to ring City Council. As it was Saturday that meant having to wait until Monday before I could get in touch with them and there was no way I was setting foot back in that house until I was satisfied my baby would be safe.

Jeffrey's friends let us stay with them over the weekend. He had met them when he worked in the Hutson's. We were very grateful for their support. We had the house fumigated and moved back into it after three or four days.

Jeffrey and I argued non stop about stupid things. The arguments grew nasty. I remember one Friday evening my sister Robyn called in to see me. Later on that night we got a bottle of cider each. Cathy was in bed. Robyn and I were sitting enjoying a drink together when Jeffrey came home from work. He called me out into the kitchen and told me to get rid of my sister. He lifted our cider and poured it down the sink.

Robyn quickly left, not knowing where to look. I asked what was going on with him; had he lost the plot? He went crazy, accusing me of being an alcoholic, and stormed up to bed, leaving me sitting in the living room. The next morning, when he came into the living room, I asked him what he thought he was doing, embarrassing me in that way. That led to a screaming match between the two of us. He lifted Cathy and headed for the front door. I came after him and pleaded with him to stop but he just kept on going.

After he'd gone I sat and cried, not knowing what to do. I thought he would calm down and come home and apologize for what he'd done. He did come back a few hours later and threatened me. He said that if I ever invited my sister back he would take Cathy away from me and I would have no chance of getting her back because I was an unfit mother who drank too much.

I didn't realize at the time that he was the sick one. I was very insecure and had no confidence in myself, nor had I anywhere or anyone to turn to so I put up and shut up.

Jeffrey became very friendly with a few of our neighbours. They began to ignore me; every time Jeffrey and I walked up the street they would smile and say hello to him and walk on past me as if I were invisible- that hurt. I felt betrayed by my husband.

On another occasion, after another row, he left and said that he wouldn't be back. I wasn't worried as I didn't want him back. I got myself and Cathy dressed and went out for a walk to the shops. I felt free and very contented with it being just the two of us. When we arrived back home I fed Cathy and put her down for her afternoon nap. While she was asleep I was busy taking down curtains and cleaning windows when Jeffrey walked into the living room. He said he was sorry and I accepted his apology. Although I was happy enough to be on my own I still wanted my marriage to work.

One evening, after coming home from a visit to my mother's house, Jeffrey was sitting chatting with a guy I had never met before. Later on Jeffrey told me that he was an old friend who needed somewhere to stay. I asked Jeffrey to get rid of him. There was something about this person that I didn't like. Jeffrey refused. He didn't bother to ask me what I thought; he just went on ahead and did what he wanted.

I asked the guy to leave, which he did. That of course meant I was in for it, big time. Another row followed, which led to yet another fight. No one knew what it was like for me, living with a man who only cared about suiting himself and everyone else. Everyone except me, that is.

On the Move Again.

Shortly after Cathy's first birthday Jeffrey wanted to move house again. He somehow found out about a woman in New Road wanting an exchange to the Force Road area. We went to see the house in New Road and I fell in love with it.

The house had three bedrooms, a bathroom and a large hall. The living room was a good size with a dining room and kitchen. Catharine, the woman from New Road, came to look at our house and decided she liked it. After a few weeks we had moved again. We worked really hard to get the house the way we wanted it. The neighbours were very friendly. Ruth, my next door neighbour, was a lovely woman. She was like a mother to me.

One evening, Jeffrey became very upset. We were in our bedroom, sitting talking, when all of a sudden he started pulling at his face with his nails, digging his nails hard into his face, so hard that he drew blood. I tried to get him to stop and asked him why he was causing harm to himself. He was crying almost uncontrollably. I was unable to get him to talk about why he was behaving in this way.

I held him and told him that everything was going to be alright, even though I didn't understand what was going on with him. I continued to sit with him and asked if he would like a cup of tea; he thanked me and said yes.

His sister Colette called to see us the next day. She asked him what had happened to his face. He lied and said the cat had scratched him. She looked over at me, and before she said another word I looked her straight in the eye and told her it wasn't me. Colette asked Jeffrey again what happened to his face; he started laughing and lied again, saying it was the cat. I looked at her and said to her that I knew people would think it was me. I am sure she believed it was me.

Expecting My Second Child.

I became pregnant with our second child who was due on the sixteenth of November 1977. Jeffrey was out of work again and I found it hard trying to make ends meet.

Our neighbour across the street, Mrs Moore, whose daughter had lost her baby, called me over to her house. She offered me a pile of brand new baby clothes and a sterilizing unit. She asked me if I minded; I thanked her and told her I would be perfectly happy to accept them.

Sam was born on the 25th of November at the Belfast Hospital. He weighed in at 7lb 8 ounces. He arrived late and his skin was red and wrinkled because he was overdue. This made him look like an old man. The midwife took him away to give him a bath and on his return the redness was gone and he was perfect and beautiful. While I was in labour the midwife was asking me questions. She wanted to know how many children I had, what sex they were, and if I had another girl I would have plenty of clothes to pass on. I wasn't in as much pain bringing Sam into the world. When I learned from the midwife that I had given birth to a son I was over the moon. I really wanted a boy and I had got what I wanted, a gentleman's family.

I was left for hours on my own after his birth with no tea and toast, no aftercare or anything. Jeffrey wasn't as close to his son as he was to his daughter. This made me even more overprotective and sensitive to my baby's needs. I would sit for hours nursing him and giving him the love he needed. Jeffrey's brother Tom came home from Africa when Sam was a few months old. I remember one day when he came to visit Sam he had fallen asleep under the chair. Tom laughed at the sight of my baby sleeping under the chair. I got up from my chair and was on my way over to pick him up and put him to bed when Tom said that I should leave him be. I wasn't leaving my son lying on the floor for anyone.

I chose the name Sam because I didn't want him to be named after his father. Sam was christened in St Augustin's Chapel in Belfast. Jeffrey's brother Paul was his only godparent.

I became very ill after Sam's birth. I lost an awful lot of blood and was in excruciating pain caused by a bowel infection. I had never suffered pain like it in my life. I believe it was due to the neglect I suffered after Sam's birth.

The doctor had to be called out to the house. He put me on a course of antibiotics and painkillers. It took me a couple of weeks to recover. It was a very painful experience, one I hope never to have to go through again.

Jeffrey was unemployed and things were tough. I found it so hard trying to get by on social security. He had applied for a couple of jobs and was turned down but then he got lucky and found a job. But it didn't last long.

A month maybe? Here we were, once again, back on state benefits.

Jeffrey said that he wanted to move again, back up to New Road. I did not want to move anywhere as I was happy where I was. The night before we moved we had a party and he invited a few friends and neighbours round.

Ruth, our next door neighbour, asked me if I wanted to move. I told her I was happy in New Road. She said that I should stay and tell Jeffrey that I didn't want to go. I felt I was unable to stand up for myself. I presumed it was up to him that I had no say in the matter. That's how I was then.

We arrived in Greenvale and started to unload the van. I had Cathy and Sam to look after as well as unpacking our belongings. It was hard work that went on for days. I didn't like the house or the location.

I remember opening the front door one Sunday afternoon and, to my surprise, standing there on the front door step was a young woman from Glenmore called Marian Smith. She said she had my brother Frederick in the back of her car. She continued, "Your mum asked me to bring him up to you". She told me that he was unconscious in the back seat. I knew what she meant. I called for Jeffrey to come out and help us get him into the house. We managed to get him indoors. Jeffrey laid him on the settee. I thanked Marian and said goodbye.

I felt embarrassed and really angry. I was very annoyed with my mother for dumping my drunken brother on me. When Frederick woke hours later he hadn't a clue where he was. He still seemed drunk to me. Jeffrey tried talking with him but Frederick wasn't listening. He left not long after that.

We had just finished decorating the living room. It looked really nice but I never had the chance to enjoy it. The very next day we were on the move again. We had been in Greenvale for only two weeks. Jeffrey found a ground floor flat in Glenmore Gardens. All I remember about that particular day was Jeffrey coming in very early in the morning saying he had got us a flat and to start packing right away. I didn't have a chance to ask any questions; he started to pack immediately. I followed him upstairs and said I didn't think it was a good idea moving again, especially when it meant living across the street from my parents' house. I knew it was a bad move. I knew it in my gut but Jeffrey had a way of getting what he wanted; he was able to get his own way every time.

There I was, living back in the street I was so desperate to move away from with my two children. Our neighbours who lived above us, the Cunninghams, were great people. Jean loved to take Sam out in his pram and go for a walk. She used to buy him clothes and on their return Sam's mouth was dirty from the chocolate she had been feeding him.

My younger sister Amber married a guy from Stewart Hill. He was a good few years older than her; she was sixteen at the time. On their return home from their honeymoon my mother sent my sister Robyn over to get me. She wanted to have a chat with me. Robyn told me that our mother didn't want Amber and her husband living with her. I didn't want them living with me either; they were not my responsibility.

I went over to my mum's just to hear what she had to say. She tried to lay a guilt trip on me, telling me that she hadn't room for the newlyweds and as I was Amber's big sister it was my duty to have them live with me. I said that I was sick to death of her dumping her responsibilities onto me. I reminded her that she had in fact got room, plenty of room, and that once again my parents were avoiding their duties. I left and went back home. My sister Robyn came over with me and we sat talking for hours until she left and went back home. She was no sooner away when she was back, saying that mother was fighting with Amber. She was crying. I told Robyn to tell Amber and her husband to come over and stay with me and that's what they did.

I didn't ask Amber for any money towards their keep. They had been staying with us for a few weeks when I knew I couldn't go on feeding them both, so I asked Amber to help by giving me a few pounds to help with the food bills. She looked at me as if I had asked her for the Crown Jewels and said that she and Noel couldn't afford it. I knew they had got it to give and I also knew there was no way she was going to part with a penny. She was too selfish. My mum spoiled her rotten. Amber was too used to getting her own way.

It used to annoy me when she came back from town with fancy clothes and makeup and boast about how much it had all cost. She was starting to take over my home. I would be sitting watching a TV programme and she would walk over and turn to another station. (No remote controls in those days.) Her husband would ask her to turn back to the station that I had on and she refused.

I'd had enough. I really tried to help her but all she did was throw it back in my face. I couldn't take any more and I asked her to leave. Mother was furious with me but I didn't care.

Jeffrey and I had some pretty bad fights. On one occasion he grabbed me by my hair and threw me onto the hall floor; I attempted to get back up when he came out from the bedroom with a pillow in his hand. He got on top of me and tried to smother me with it. I fought like crazy. I really thought he was going to kill me. He took the pillow away from my face and got up from me. I got myself up, opened the front door and ran as fast as I could across the street to my mother's house. I opened the door and went into the living room where my brother Frederick was sitting watching TV. He got up from his chair and came over to me, asking me what had happened.

It took me a few minutes before I was able to speak. The tears were blinding me and my throat was sore. My mother came in from the back where she had been hanging out washing. I told them what Jeffrey had done to me. My brother Frederick went crazy, asking me where Jeffrey was. He put his boots on and ran across the street. When he returned he asked me what I was playing at: he said that Jeffrey had told him that I started a fight with him and scratched his face with my nails, calling him names. He told my brother that I was crucifying him.

Again Frederick asked "What are you doing? Jeffrey is in a terrible state- the man's a nervous wreck". I couldn't believe what I was hearing. I was totally stunned. I asked Frederick to please think about it, why would I lie? What reason would I have? I pleaded with my mother and Frederick not to be taken in by his lies. I knew they didn't believe me. Why would they, not after the grand performance that my husband had put on for them both. I left my mother's and came back over to the flat. Jeffrey was sitting there. I walked on past him, not speaking a word and that's the way it stayed for days.

Needless to say, I stopped speaking to my mother and my brother. Okay, Jeffrey is a master at fooling people. Nevertheless, I was visibly shaken when I went over to them looking for their help and protection. My throat was hoarse and tears were streaming down my face. I never thought in a million years they would take his side. After all, they were my family.

I asked my sister Robyn would she go over and get my payment book from our mother. I had a cheque to pay off which I had been paying at three pounds a week. When she returned with my payment book I noticed that there were a lot of payments that hadn't been paid. I had been sending my three pounds over to my mother's every week. I never found out what had happened to the money. I didn't really care. I just wanted to get as far away as possible from my so-called family as quickly as I could.

The Attack on My Home.

One evening as Jeffrey and I were about to go to bed there was an almighty sound of breaking glass coming from our bedroom. I rushed into the bedroom and saw that Sam's cot was covered in broken glass. I became hysterical. I lifted Sam from his cot and went into the back bedroom (Cathy's bedroom) to check that he was alright. Thank God he wasn't hurt. There wasn't a mark on him. He had been wakened by the noise and he was crying. Cathy was fast asleep. I didn't want to waken her. I thanked God they were both okay. I cradled Sam in my arms, trying to comfort him. All I could think about was that my infant son could have been injured or worse.

The living room window and the second bedroom window came crashing in. All the windows at the front of the flat had been smashed. I suspected that my mother and brother Frederick were behind the attack on my home.

I left Jeffrey with our two children and ran across the street to my mother's house. The living room light was still on. I banged on the front door until someone answered. Frederick opened the door to me and I pushed past him. He demanded to know what was going on with me. I asked my mother and my brother Frederick had they anything to do with the attack on my home and my children; they both denied having anything to do with it. I didn't believe them; they both looked guilty to me. I knew my mother was mad as hell with me because she could on longer manipulate me. I was beginning to see through her. I was no longer the innocent, gullible little girl.

I didn't want to believe that my family could have anything to do with that night. Jeffrey told me later that two of our neighbours had been asked by Frederick and my mother to teach us a lesson. To this day I still don't have any proof that this was true. I confronted one of the guys who were supposed to have been involved in attacking my home a few years after it happened. He strenuously denied any involvement; he said that he and his friend were wrongly accused and I believed him.

I wonder if the person responsible for the vicious attack on our home and children that night was closer to me than I had originally thought! Had Jeffrey upset or done something to annoy the wrong people?

After the attack it was me who wanted to move as I no longer felt safe living in Glenmore. We had the windows put back in and started making enquiries about getting out of there. Jeffrey's brother Mike was living in Springdale, just at the peace line. It was very close to a predominantly Protestant housing estate. Jeffrey said he had a house for us to move into next door to Mike. I said I didn't want to move to Springdale. I didn't want to live in a house with grills on the windows where I would feel frightened for our safety and that of our children.

Shortly before we moved, Amber and I were at the Glaze shop, not far from the flat. I had Sam with me in his buggy. Amber and I made friends after the assault on my home. She called to see if we were alright. When we left the shop, Sam was still sitting in his pram. Amber and I were walking away from him when the manager of the shop came after us; he asked me was the baby in the pram mine? I looked at him and said no. It wasn't until we were a few yards away that I suddenly realized there was something missing, my son! I ran back to the shop with Amber running behind me. When I arrived at the shop my son was sitting in his pram, smiling and totally unaware of what his mummy had done. I nearly hugged him to death. I couldn't take it in that I had forgotten him. It must have been the stress I was under at the time that caused my temporary memory loss. I'm not sure why Amber didn't notice when the manager asked me about my child.

Number 9 Willow Parade became our new address. I hated living there with a six foot fence around the house as well as grills on the windows and front door. It wasn't long before our house came under attack from a gang of Loyalists. All they had to do was cross the street-easy access. There were around a dozen of them and they began to pelt our house with bricks and bottles. This would go on for hours, sometimes on a nightly basis.

Mike got Jeffrey a job which was great. It really helped with our financial situation. Every Saturday Jolene, Mikes's wife and I would go shopping in town. We would spend hours going around all the different shops. Jolene must have spent a small fortune. She was able to buy a lot more than I was. We would return home around six o'clock. It was always the same when I walked into the house; Jeffrey let the kids go mad and their toys would be lying everywhere. I would put away the shopping and afterwards get Jeffrey and the children something to eat. When bath time came I took care of that too and put my two children to bed. After that I cleared up the mess and tidied away all their toys until the next time.

Our home was coming under constant attack. I was fearful for my children. It got to the stage where I didn't want to put the children upstairs to sleep. I wanted them in the living room downstairs so we could make our escape out the back door if need be. On one occasion our front door came under a barrage of missiles. It only stopped when they succeeded in breaking the door down onto the hall floor. I went running upstairs to my children to make sure they were okay.

Jeffrey and Mike were at the side of the house throwing bottles at the thugs, trying to stop them from causing any more damage to us and our home. A neighbour rang for the police who arrived some time later. Meanwhile, the gang retreated behind the derelict houses just across the street and then disappeared back to where they had come from. I shall never forget that night- it was very scary. I really thought that when they broke down our front door it was all over. I thought they were going to kill us.

When the Army arrived they boarded up the front door with planks of wood to make it secure for the night. We were left alone for a short time and then it began again, only this time Jeffrey, Mike and a couple of our neighbours were ready for them. I myself was getting really fed up with my home being attacked so I joined them. We had saved up empty milk bottles and lemonade bottles and went around to the side of the house. I wasn't much use because of of my poor eyesight so I left and went back into the house.

After a while I heard Jeffrey calling my name. I looked out the window and saw him waving for me to come out of the house. I came out by the back door and round to the side of the house. Jeffrey told me to go back into the house and get his knife. He was shouting at the top of his voice for me to join in after what this man and his gang had put me through. I jumped over the fence and there lying on the ground was a man covered in blood. Jeffrey and the rest of them had managed to get this man and beat the crap out of him.

He was the ringleader whose name was Dave. As I came closer I couldn't bring myself to hurt him. Jeffrey took the knife from me. I asked them to leave the guy alone as he had had enough. He lay on the ground, unconscious. Someone rang for an ambulance and within minutes it had arrived and he was taken to hospital. Dave's shoe hung from a telephone wire that could be seen from the other side of the peace wall. A reminder to Dave's gang, if you will, of what happened that night.

The next day the police called to our house and questioned Jeffrey about the assault. The police said they wouldn't blame Jeffrey for putting Dave into hospital. They were trying to get a confession from him but he was too clever for them. When Jeffrey was summoned to court the judge dismissed the case. Apparently Dave had a record going back some years of assault and battery and his own people wanted him removed from their community. He was known to everyone as the bad boy.

I was preparing breakfast one Saturday morning when one of our neighbours called to the back door. He told me there was a suitcase sitting on the front doorstep with wires coming from it. He said he would call the police. I ran upstairs to wake Jeffrey and began getting the kids dressed when there was a knock at the back door. Jeffrey went down to answer it. The police had arrived with the bomb squad. They said we should get out of the house immediately and that they would let us know when it was safe for us to return.

We stayed with friends of Jeffrey's who lived nearby. It was only a few doors away from our house; that meant we were able to see what was going on. After a few hours or so we were able to return to the house. It turned out to be a hoax. The police said that for our own safety we needed to leave right away. They told us that they had informed Social Services of the ongoing situation and that it was no longer safe for us to live there.

Two social workers from Alice Street called to see us and offered me and the kids accommodation in a nearby hostel. I asked why Jeffrey couldn't come with us. I was told by the social worker that men weren't allowed in the hostel; it was for women and children only. I was not happy about leaving without my husband. I was scared and unsure where Jeffrey would live. I said I would only go to a place where men were allowed to go. They told me this was all they could offer and that I had no choice, that my life and the lives of my children were in jeopardy.

We were given a few hours to pack our belongings. I took what I needed for the kids and we were driven to the hostel by Social Services. The social workers helped me in with my bags and introduced me to the warden, a nun called Sister Anne. She showed me to the first flat on the second floor. It was so clinical and cold-looking. I stood in the hallway, not quite believing that this was happening to me and my children. It felt almost like a bad dream except it was real, very real.

Sister Anne explained the rules to me which where what you would expect, living in a hostel. They included no men allowed in after nine o'clock at night, no alcohol, no pets, no family members or friends allowed to stay overnight. No staying out all night. All residents had to be in the hostel no later than ten o'clock at night.

My first week in the hostel was hell. I had really bad nightmares. I would wake up with my eyes wet from crying and a sore throat after screaming and shouting in my sleep. I missed my husband. I felt very alone and frightened. The ugliness of living in Willow Parade came back to haunt me in my dreams.

I learned after one week that there were men living in the hostel with their wives. One married couple happened to be a cousin of Jeffrey's and her husband. I asked Sister Anne why my husband was not allowed to stay with me. She said I should ring my social worker to ask the reasons why. Sister Anne really liked Jeffrey. He turned on the charm with her too, and it worked. He would brush the balcony and stairs for her and do any other odd jobs that needed doing.

When I got through to my social worker to ask him why my husband wasn't allowed to stay with me while other husbands were, he told me it was because Jeffrey and I were intimidated and that they feared an attack on the hostel. They felt it would be safer for Jeffrey to stay away. Why the hell was it okay for me and my children to stay there then? Sister Anne told Jeffrey he could stay with me and the children and not to let on to anyone.

Jeffrey was waiting for a job interview at a children's home in Belfast. Sister Anne said she would be more than happy to give Jeffrey a reference. She went further; she said that she would ring Sister Kerry (the head nun at the home) and try to get Jeffrey a start as soon as possible.

Jeffrey's brother Joe worked in the home at the time when my sister Robyn had her second baby whom she gave up for adoption. Joe was able to tell us all about it. Of course he should have said nothing; it wasn't his business to. He got into a lot of trouble with his employers for breaking confidentiality, and rightly so.

Jeffrey was pestering me to visit Robyn's baby at the home. He wanted us to adopt her. He just wouldn't let it go. Day and night he would argue his reasons why we should try for adoption; he was being totally irrational. Of course he had his own agenda, not that of the child.

I knew in my heart I couldn't love her like I loved my own children. Besides, it would have been cruel on both Robyn and her baby. Robyn had made her decision to have her baby adopted. My mother didn't want another baby to rear as she had her hands full with Robyn's first child, Kevin. As soon as Kevin was born my mother took over. She fed him, changed him, did everything and then complained when Robyn did nothing.

My Life After the Hostel.

My life was falling apart. I was living in a hostel because I had made myself homeless by moving from place to place. Jeffrey tried everything in his power to get me to change my mind about Robyn's baby. Thank God I had the sense to do what was right for us all, including my own children. I know that I made the right decision.

My social worker rang me and said the Housing Association had a flat in Moypark for us. I said I did not want a home in Moypark; I reminded him that the Housing Association gave us A1 priority which meant a house in about five to six months' waiting time in an area of our choice. We had been told by the police to leave our home and we had seventeen police reports as evidence of intimidation, so there was no way I was settling for a flat in Moypark or anywhere else. I let him know this and I asked him, would he? Here was a middle-class man with no clue what it was like to have come through what we had; he made me sick.

The Housing Association restricted the A1 priority because of the number of times we had moved. We had become known to them as professional squatters. A second offer was made to us; this time it was a house at the top of the Willowbank Road with very few Catholics living in the area. It was mostly Protestant people. I turned it down right away.

My social worker wasn't pleased with my refusal to move. He said I would be evicted from the hostel. I couldn't believe this man. He insisted that I had no choice because of our record with the Housing Association.

I got up from the chair I was sitting on and told him to get out. I let him know that if he tried to have me and my children evicted I would let the media know. Had he forgotten why we were in the hostel in the first place? He wasn't helping me or my children. I asked him again, would he live in that area? He refused to answer me. Sister Anne came in and said she had heard me berating him. She said she wished everyone would speak their minds to their social workers, and then maybe they would get rehoused quicker.

Finally, after eight long months, we were offered a three-bedroom house in Jamestown. Jeffrey and I went to view the house, number 6 Kennedy Gardens. Again it needed a lot of work done but I didn't care. At last I had a place I could call my own. We moved into number 6 on Good Friday 1980.

Jeffrey started work in the children's home soon after the move. We were both happy getting our new home decorated and also that he'd got a job. He was paid monthly in his new job. He had to do a lying month which made it very difficult for us as a family to survive financially, but somehow we managed.

I was lonely without his company, even though we were not the happiest couple in the world. I hadn't any friends. We didn't stay around anywhere long enough for me to make friends. Jeffrey had to sleep over two nights a week and I found it hard. We never spent any time together; it was like we were living two separate lives under the same roof.

Cathy started primary school in September of that year. It felt so strange for me, leaving her into her class. Cathy was very excited and let go of my hand as soon as she met her teacher and skipped into the classroom, waving me goodbye. She was such a wonderful child; she always had a smile on her face. What a great kid she was. She excelled at school. Every other day she would come home with either a certificate or a medal. She was very bright and wonderful.

I was getting Cathy ready for school one morning when I heard on the news that my idol, John Lennon, had died. I couldn't take it in. He had been shot five times at close range outside his Dakota apartment. It was the morning after our sixth wedding anniversary. I was incredibly sad and I felt that there was no one I could talk to about how I felt, no one I could share my grief with.

On my way to and from school with Cathy and Sam, I became friendly with one of the other mothers. Her daughter was in Cathy's class. It was the only time I was able to have a conversation with another adult.

1980 was also the year of the first hunger strike but it ended when the government and representatives of the prisoners came to some sort of arrangement. I remember for the first time in my life becoming interested in Irish history. I wanted to understand why men were prepared to die for their country.

Jeffrey would come home from work and see me with my face in a book on Irish history; he wasn't interested in books, only in hating and blaming. I remember our class being asked by our history teacher if we wanted Irish history or American history and we all wanted American history. It seemed more glamorous to us. God knows why.

I felt so empty inside. Jeffrey was working and when he wasn't we did very little together apart from argue. My sister Robyn was drinking a lot so I didn't see that much of her which saddened me a great deal.

Amber was living in Diggen, as was my brother Frederick, while Alvin was in Southeast. I spent my days looking after my children and keeping our home spotless.

Jeffrey had got an out-of-court settlement of £7,000. When he was working with Mike he contracted a skin complaint caused by working with cement.

He gave my mother £100 and his mother the same amount. He spent a lot on our house, buying new carpets and furniture and before long it was gone. I had a beautiful home that did nothing to fill the emptiness I felt inside.

The year that very nearly broke me.

In 1981 things took a turn for the worse. Jeffrey told me about a young man he had come to know who had been on visits to the home where he worked. His name was Paddy from Diggen. Jeffrey said that he felt sorry for Paddy because he and his parents didn't get on. The reason he came to Belfast was to get away from them. He was living with his uncle in Belfast and was very unhappy living there.

The next day, Jeffrey introduced me to Paddy. Two weeks after that he had moved in with us. Jeffrey made this decision without talking it over with me; his usual behaviour. I let him get away with it because I thought so little about myself. My opinion didn't matter. I felt I had no voice so again I kept quiet.

I really tried to get on with Paddy but as hard as I tried it just wasn't working. He made no effort whatsoever to get on with me. He took over my home and my husband. He wasn't contributing towards food and was living off us. I was not happy about it so I asked Jeffrey to speak to him. The next week Paddy came into the house with a shopping bag from Spencer's with all this really expensive food. It must have cost a bomb. He seemed to be the only one who enjoyed it. Jeffrey and Paddy would sit up to all hours of the morning. I remember one particular night I was unable to sleep. It was after two thirty in the morning. I came downstairs and walked into the living room. Jeffrey and Paddy were sitting opposite each other. A deathly silence filled the room the moment I entered.

I asked what they were doing still up. They told me they had been watching a programme which went on until after one and that they were so busy talking they hadn't noticed the time. I had a feeling in my gut that things were wrong, very wrong. I accepted what I was told and went back to bed alone.

I felt an emptiness inside me that was almost too painful to bear. There was absolutely no one I could talk to about how I was feeling. I grew deeply depressed and felt numb; I was operating on automatic pilot. Deep down in my soul I knew what was going on between Jeffrey and Paddy. But the reality was too much for me to cope with, so I put it to the back of my mind and continued to pretend that everything was fine. I was in complete denial. After all, I was from Jameston and Jeffrey was a Force Road man. This wasn't happening to me; I had two children to bring up so I had to get on with it the best way I could.

One Friday morning I had just got back from taking the kids to school. Jeffrey was sitting at the breakfast table. He smiled at me and said that I had been looking a bit down recently. He suggested I should go away for the weekend to Diggen and see my sister Amber. I asked about the kids; he told me not to worry, that he would look after them. He seemed so sincere and kind. I said that I wasn't that keen to go on my own. He got up from his seat and walked over to me, gave me a hug and said he wanted me to get away for the weekend and enjoy myself. That was that. He was not taking no for an answer. I packed a bag and left for Central Station. Amber was pleased to see me. It was good to get away. All the same, I couldn't help wondering what Jeffrey's motive was. He was almost desperate for me to leave but, as usual when thoughts of that kind came into my head, I didn't entertain them for too long for fear I would be right.

I returned from Diggen around five thirty on Sunday. The kids were pleased to see me and me them. Jeffrey was his usual self. Paddy had gone to Diggen for the weekend, Jeffrey told me. Later on that evening, when I was putting the kids to bed, Cathy very innocently said that Paddy was sleeping in Daddy's bed. My heart started beating very fast. I tried not to let my child know that there was anything wrong with her mum. I kissed her good night and tried to pull myself together before going downstairs to confront Jeffrey about it. I went into the bathroom first to try and calm down. My heart was racing and my head was aching. I was being forced to acknowledge the truth and I wasn't ready to handle it. I went downstairs to the living room and asked Jeffrey what was going on. He looked at me and asked me what I was talking about.

I said "You know damn well what I'm talking about, what's going on? Why was Paddy sleeping in my bed with my husband?" He said that I was insane like the rest of my family and told me to shut up. I said I wouldn't. He got up from his seat and lunged towards me, grabbing hold of my hair. He threw me to the floor and started beating me. I was crying, begging him to leave me alone but he kept on hitting me. I curled up into a ball to try and save myself. Then finally the beating stopped.

The next day I told Jeffrey I wanted Paddy out of my home. I was shocked when he said he agreed with me. He then said that Paddy was very disturbed and it had taken a while before he realized just how screwed up he really was. I was so relieved that my husband was taking my side and not Paddy's. I even began to doubt myself, telling myself that Jeffrey wasn't gay. It was Paddy's fault that things were bad between us. It was easier this way. I didn't have to face the truth when I wasn't ready to.

I told my sister Amber about Paddy and Jeffrey sleeping together and she told me that her husband had slept with men; it doesn't mean that there's anything going on. That was all I wanted to hear; it made it even easier to lie to myself.

After about a week Jeffrey came home from work and told me he had met Paddy in town. He said he felt sorry for him because he looked so depressed. His parents didn't want to know him and his uncle had turned his back on him too. I knew this was a pack of lies but I was prepared to do whatever it took to hold on to my marriage. I was desperate to keep my family together. I knew what was coming next.

Jeffrey asked me if it would be alright if Paddy came back to live with us. He promised it would only be for a short while. I was reluctant to say yes. I felt under so much pressure- I felt he had backed me into a corner. The very next day Paddy was back living with us. He was the same arrogant selfish person, letting me know that he didn't care one bit about my feelings. He was back living in my home and he knew there was nothing I could do about it.

I knew only too well what Lady Diana meant when she said on national TV that there were three people in her marriage; the same was true about my own. Only it wasn't another woman!

One morning while I was getting the kids ready for school I had a gut feeling that I should leave the back door open so that when I returned there would be no sound of me coming into the house. I didn't leave it open though. When I got back home from leaving the kids at school I was regretting closing the door. I opened the door as quietly as I could and walked quickly through the living room to the bottom of the stairs. I heard the sound of running feet above my head.

When I reached our bedroom Jeffrey was pretending to be asleep. It was so obvious what had been going on. I pulled down the bed clothes and around his ankles were his underpants. I asked him what was going on. He didn't answer me. He just lay there with a terrified look on his face. I went into the box room where Paddy was. He too was pretending to be asleep. I think the reason I closed the door shut was because deep down I knew what was going to happen when I left the house. Part of me wanted to know for sure and the rest of me couldn't handle the truth.

Since I hadn't actually seen them in the act I managed to convince myself that nothing had happened, so I came downstairs and carried on with the daily chores. I was an expert at putting what was too painful to deal with to the back of my head. I was so good at denial; it's what got me through my painful childhood and the emotional and mental pain of being stuck in a loveless marriage.

A couple of days later Jeffrey told me Paddy's parents had invited all of us down for the weekend. Of course, Jeffrey accepted the invitation. On Friday we packed our bags and headed for the train to Diggen.

When we arrived later that evening Paddy's parents made us very welcome. They were such a nice couple and I wondered how they ended up with Paddy for a son! We stayed in on Friday night and talked for hours. It was a pleasant enough evening until Jeffrey and I went to bed. He was very cold towards me, more so than usual. I needed warmth but all I got was a chill.

The next day we walked into town. Jeffrey and Paddy stayed very close together while I was left to take care of the kids. They hardly took any notice of me at all or my children. Paddy's mother had dinner ready for us on our return. After dinner, Jeffrey and I put Cathy and Sam to bed. Paddy's parents were looking after our children for us. Jeffrey and I began getting ready to go out for the evening when Paddy's mum knocked on the door. She handed me a necklace to keep. It was a silver necklace in a red velvet box. I thought, how sweet of her, and thanked her for the beautiful gift.

We went to a night club in town. The music was deafening. I never cared that much for discos; I preferred live music. I was determined to make the most of it as I didn't get out that much. Boy, did it all go wrong! Paddy was acting really strangely. He seemed very upset and was crying. When I asked him what was wrong he snapped at me and stormed off to the toilets. Jeffrey went after him. They were gone for a long time. I was left sitting there, feeling like a spare part. I became very anxious and became even more upset as time went on. I got up from my seat and went down to the gents' toilets to see if I could find my husband. When a man came out from the toilet I asked him did he notice a guy with ginger hair helping another man with blonde hair? He said he would go back in and check for me. After a minute or so the guy returned with Jeffrey. I thanked him and asked Jeffrey what the fuck was going on. The tears were blinding me by this stage. Jeffrey put his arm around me and walked me back to my seat.

He said Paddy was feeling really sick and as soon as he could he would come back and be with me. I knew he was more concerned about him than me and that he was feeding me more of his lies.

I was in this strange place, crying my eyes out in front of everyone. I was so upset I didn't care who saw me; I really didn't. Jeffrey returned with our coats and said Paddy was waiting outside for us. He was trying to reassure me, telling me everything was going to be alright. (Where have I heard that before?)

When we met Paddy outside the night club he was still pretending to be ill. I went over to him and said that his act didn't fool me. He turned on me like someone possessed. He went to strike me and I moved quickly out of his way. He came after me, screaming and shouting abuse at me. I will never forget the look in his eyes; he looked like he wanted to kill me. I threatened him with my brothers; everyone was looking at us. Jeffrey was holding Paddy back, trying to calm him down.

Eventually things did calm down and we were back at Paddy's parents' house. The next day, Sunday, I begged Jeffrey to leave Diggen. I knew

I couldn't take another minute in the company of this man who hated me so much. Jeffrey said we would be leaving after dinner; he didn't want Paddy's parents to know anything was wrong. They would have had to be deaf, dumb and blind not to notice that something was wrong. You could have cut the atmosphere with a knife.

I stayed in the bedroom all morning as I couldn't face anyone. Sam and Cathy played outside while Paddy and Jeffrey went for a walk. It was the longest morning of my entire life. The hands on the clock moved very slowly. I prayed to God that dinner time would come quickly. Finally it did and I was able to leave. I felt so relieved to be leaving that house in Diggen and Paddy. All I wanted was to get back to my home with my children and to be left in peace to get on with my life.

As the train pulled away from the station I cried. I had never felt the need to get away from a place so badly in all my life. Jeffrey was crying also. It was later that I realized his tears were for the man he loved and was leaving behind. It also became clear that Paddy wasn't mad. He was in love with a pathological liar, a married man with two children.

We arrived home and carried on as normal. We didn't say much about the weekend. Over the next few days Jeffrey seemed to be in better form. He said things were going to get better for us all. I told him I never wanted to see or hear of Paddy ever again and he assured me that that would never happen. I asked Jeffrey why he thought Paddy behaved in the way that he did. His reply was that he was insane. Same old answer.

On Tuesday morning I was gathering up clothes for washing and, when emptying Jeffrey's pockets, I found a letter. I opened it and began to read it. As I read on, it soon became clear that it was a love letter from Paddy to Jeffrey. I felt sick to the stomach. I had in my hands the truth about what really went on that weekend. It was right in front of me in black and white. Paddy was begging Jeffrey to leave me and his children. The letter went on to say how much he loved him and couldn't bear to be without him.

I fell back onto the bed and cried. I felt so hurt and betrayed. In my mind I was trying to make sense of it all. My head felt like it was going to explode. I could not accept this truth right before my eyes again, so I chose to believe what Jeffrey had told me, that Paddy was insane. I pulled myself together, telling myself that no way was I married to a man who was gay. I was from Belfast; we both were. This only happened to people living in Southeast, not here in a staunchly Nationalist area of Belfast. Crazy, what we tell ourselves when the truth is too hard to handle.

When Jeffrey came home from work he knew by the look on my face that something was wrong. He looked scared, as if he had something to hide, which of course he had. He sat down beside me and put his arm around me, asking me repeatedly what was wrong. I told him I had found a letter in his trouser pocket; he asked if I still had it. I told him I did. He asked me for the letter which I got and began reading it out to him. When I finished reading it he took hold of me and begged me not to believe a single word. He took hold of both my arms, looked me straight in the eye and said it was all a pack of lies.

He pleaded with me to believe him, asking me if I now believed him that Paddy was insane. He was extremely convincing; he said that he loved me and our children and would never do anything to hurt us. I just wasn't able to handle the truth which I knew deep down inside. I was fragile and vulnerable. I chose to deny the awful truth, that my marriage to this man was a lie. I had done what I'd always done throughout my life when faced with emotional and/or physical pain; deny it was happening. That's how I survived. I told him that I believed him and wanted to forget all about Paddy.

I carried on preparing the dinner. Later on that evening, at around seven, the phone rang. I answered and could hardly believe my ears. It was Paddy asking to speak to Jeffrey. In a calm voice I said no and asked him to leave us alone to get on with the rest of our lives. That was the last I heard of him.

My First Job in over Nine Years.

As the weeks and months went by I carried on with the pretence that everything was fine. Jeffrey, as far as I could tell, did the same. He became friendly with a woman he had met at work, Caitlyn, a very nice person. Through her I got to meet her sister Christine who worked as a cook supervisor at a primary school in Turfroad.

Christine got me a job in the kitchen as a dinner lady. I was very nervous and excited at the same time; it was my first job in nine years. It felt good being back in the workplace, meeting people and making friends. I enjoyed the work and took pride in my job as kitchen assistant. I worked part time at first as I needed to collect my children from school. After a while, I went full time. Beth, the head cook, went out on the sick for almost a year. Mary, the assistant cook, stepped into her shoes as head cook and I was doing the work that Mary did but without any extra pay or title. I didn't mind; I loved it.

We worked well together. She was a brilliant co-worker and such fun to be around. Mary taught me a lot about cooking and how to laugh at life. She loved fooling around and pulling pranks on her work colleagues. Her home was old-fashioned in its design, both inside and out. She had really unusual but beautiful furniture. She gave me an old-fashioned oil lamp which I kept for years until it broke. After a year or so Beth came back and I went back to my old job as kitchen assistant and continued working there for a further three years until I had to leave. I loved the job and I loved to cook. I was sad about leaving.

Jeffrey was suspended from his job at the children's home because of allegations of sexual abuse towards one of the boys in his care. Of course there was an investigation which took over a year, after which he was cleared of any wrongdoing.

At the time I couldn't believe what he was telling me. I refused to believe there was any truth in these allegations. Jeffrey was so distraught- we both were. We called up to see his brother Peter who worked in a home for boys on the Caveview Road. Jeffrey told Peter what had happened. Peter sat very calmly and asked Jeffrey had he abused this boy? Jeffrey swore to God that he hadn't laid a finger on the boy. I remember thinking at the time, how could his brother ask such a thing! I then began to wonder about it seriously but then I dismissed my thoughts about it. Jeffrey always talked about this boy. He seemed fond of him. He told me that this kid was very insecure and had a lot of emotional problems. He felt sorry for the boy.

After the investigations were over and Jeffery's name was cleared, he left his job which meant I couldn't return to mine because he would be claiming benefits. I was saddened by this turn of events. When I was working at the school it gave me a sense of worth, something I hadn't felt since my first job at the age of fifteen in the supermarket. I was forced to go back to housework and my four walls. All Jeffrey did all day was lie in bed until midday. It was difficult for me to get used to my new way of being.

Singing in public for the first time.

My brothers called to see me one night; they brought their guitars with them and we had a sing song which I enjoyed immensely. Alvin was recording the songs on an old tape recorder of mine. The next day, while I was cleaning the house, I listened to the recording. I couldn't believe that my voice sounded so good. I was amazed. I had always loved music and I believe it was my love of music that kept me sane, growing up in such a dysfunctional family.

The radio was my friend as a child. I loved Motown music artists like Stevie Wonder and Marvin Gaye. I loved their voices; they sang from their souls. They had lived it and it thrilled me to the bone when I heard them sing.

Alvin called in the day after and asked me for the tape. He wanted to bring it home to Crossblakes where he lived at that time with Elaine, his girlfriend, and Rose, Elaine's daughter.

A week or so later Alvin called in and asked me if I would like to form a duo with him. I was delighted and said yes. I asked him did he really think I was good enough? I wanted to know why he had asked me. He said that Elaine was listening to the recording and said I had a great voice and that we should get together.

I was so excited. I could hardly believe that my big brother, whom I looked up to, was asking me to join him in forming a duo. I had Elaine to thank for that; nobody else in my family thought I had talent, not even me. Alvin suggested we enter a talent competition. The first prize was £500. He thought it would be a good idea if we were to enter separately; that way we would have a better chance of winning. We needed money to buy a PA system, mikes etc to get started. I was so nervous.

The very first time I ever sang in public was on a night out with my mother. We went to a local pub. I think it was the first and last night we ever went out anywhere together. I remember ordering vodka and orange for her. She didn't drink at all. I did so because I was curious as to what it would be like to see her tipsy. Very wrong of me, I know. She had three drinks and didn't seem to notice that there was vodka in with the orange. It made her so relaxed. She seemed to be enjoying our evening out together.

My mother asked a member of the band if he would ask me up for a song and when my name was called I began shaking. I didn't want to go up. I felt sick with nerves but the crowd was cheering me on and my mother was urging me to sing, so I got to my feet and went to the stage. I sang a Neil Young song called 'Four Strong Winds'. It's an old country and western classic. The crowd loved it. I couldn't wait to return to my seat and get my feet back under the table. The crowd were still clapping and cheering for me to get back up and sing another song. People were coming over to me, asking me where I sang. When I told them that was my first time singing in public they said I had a voice of an angel and should not waste my talent; I could make a living out of it.

Alvin and I arrived at the Kilmore Social Club. It was the first night of the talent competition. He was on first; he sang one of his own songs and a cover version of Bruce Springsteen's 'The River'. I thought he was brilliant. Then it was my turn to get up and sing. I had been thrown in at the deep end and I was so nervous. I sang a Leonard

Cohen song called 'Bird on a Wire' and Jennifer Rush's 'The Power of Love'.

In retrospect, the Leonard Cohen song wasn't a good choice but it didn't seem to matter that much because my second choice brought the house down. People were coming over to me and telling me that I was the best singer they had ever heard. I felt so overwhelmed. Jeffrey's brother Joe came with me that first night to offer me support. He said he was very proud of me. For the first time in my life I felt good. I had found something I was good at.

I got through the heats and made it through to the semifinals. It was like a dream come true for me. This was something I thought would never happen to me. This was real and it felt so good.

Unfortunately, Alvin never made it to the semi-finals. On our way to the semi-finals my mother came out from her flat, down her path and shouted over to Alvin, "Good luck, son". Mother lived across the street from me at the time. I remember how much it hurt and wondered why she didn't wish the same for me. Still, I had Joe with me for support; he believed in me, and Alvin did too.

A friend of Tom Gracey's was a judge at the competition, a man called Tom Maginnis. He said he thought I had a lovely voice but I lacked confidence. He asked me to come up to the D.D. Club on Sunday night and sing a few songs until the finals. He suggested practising singing songs in front of people in the club- it would help me to overcome my nerves. I took his advice as he had been in the music business a lot longer than me. He was front man in the band Match, one of Tom Gracey's first bands.

For my first night in the D.D. Club Jeffrey came with me along with Joe and his wife. When I came back to my seat after singing, Jeffrey was laughing and told me that every time I hit a high note he would shake, believing I would mess it up. He was more of a hindrance than a support; thankfully, not everyone else shared his lack of belief in me.

On the night of the finals I was sitting with Joe, my sister-in-law Jolene, her sister Aine and Alvin. I was a bundle of nerves. Alvin suggested drinking an alcoholic drink rather than a soda water and lime to steady my nerves. I told him that I wanted to stay in control so I would be able to remember the words. When I came down from the stage people were clapping and telling me that they thought I sang brilliantly.

I felt so good. I didn't worry about the results but Alvin and Joe were anxiously waiting for the judges to decide who the winner would be. I was sitting next to the singer, whose name I forget, from the band The Freeworld. I thought he sang very well. He had a very powerful voice and I thought he was in with a good chance. Then the moment had arrived. The compere invited the person who had come fourth onto the stage first, third place went to the singer from the Freeworld, I came second and the woman who sang Country & Western songs came first. I was over the moon. I could hardly believe it; Rebecca Waites coming second in a talent competition. People were coming over to congratulate me, shaking my hand and telling me that they loved my voice; it was totally amazing, one of the best nights of my life.

I was able to sit and relax and enjoy this great feeling. I had never known what it was like to be this happy, in fact I don't believe I had ever felt that good about myself before. This was something that I really enjoyed. I had a talent that people loved and appreciated. I had to reach the age of twenty-eight before I realized I had got something special, something that I loved to do.

Alvin asked me to open the envelope to see how much I'd won. I counted out £75.00. I was very pleased with the money I'd got. Alvin went crazy and asked the guy who came third how much he'd won.

Both he and Alvin were not amused. They started complaining about the judges. They both thought we all had been ripped off. The singer who came third got up and left the club. He was furious.

The next day Alvin called in to see me. He was still fuming but I wasn't bothered at all. Alvin said that he would write a letter to the club to complain about it.

£265 pounds was paid out in total; my £75, £100 to the woman who came first and £50 to the singer from The Freeworld. The four runners up got £10 each.

Alvin wanted to know where the rest of it had gone. He assumed the remaining £235 had gone into the judges' pockets. I tried to calm Alvin down but he kept going on about the money, reminding me of the reason why we had entered the competition in the first place. The reality was I got £75 pounds and as that wasn't enough to buy the equipment we needed I decided to pay a telephone bill with the money. Neither one of us was working at the time so there was no way we could have got what we needed on hire purchase.

I was frustrated at Alvin's refusal to accept the fact that we weren't in a position to buy a PA. I felt that because of his constant moaning I was unable to enjoy the satisfaction that doing well had brought me. It was my money won fair and square; it was up to me to spend it whichever way I chose to. If either one of us had come first in the competition and won £500, things would have been different but that's not what happened.

He stormed out in a huff and returned a few days later.

We made a start on a few songs. Going over and over the same songs was driving me crazy. Alvin was always a perfectionist. I am one too, but he took it too far. At first Alvin was calling up to my house on a weekly basis and I would call at his house in Crossblakes to practise the songs but sadly this didn't last. He started missing weeks and not ringing to cancel. He was becoming very unreliable so my hopes of us becoming a duo ended before it had even started.

I became interested in learning to play the guitar. A friend of Jeffrey's, Don Ray's girlfriend, offered to give me a few lessons. It was just a few basic chords to get me started. I was very enthusiastic and eager to learn. I bought my very first guitar from a mail order catalogue and it didn't cost too much. The neck of the guitar was extremely wide which made playing difficult. Alvin gave me a few lessons as well but his teaching methods were harsh. It was like being back at school and being taught by a strict teacher who was only there for the money.

By the time I got my Yamaha guitar which my husband Jeffrey had bought from his brother Joe, my enthusiasm had gone. The old negative chatterbox inside my head began playing the same old tapes; I wasn't good enough so don't bother. Wrong thinking altogether. What's known in AA as 'stinking thinking'.

If I had believed enough in myself and practised I could have become good but that's how I was in those days.

I still lacked confidence in myself.

When I was twenty-nine I decided to make that year the best year of my life, before I reached the grand age of thirty. I wanted a better life for me and my two children. I needed a job. My heartfelt desire was to sing in a band so I bought the local paper and began to read the job section. I noticed straight away, female singer wanted for a five-piece band. I rang the number and spoke to a guy called Joe Hernery. He asked me had I any experience of singing with a band? I told him about winning the talent competition and he asked me to come over to the block leisure centre the following day for an audition.

He asked me to learn the words of three songs, 'Like a Virgin' by Madonna, Whitney Houston's hit record at the time, 'Saving all my love for you' and 'The Power of Love' by Jennifer Rush. My adrenaline was pumping like crazy; I knew I could sing these songs with ease but I was very nervous about singing in front of strangers. I took my daughter Cathy along with me for support even though she was only twelve at the time. We found our way to the room in which the auditions were being held; my heart was beating like a drum. I began to perspire; I managed to hide just how nervous I was. I didn't want to blow my chances; I wanted to succeed.

Joe introduced us to the rest of the band and we talked about the songs we liked and what songs they were working on. I sang the songs and was able to give Freddie, Jim's brother, the key in which I sang 'The Power of Love'. They were struggling to find the right key. I knew it was in the key of G because Alvin and I had gone over it so many times before the talent competition.

I didn't hang around long after the audition. Joe walked us out of the building and said he would ring to let me know in a day or two if I had got the job. I sang well and I felt I had made a good impression. I had a good feeling about it. Cathy and I made our way home. I was feeling confident and in a brilliant mood. I couldn't wait to tell Jeffrey all about the audition. I was so excited and when he didn't share my enthusiasm I felt deflated. I could tell he was shocked that I had actually gone for it.

The following day Joe rang me to offer me the job as singer of their band. I was ecstatic and ran up the stairs to tell Jeffrey my great news but he didn't share my joy; he just said "That's good."

I had to meet the guys the next day for a rehearsal. I didn't let Jeffrey's lack of support spoil my happiness. I had found people who saw me as something more than an object. People who wanted me in their band. They valued my talent and obviously believed in my ability or I wouldn't have been successful. I felt that I was now able to begin living for me and doing what I liked to do instead of just the role of a loveless/lonely wife. A door was opening up for me with new life experiences to explore. I was not going to let anyone take it away from me, especially Jeffrey.

Despite my new adventures and discovering ways to express myself through music, I could never quite get away from the nagging feelings just below the surface about the deep unhappiness I felt being in a loveless marriage.

Over the next few weeks the guys and I got together to practise songs. They would come up to my house or we would meet in the leisure centre. Whenever the guys were around, Jeffrey was as sweet as pie. He would make us tea or coffee whenever we needed it. He acted the perfect husband. I was relieved he didn't show his true colours in front of them.

For the first time ever, Jeffrey began to notice me, particularly in the bedroom. We didn't ever make love; we had sex. It never felt good, just cold and calculated. To be brutally honest, he was just relieving himself. I would never initiate having sex with him as I hated it with a passion.

After a while the band split from a five-piece to a three-piece, which I preferred. I had a bigger say as to the songs that I wanted to sing. I never felt like singing pop songs as I was more geared towards American folk, laid back and easy listening stuff. Jeffrey got us our first gig at Temps Restaurant in town where he worked as a waiter. His boss paid us £30 which was shit money. He said that if he liked us he would pay us more.

When we arrived at the restaurant it was packed with people dining out on a Sunday evening. I was as nervous as hell. Jack asked me, "Are you nervous?" He had sung in other bands, as had Joe. After the second song I began to relax more and enjoy the songs I was singing. We gelled well together. I sang lead vocals, Joe played bass and Jack played rhythm guitar. People clapped every song; there was a great atmosphere in the place. It was quite intimate which made it all the more enjoyable. While we were on our break a man came over to talk with me. He said he loved my voice and asked me if I would be interested in doing some cabaret in the Range Club on Sunday nights. He said he could guarantee my safety, and I would get paid £50 for singing four songs. I thanked him but turned down his offer. I believed he was sincere enough, but I wasn't going to take the risk. He gave me a phone number and asked me to think it over, and if I changed my mind to give him a call. He went on to say that he would collect me and personally see to it that I would come to no harm. He had tattoos all over his arms and wore dark glasses. I had a feeling that he was genuine enough, but in those dark days I wanted to play it safe. I told him I would give him a ring but I never did. I thought it better to stick to playing in my own area or in the town and stay out of Loyalists areas.

There were a lot sectarian murders at the time and I didn't want to become another murder victim. A school friend of mine's sister was murdered in the early 70s. She was in a taxi depot. She was waiting to get home but unfortunately, she came home in a box. That stuck in my memory. She worked in the same stitching factory as me when I was fifteen.

The next gig we played was at Mount Social Club in Belfast. The place was packed with civil servants of all ages. We went down a treat; the crowd loved us. I was having a ball and loving every minute of playing. What made it even better was getting paid for something which I thoroughly enjoyed doing.

We would usually rehearse on Wednesdays, and this particular Wednesday Joe called for me. We were going to Jack's house to practise. When we arrived, we discovered that Jack was still in bed. As always we would hammer at the door to get him up. He finally. Opened the door and let us in. After making us tea, he asked us if we fancied going to the pub for a drink. It was such a scorching day outside and I quite fancied the idea. The only time I got out socially was either playing or on occasions like this. I didn't want to turn his offer down. The pub was literally up the street from where Jack lived. We sat down and Jack asked me what I'd like to drink. I asked for a soda water and lime. Jack suggested I try a Guinness; I told him I would be ill if I drank Guinness. He said to trust him and give it a try. To my surprise I really enjoyed it.

I knew something wasn't quite right with me. I had a feeling that I was pregnant but I kept it to myself. I hadn't missed a period or anything like that, but somehow I just knew. I got my suspicions confirmed by my doctor a few weeks later.

The due date he gave for my third child was 16/04/87. It felt strange as it was nearly ten years since my last child was born. I was thrilled but nervous. Here we were, starting over again. It was a little crazy given that Jeffrey and I weren't what you would call happy. Even so, it did seem to bring us closer, even if it was only for a short time. I was thrilled with the news; it certainly took me by surprise.

I had found myself a life and I think that Jeffrey felt threatened by that. It made him insecure. After all, he liked to be the one in control. He was jealous of my voice and the guys in the band.

I once accompanied Jeffrey to a talent competition. He wanted to go to the pub not far from where we lived. He had taken a couple of vodkas before he was called to sing so as to settle his nerves.

He never made it to the heats. I felt sorry for him; I knew he was very disappointed. This was before I went for my audition, before Elaine noticing my voice, and before mother had asked for me to sing.

I was twenty-nine and pregnant with my third child. I decided to let the guys in the band know because I wanted to leave. When I told them my news they congratulated me and asked me not to quit just yet. They wanted to continue playing for the rest of the summer and early autumn but I had made up my mind. It somehow didn't feel right so I returned to being a boring housewife again. We kept in regular touch with each other and on one occasion Jack and I went out for the night. He told me of a band that played in Pin Street. The band were called Pageboys, they played there every Wednesday night. They were pretty tight and played some great music. Towards the end of the night a fight broke out and the guitarist, who was a protestant, got beaten up. Someone in the bar found out and started murder. They never played there again.

Jack was making plans to marry his fiancee who was the same age as me. He was 25, good looking and had a great personality. Joe always maintained that Jack had a thing for me. Maybe he did, we just got on so well together. My daughter Cathy didn't like him; she was twelve at the time, going on thirteen. I don't know if it was because her father and I didn't get on so well, or that she simply just didn't like him.

Jeffrey started work in the Northern Bar in Belfast. Yet another change of job. He never seemed to stick at the same job. Not long after he started, his boss, Jean, promoted him to manager. Things were beginning to go well for us financially. Not only did Jeffrey receive a wage increase, he continued to sign on at the Social Security as well. Of course that meant we were better off than we had ever been.

I was concerned about his safety; the pub was situated in the back streets of Belfast city centre. Three innocent Catholic men were murdered in the 70's and 80's while they sat drinking in the bar. I was delighted that Jeffrey had been given a position of responsibility and not having to worry about our finances with our third child on the way was great, but it didn't stop me worrying. I feared for his life. I wanted my husband around and I prayed to God he would be safe.

The owners had installed cameras outside the pub which enabled the bar staff to watch out for anything or anyone acting suspiciously coming into the premises. There was also a panic button behind the bar counter for the staff to use if they felt they were in any danger. This alerted the nearby police station.

Jeffrey tried to make a success of the pub by bringing in solo artists to play in the lounge upstairs on certain nights of the week, but it never really took off. The pub had its regulars who drank mainly during the day but people were afraid to drink in the pub at night. On the occasions when the lounge was in use I would go down the next day and clean up after the night before without getting paid. I wanted to help my husband to be successful at his new job in any way I could. I suggested making stew, soup and salad rolls to sell in the bar. I thought it might help. People get hungry when they drink, especially at lunch time. As it turned out, very few people wanted to eat at lunch time. The locals weren't interested in the food, only the alcohol.

Marvin employed an American female folk singer called Tina. She played on Saturday afternoons in the lounge upstairs. She had a really nice voice, very powerful. I introduced myself to her and told her I had played in a band for a short while myself. She asked if I would sing a few songs when she was on her break and I said I would. I enjoyed the session that afternoon.

Tina invited Jeffrey, the kids and me for dinner one evening. She lived in the Dori flats at the time with her husband who she treated abominably. I felt really sorry for the guy. She complained about me not liking garlic bread and about my children leaving their vegetables. I found her manner very abrupt. Once dinner was over she picked up her guitar and started singing. She sang a song which made the hairs on the back of my neck stand up; it was a song about one of the hunger strikers. I asked her for the words to the song and the chords which she gave me. She knew them off by heart.

We later found out that the couple had split up. People who knew her husband said that she had married him so that she would be able to live in this country legally. I never saw her much after that night; I found her too overpowering.

As Christmas was approaching, I thought it would be a good idea to buy some decorations for the bar. I wanted to create a festive atmosphere for the punters. I really enjoyed helping Jeffrey in whatever way I could. By the time I had finished, the bar was looking very Christmassy. Jeffrey told me that the money for the decorations had come out of his own pocket. He said his boss wasn't that bothered about decorating the bar. According to him, she told him, "If you want to decorate the bar that's up to you".

By this stage I was getting pretty big as I was five months pregnant. My baby kicked quite a lot which made me think I was having a boy. I was carrying a very active baby- the kicks actually hurt at times.

I didn't go down to the bar as much after Christmas because I felt uncomfortable with the extra weight I was carrying around. I felt like I was getting in the way so I spent more time at home.

My neighbours at the time, the Ramseys, who lived next door in an upstairs flat, were causing me a lot of stress. Jackie Ramsey's daughter Paula taunted my two children every time they went out to play. She would say things like "I hope your ma's kid is born a spastic".

She said some pretty mean things and would throw eggs at my daughter Cathy's head; I was coming to the end of my tether. One day, while Jeffrey's sister Bernadette was up visiting, I sent Cathy to the shop. When she came back from the shop she was in floods of tears with eggs dripping from her head. I lost it- that was the final straw. I had tried talking with Jackie about Paula's behaviour but to no avail. In a fit of anger I said I would put a stop to it. I was putting on my shoes, getting ready to confront Jackie. Bernadette tried to stop me from going to their flat but she didn't succeed. I was banging on their front door when Bernadette came up the path behind me. She tried to calm me down but I just continued banging on the door.

Finally Anne, Paula's older sister, opened the door and I asked to speak with their mother. I was told she was sleeping. I shouted that I didn't care a toss if she was sleeping or not and added, how nice it must be to be able to sleep while my children and I were being tortured by an out-of-control, undisciplined child. Anne just stood there and said nothing. Her mother stayed upstairs. I'm glad she did. Bernadette and I left as there was no point staying there. In those years the fighting that went on between my children and the children in the street was crazy.

I fought verbally with a lot of my neighbours in the street over my children. One day, after an argument with one of my neighbours, I came back into the house, sat down and for the first time started to question my part in all of it. I thought to myself, they (my neighbours) can't be all wrong- what was I contributing to all of this madness? For the first time in my life, I started to examine my part in what was happening and to take responsibility for the part that I played.

I remember telling my sister Amber about it and she said that she didn't think she would be able to admit if she were in the wrong. I was very glad the light went on in my head. It gave me a sense of peace. The fighting still went on between the kids but I distanced myself from it. I allowed my children to fight their own battles.

When I was a child I wouldn't have dared go into the house crying to my parents. Any time I got hit by anyone in the street I knew not to go to them. My father would have given us a slap and sent us back out to fight our own battles. That's how it was in our house. My father was a very violent and aggressive man. His way of solving a dispute was to use his fists.

On Easter Sunday I felt twinges of pain. I was able to handle it but as evening drew nearer the pains were coming more regularly and I wanted to get to hospital. Jeffrey and I got a black taxi down to the Maternity Hospital where I was examined by a doctor who said that I was in the early stages of labour and that we should go home and return in the morning.

We both returned home and when I tried to get some sleep the labour pains prevented me from doing so. I knew I needed to get back to the hospital. Jeffrey and I made our second trip to the hospital. We hadn't even been back in the house two hours when it was time to leave for a second time.

I was admitted to a ward, examined a second time and given two paracetamol for the pain, after which Jeffrey left to go home. The pain was getting really bad. I asked the nurse for an epidural but I was told that I was too far into my labour and that it wouldn't be safe for me or my baby. As I lay in the bed in agony a woman in the next bed to me began telling me how to breathe with each contraction. She was an angel; it would have been so much harder without her help.

At nine thirty in the morning the midwife arrived to take me to the labour room. Just as we were leaving the ward Jeffrey came in and within minutes we were in the labour suite. I got up from the chair, helped by the midwife who was leading me to a bed. I insisted I was having my baby in the birth chair. She then helped me to a Parker Knoll chair which I was very relieved about. I had had back labour with Cathy's and Sam's births and I wasn't about to repeat the same painful experience again. The sitting position is a more natural way in which to give birth, not lying on my back.

I was on the easy chair for just ten or fifteen minutes. A few minutes before I was about to give birth the midwife asked me to walk over to the birth chair but I told her that I couldn't make it. I was in a lot of pain and didn't believe I had the strength to walk the few yards. She and another nurse helped me over and I had just sat down on it when I was told to push. A few more pushes and my third child was born. Our second beautiful baby girl was born on Easter Monday 1987 at twenty-four minutes past one in the afternoon, weighing 7lb 10oz. The midwife immediately took her away from me. I asked her "What's wrong with my baby?" She assured me that I needn't be concerned my baby had swallowed her own excrement while in the birth canal and they needed to attend to this.

After they had cleaned my baby and taken care of her needs the midwife brought her over to me. As I held her in my arms I felt a mixture of emotions welling up inside me; joy, sadness and bewilderment. I was unable to stop crying. The midwife took her from me and asked me what was wrong. I was unable to answer her because I didn't know why I was feeling the way I was.

As I was leaving the labour suite I heard the midwife say to the ward sister, "Keep an eye on her". When I reached the ward with my baby in her cot beside me I felt so down, particularly when I looked over at my husband. In retrospect I believe it was probably because I was in so much pain emotionally. I knew deep in my heart we wouldn't last but dared not acknowledge it to myself. Again, my defence mechanism was to deny the truth.

At the time I was unable to comprehend why my feelings were all over the place. I was thrilled with my new baby daughter; she was perfect with a mass of blonde spiky hair. I tried to breast feed her but had to give up the idea because it was too painful. I was in a mess, both emotionally and physically. Her birth had taken a lot out of me and I hadn't slept in nearly 72 hours. That first night after she was born I couldn't sleep with the noise of all the babies crying. Of course my ex husband saw this as a wonderful opportunity to put me down by saying that I didn't care about our baby. He told me to snap out of it and start behaving like I cared. By this stage in my life I had got well used to stuffing down my feelings. I did what I had done as a child and carried on regardless.

I had said to the midwife right from the very start that I wanted to be discharged seventy-two hours after the birth of my baby. I was told that provided there were no complications I would be able to leave. On the second day after the birth I asked to speak to the ward sister about leaving hospital. She strongly advised me not to. Her reasons were because it had been such a long time since I had last given birth and also because the birth had taken a lot out of me.

Three days later, after the visitors had gone, I lay on my bed and fell into a deep sleep for about three hours. When I awoke the woman in the next bed told me that I had lain perfectly still the whole time and hadn't moved at all. I think that was the best sleep I've ever had in my life. I felt so much better afterwards. I ended up staying in hospital for five days. I still felt very down and I couldn't understand why no one from my family had come to visit me and my baby. Robyn, my sister, told me afterwards that Jeffrey told them I didn't want any of my family to visit me, which was a lie.

The day after we arrived home from hospital Jeffrey returned to work. I hardly saw him at all. I found it very difficult and tiring looking after my newborn baby as well as my two other children. Having to cope on my own, doing all the things I had done before like running a home and seeing to all their needs left no time for me.

Our daughter was christened in St Mill's Chapel when she was six weeks old. Jeffrey's sister and her husband were her godparents. Betty cried non stop; it was quite difficult for me as I didn't understand why. I tried everything I knew to help her. I took her to the doctors who found nothing wrong with her. It seemed worse every time I put her in her pram. She would cry from the minute I put her in and wouldn't stop. I was at breaking point. I got no help from Jeffrey or anyone else. He worked day and night which meant I had the night feeds to attend to as well. I was exhausted.

I knew there had to be something wrong with my baby for her to continually cry so I went back a second time to my doctor. This time she said Betty had thrush, which was the cause of her discomfort. The reason for this was that I had been given antibiotics in the last week of my pregnancy because of a urine infection. I was given medicine for her and within a week she settled down. She still didn't like being in her pram. I remember one morning I was taking her to the baby clinic. She cried most of the way and people were looking at me so I gave up and returned home.

Betty had received many presents from friends of ours, not to mention all the people Jeffrey worked with. Jean, Jeffrey's boss, had bought her an easy chair. The house was coming down with presents. Her big sister Cathy and brother Sam were over the moon with their new baby sister.

I was standing by the sink looking out of my kitchen window one morning when Jeffrey came up behind me; he stood there for a moment and told me that he was gay. I didn't look round at him, nor did he make any effort to face me. He continued on with the words "I'm sorry, I can't help it".

He had confirmed the truth about himself. I wasn't able to accept it. I walked past him without saying a word and made my way to the stairs. It had been just seven weeks since I had given birth to our third child. I wasn't able to cope with his confession. At that particular time I would have preferred that he continued to say that I was insane like the rest of my family. He stripped me of my defences; I felt physically sick and numb.

Neither one of us spoke another word. When he left for work later that afternoon and I knew for certain he was gone I asked a friend if she would mind Betty for me until Jeffrey got home from work that evening at six o'clock. I knew I needed to get away so I made plans to take Cathy and Sam with me to Castleville.

My head was in a total mess. When the bus stopped at St Peter's Chapel on the Force Road to collect other passengers I noticed a man staring at me. It took me a minute to realize that it was Johnny Watson with his wife. When we arrived in Castleville I found a B&B and booked the three of us in. A while later we went out to have a walk around the town. Most cafes were closed so we went into a restaurant to get a bite to eat. Cathy told me a man was staring at me. We had only been in the place less than an hour when I decided to leave.

We went to the seafront. I sat down on a bench while the kids went off to play nearby. I was sitting there in a trance. I felt so unhappy; I didn't know who to turn to or where to go. A woman came walking towards me. She stood in front of me and said "Things will get better - don't give up". I didn't engage in conversation with her. I felt she had a lot of compassion for me, the 'lonely stranger' sitting on a bench.

The next day I rang home. I hadn't enough money with me. Jeffrey answered the phone and asked me where we were and were we all right. I told him that I couldn't believe what he had said and I needed to get away. He begged me to return home and said he didn't mean what he had said; he told me everything was going to be all right. He said he would send our friend down on the next available bus to get us home. I felt relieved. He knew I wasn't ready to deal with the truth and when we returned home we continued on living the lie.

Jeffrey left the house one day to meet his boss Jean; he said she wanted to discuss matters with him regarding work. When he returned later that evening I knew there was something wrong. He looked like he had been crying. As soon as I put the kids to bed I came downstairs and found him sitting in the dining room with his head in his hands. I knelt down beside him and asked "What's wrong?" He seemed unable to stop crying. I was beside myself; I waited what seemed like an eternity, then he finally began to tell me why he was so upset.

Jeffrey thought he was going to a meeting with his boss Jean to discuss work business. He was to meet her at the Springhead Road but instead Jean's husband turned up. He drove up with another man who was sitting in the back of the car. Jeffrey was told to sit next to the man in the back. He began talking to Jeffrey about a robbery that had taken place in the bar a few days before. The car stopped and another man got in. Just as they were taking off, this man put a hood over Jeffrey's head.

They took him into a house and started to interrogate him about the robbery at the bar. He was still crying as he continued to tell me what had happened. They asked him where he got the money for all the presents for his new baby and why all of a sudden he seemed to be flush. Jeffrey said it lasted for hours. They kept the hood on his head the whole time.

They questioned him over and over about what happened on the day of the robbery when he handed over £1000. Jeffrey told them about a man coming into the bar holding a gun and demanding the takings. He was questioned about why he didn't press the panic button until after the robber had left the premises. He told his interrogators that he froze; he thought he was going to die. He was eventually released, and to my knowledge that was the end of it. They must have believed him, otherwise he would not have been able to tell the tale.

I could hardly believe my ears. I was horrified at the way in which my husband was treated. I felt so sorry for him and my immediate reaction was to go down to Jean's house to maintain my husband's innocence and to protest very strongly about the way in which they had abused him both physically and mentally. Jeffrey said that he wouldn't go back to work for them. I doubt if they wanted him back. I agreed with Jeffrey that he should stay away and take it easy for a while. I didn't want my husband to have anything more to do with these people. Later on that night, as I tried to sleep, I couldn't get the images out of my head of my husband being tied up with a hood over his head for hours.

The next day I phoned the bar and made an appointment to speak with Jean about what happened. She agreed to see me at seven o'clock that evening. Jeffrey wasn't that keen about going down but I persuaded him to come with me and he reluctantly agreed. I felt it was important for him to stand face to face with this woman and her husband. I wanted an explanation and an apology. How very naive of me to believe I would get either.

When we arrived Tim and Jean were behind the bar serving. It wasn't that busy. Tim came from behind the bar and escorted us out into the back hall of the pub. I asked him what was going on, why was my husband treated like a common thief? He looked me straight in the eye and said "Jeffrey knows fine well what's going on".

I began to get angry and told him that he was wrong to believe my husband was guilty. Jeffrey had worked very hard to build up his business. He spent every waking hour working in his pub.

Tim wasn't interested in anything I was saying; his mind was made up. He believed Jeffrey had robbed him- he didn't say it but he didn't have to. After I told Tim what I thought about the way he treated my husband, Jeffrey and I walked out of the bar. That was the last time I set foot in the place. The next day Jeffrey and I threw everything out that they had bought for Betty. We never talked about it again.

The end of my marriage
was drawing near.

In 1989 we were all invited to America for a two-week holiday. Jeffrey had somehow got involved with a man named Jeff from America. Jeff had sent tickets for the five of us to visit him and his family in New Jersey. He had stayed with us for a week in 1988 when he was over visiting. I was excited about going as I had always wanted to visit New York. I was still miserable in my marriage and I knew it wouldn't make our marriage better, but I didn't want to miss this opportunity to get out of Belfast for two weeks.

All we needed for the trip was spending money. I was out singing four to five nights a week but Jeffrey wasn't getting the money he used to when he worked in the Northern bar. I had saved money for clothes for the kids and had enough spending money for us all.

One night, after a gig in The Mount on the Force Road, a well-known Republican approached me. He came over and complimented me on my singing; he told me he was a friend of Christy Ivin's sister who would be able to help me in my music career. (Christy Ivin is a famous Irish musician). He asked me to make a tape so he could let Christy's sister listen to it. He then asked me if I would like to sing at the August Festival. I would have loved to but as luck would have it, the dates clashed with our holiday. I would have shared the same stage as Mary Black and other famous people.

My brother Alvin wasn't that keen for me to get involved with anyone from that background. His fear was that if I were to receive help from them, what would they want in return? Alvin was wary and quite suspicious when it came to getting offers from well-known Republicans.

The day finally arrived for us to go on our holiday to America; the kids were as excited as I was. Jeffrey had ordered a private taxi to take us to Diggen Airport. Betty was eighteen months old at the time. I bought her a beautiful sailor suit; she looked absolutely gorgeous in it. Cathy wore a similar outfit. Everyone turned their heads to look at Betty. One man asked if he could take a photo of her.

I enjoyed the journey; this was my second time on an aeroplane. The first time was when I took Cathy over to visit Marie, Jeffrey's sister-in-law in Southeast. I absolutely loved New York, the Empire State Building, St Patrick's Cathedral and the Twin Towers (tragically, no longer there). We went to the very top of the towers. I took photos of the people and traffic below. It was truly an amazing experience. I had to get to the Dakota building where John Lennon lived and, sadly, lost his life. I have a picture of me standing outside with Betty in my arms.

Mr and Mrs Smiley, Jeff's parents, let Jeffrey and me have their bedroom. I woke up the following morning having had really frightening nightmares. All I knew was that the dreams were about something bad and ugly- the images of the Devil terrified me. The feelings that were left with me when I woke the next morning were feelings of fear.

When Jeffrey and I arrived back home things just went from bad to worse between us. He started bringing home animals of every kind without asking me how I felt about it. When he went to work I was left to clean up their excrement and urine. He had over fifty pigeons and hired a guy to build a shed out the back to house them in. There were chickens, a rooster, birds in a cage inside the house as well as a cat and two dogs. He was living at the same address as me with our three children but he was making decisions that didn't include me and it was driving me insane. I felt invisible, taken for granted, unloved, uncared for and terribly alone.

My children and my love of music were the only good things in my life. Jeffrey would always find ways to start a fight with me just before a gig. It brought me down and my eyes would well up with tears. I knew I had to get myself together before leaving the house and somehow I did. When I returned home from the gig I was in top form. Music was my escape from the hell I was living in. He could never quite work out why I hadn't completely gone to pieces with his violent outbursts.

Music had always been my saving grace over the years. It kept me from going crazy. It was a way in which I could express myself and, in doing so, gave me some relief, something which helped me to carry on.

In 1989 Jeffrey told me he was going to America to work for a few months to earn some money. He and his sister Colette left in March that year. Jeffrey told me he'd be staying with an old friend of his. When Jeffrey left I had to claim social security to support myself and my three children. I registered myself as a one-parent family. Initially, I found it hard living on very little money. Easter was approaching and I needed to get my children sorted out with clothes and Easter eggs. I wasn't receiving any money from Jeffrey. All I had was the money I was getting from the social security. I found it difficult paying the bills and providing for my children.

I met a nun, Sister Mary, when I was at the mother and toddler group a few months before Jeffrey left for America. I was at my wits end so I decided to ask Sister Mary for help. I didn't really relish the idea but I had to do something. When Cathy was making her confirmation I met Sister Mary for the second time in St Augustin's Church. I didn't like her at first as I found her quite abrasive and bossy- that was my impression of her then. As it turned out, she became my rock; she was there for me always. I really don't believe I would be here today if it hadn't been for her sincere belief in me as a valuable and worthwhile human being.

Just before Betty's second birthday she had become very ill. She had a very high fever and was burning up. I rang for a doctor at around noon and we waited over two hours. I was beginning to panic. I didn't know what was wrong with her. All I knew was that she was very ill and needed a doctor. She just lay still in my arms, so helpless. I rang a second time and not long after that the doctor arrived. On examining her he told me that he suspected meningitis. He removed her clothing and told me to wash her down with a cool facecloth. Her temperature was 104/5, dangerously high. We waited for the ambulance to arrive and after about fifteen minutes we were on our way to the Hospital for Sick Children.

As soon as we arrived the doctor in the hospital examined her. There were nurses there too. When the doctor finished his examination he spoke with me and said he didn't feel that she had meningitis. I asked him was he sure? Was there a test which could rule this out completely? I needed to be reassured that my child was getting the best possible treatment. I didn't want anything to be overlooked. He agreed to carry out a test which involved putting a needle into her spine to drain out some fluid; this would let them know for certain if she had meningitis. In the meantime, I continued to wash her down with cold wet sponges from head to toe to try and bring her temperature down. There was a fan placed beside her bed too.

After what seemed like forever, the tests came back negative, thank God. My baby was sick but not critical. We didn't leave the hospital until after ten thirty that evening. Cathy and Sam were tired from the waiting and the worry over their little sister. I knew she'd be okay. Her temperature was coming down. The relief I felt from knowing that she was okay was like nothing I had ever felt before. She remained in hospital for three days after that. On the day of her release from hospital I bought her a beautiful outfit; a pink top and shorts to match with pink shoes. She was gorgeous despite the fact that she had lost weight and looked a little pale. We were so happy to have her back home. Sam and Cathy were great with her, watching over her and playing with her.

Easter had arrived and I managed to provide clothes and Easter eggs for all three of my children. Things weren't too bad. Jeffrey was still in America and I was enjoying my newly found freedom. There were times when I missed my husband or the idea of a loving husband being around. Cathy was an adolescent now with all the hassles which that can bring. She was no different from any other teenager, wanting to grow up too quickly, believing she knew everything and experimenting with make-up. Even so, I was managing fine.

In June of that year (1989) Jeffrey wrote me a letter to say that he was coming home. The kids were so excited that their dad would soon be home. I went out to the shop and bought a cake for his homecoming. I put up welcome home decorations and cleaned the house from top to bottom. I cut the grass in the front and back gardens too. I wanted everything to be perfect for my husband's return.

The children and I got a taxi into town. We waited for Jeffrey at the train station and as he stepped off the train and began walking towards us he seemed pleased to see us all. When we got home he had bought lovely presents for us all, including an American doll for Betty called Uncle Sam. The kids were thrilled to bits with their presents and with their dad being back.

It was a beautiful summer that year. A few days after Jeffrey got home he and I were sitting in our back garden, enjoying the sunshine. I remember saying to him, "I am going to make life so good for you that you'll never want to go away ever again". He answered me back saying, "I never want to be apart from you or the kids again".

We got on for a week but that was it. Jeffrey was offered a job at the Walton Bar in town and he seemed to earn a lot of money; he was never short of a few quid. He took it upon himself to start knocking down walls in our living room. Again, it never dawned on him to talk about his plans with me. Whatever notion came into his head, whether it was to do with knocking down walls, bringing in animals or people, it really didn't matter- Jeffrey got what Jeffrey wanted.

I remember sitting amongst the dust and rubble one evening, thinking to myself, this is insane. He wants to build a palace- what for? All I wanted was some sort of normality. Looking back years later I see that his behaviour was erratic; it was his way of dealing with the emptiness and loneliness he felt inside. Behaving this way gave him a sense of control, I guess.

When the work on the house was finished it looked really good. Neighbours and friends complimented us on our beautiful home. It didn't make me any happier; in fact I became unhappier, especially when Jeffrey started bringing home more and more animals.

He asked a neighbour of ours to build a fence and make a run for the chickens. I was finding living with this madness particularly difficult. Everywhere I went I was faced with animal shit and the awful smell. It has left me with a phobia. To this day I can't bear to be around pigeons. It's not that I don't like animals; I do. It was my husband's lack of consideration towards my needs. I had always been ignored, first as a child and then as an adult. It didn't make me feel good about myself; I felt I was invisible. I was slipping into deeper despair with no support from my family. I felt alone, abandoned, rejected and a failure. I felt trapped in a loveless marriage. I had three children, no career and no money of my own. I was fast approaching thirty-three and my life was passing me by. I needed a way out.

I was in a three-piece band, pretending that my life was normal and good. The only time I felt good about myself was when I was out singing. I felt so lonely inside- thank God I had my music and my children.

One day in June 1990 I asked Jeffrey if he would come out with me as I was feeling so lonely. I was very surprised when he said yes. That afternoon he rang me saying he'd met up with an old friend whom he hadn't seen for years and would I mind if he joined us? I was so desperate to get out I said "No, not at all". I needed and yearned for a night out. Jeffrey and his friend arrived home after six o'clock that evening; he introduced his friend who seemed like a very nice guy. After dinner, Jeffrey went upstairs to get ready. I sat in the living room and had a chat with his friend. While we were chatting, I felt that something wasn't right. My gut was tugging at me; I asked him how long he had known Jeffrey. He said that he had just got off the boat at three o'clock and went into the Walton Bar for a drink.

Jeffrey had served him his drink at the bar. The guy said they hit it off like they had known each other for years. Jeffrey invited him to stay at our house until he got sorted out with digs.

Alarm bells were ringing in my head- more lies. I carried on as if everything was okay. When Jeffrey had finished getting ready I went upstairs and got ready for the evening. We went to the Pags Bar in the centre of Belfast. I was finding it more and more difficult to keep up the pretence that everything was fine. Here I was, out for the evening with my husband and a complete stranger, feeling totally lost and angry. I knew I couldn't take any more. Deep down I knew my marriage was over and I needed it to end.

The following morning I woke knowing I didn't want to go on living this lie. I hadn't got the energy required to go on living like that any longer. What happened the previous evening was the straw that broke the camel's back. I had lived fifteen years of neglect, abuse and lies; I'd had enough. I asked Jeffrey to leave; I couldn't go on living with him. He became very angry but willing to end what we called a marriage. If I had been willing to turn a blind eye to his extramarital affairs I believe that maybe he would have stayed married to me. He went upstairs to pack a few of his belongings and while he was getting ready to leave I sat down to watch a football match on TV. Ireland were playing- it was the World Cup.

I have never had any interest in football but I needed a distraction, something else to think about. I couldn't bear to think about what was happening and it was my way of coping. My mother called over that morning. I never said anything to her about what was going on. Jeffrey came downstairs and was only too willing to let her know what was happening. My mother asked Jeffrey how he was and he replied in an angry voice, "She's asked me to leave my home saying that our marriage is over. Look at her, sitting there watching a football match. She doesn't give a shit".

My mother became angry with me, asking me what I thought I was doing. Had I lost my mind? What was I doing to my husband and children? She went on to say that I was throwing away a perfectly good husband and father. She didn't stop to think why someone would want to throw away something as perfect as she imagined I had. Again, Jeffrey had played a blinder; he always managed to get people on his side.

I told my mother that we were finished. I didn't say why as I was too ashamed, and besides, she wouldn't have understood. I knew I was on my own with this one and remained that way. I got no support from her whatsoever.

A big part of me was relieved that I had finally found the courage to get out of the living hell that I had been in for fifteen years. I was managing quite well on my own. The kids stayed with their father at the weekends. He was staying in his sister's flat. She lived on the Ash Road at the time. I was still singing and out playing gigs with Jerry and Chris. We were playing two to three nights a week. The money came in handy, not to mention the escape from the loneliness that I was feeling.

I made an effort to stay friends with Jeffrey as I felt it was better for the children. We went out to a concert one evening. Jeffrey's sister was waiting in the queue with a friend of hers; she ignored me. I found that upsetting as we had been good friends. I have no idea why she stopped talking to me. God knows what Jeffrey had told her. He left me standing waiting in the queue to go and have a chat with her. I never said anything to him about her behaviour towards me.

After a short while Jeffrey was able to buy a house in Park Street and that's when things between him and me took a turn for the worse. When he moved into his new house he asked me to borrow £500 from the Credit Union as the account was in my name. I was the only one who put money into the savings. He said that he would pay me back but he never did. He also took down all the wood panelling from the hall and landing from my home to use for his kitchen in Park Street. I stupidly agreed to this, leaving the walls in my hall and landing full of holes.

Jeffrey was buying the children more and more gold jewellery and the very latest sports gear, spoiling them rotten, especially Cathy. Cathy's behaviour was becoming more and more difficult for me to deal with. As well as being spoiled, she was now a teenager who got away with whatever she wanted, God help her. I spoke with Jeffrey about it, asking for his support but as usual it fell on deaf ears. Cathy was rebelling and I needed help. He told me he'd speak with her but of course he never did. Whenever I said no to her, he said yes. As a result, she learned very quickly how to manipulate us both. That didn't matter. Jeffrey wanted control. I was seen as the bad guy and he was the wonderful dad who allowed her to do whatever she wanted. At that time Cathy was fifteen, Sam thirteen and Betty three.

Jeffrey bought Cathy clothes, continually gave her money and allowed her to go to dances, staying out late. Whatever she wanted she got. I tried at first to compete with him. I couldn't bear the thought of losing her but I gave up in the end as there was no way I could keep up with him. I hadn't the money. I remember her wanting an electronic keyboard so I bought one for her but I never saw her use it. Trying to compete with him just to try and keep my children from leaving me became impossible- I couldn't do it. I knew it was wrong; I didn't want to teach her that she had to earn my love. I loved her because she was my daughter. I was hurting big time. I knew it was only a matter of time before she would leave, and before long that's what she did. I guess I would have done the same thing had I been in the same situation as her- what teenager wouldn't?

When Cathy left I found myself becoming very depressed. My head was all over the place. I was in Robyn's, my sister's flat one Saturday evening and she was having a drink. Mike, her husband, and his friend Sean were there. Sam and Betty were staying with their father that weekend and Cathy too, of course. I ended up seeing Sean that night (he left me home.) I was craving for love and affection and he was showing me plenty of interest. My marriage had ended only a couple of months when this happened but I didn't see anything wrong with moving on with my life. I was 33 years of age and starved of love and affection all of my life. Sean was very keen on me. He was ten years younger than me and good-looking. I was enjoying the attention. I wasn't as in to him as he was to me. I did enjoy his company though.

Going back to my ex husband was a big mistake.

That was until my mother poked her nose into my business; she was furious with me. She made my life hell. I was made to feel like I had committed a mortal sin. The pressure got to me. I missed my children so much; between that and the cold shoulder I was getting from my mother, I ended up taking Jeffrey back. Sean was heartbroken- he was beginning to fall for me. I broke his heart unintentionally.

On the day Jeffrey and my children were due to return home I got busy cleaning the house and getting things ready for them all. I was listening to Fleetwood Mac's Rumours album while hoovering the living room and my gut was screaming at me NO! I didn't want him back in my life- I wanted my children, a family but not him. I knew I couldn't have one without the other. I felt sadness at the thought of him coming back into my life.

Cathy didn't want us to get back together; her face said as much when she came into the house with her father. It was impossible for me, living with this man again. I could really see how Jeffrey was teaching our children to disrespect me. One Sunday afternoon after dinner I asked Cathy and her brother to wash the dinner dishes. I saw through the living room door Jeffrey giving me the fingers in front of my children. Cathy later told me about the times he would make faces behind my back when I had asked for the chores to be done. I couldn't stand it; I was so unhappy. It was a massive mistake getting back together. Our marriage ended again, only this time for good.

Things went back to where they were before as regards buying the kids whatever they wanted. Cathy was unhappy living with me and left in September 1991. Sam, my son, left in January 1992.

One day I received a phone call from Sam's teacher who told me that he had been causing trouble in school and was involved in starting fights with other boys. When Sam came home that day I questioned him about it. I told him that I had had a chat with his teacher who said that they were considering what to do about the situation. When I met Sam's teacher, he told me that he was being very disruptive in school- his behaviour was unacceptable so he was suspended for three days. When we got home I told Sam that he was grounded and wouldn't be allowed back out again until I said so. He began shouting at me and went upstairs, changed into his tracksuit and said he was leaving. He told me that I couldn't stop him. If he wanted to go and live with his father he could. He was right; I couldn't stop him. I tried and cried but he walked on out the door. I felt so utterly powerless; there was nothing I could do.

I rang his father and explained what had happened. I pleaded with him not to let Sam out. I rang my son the following day and he told me his father had taken him into town and bought him a coat that cost £45 and a pair of runners (shoes) that cost £70. He then went on to tell me that he was allowed out and that he didn't want to live with me. He wanted to stay with his father.

My heart was broken into a million pieces. My world had fallen apart. I never saw that coming. It was bad enough losing Cathy; now my precious son had left me too. I felt totally alone and wanted to die. I didn't see the point in going on- I was devastated and broken. I walked the streets in floods of tears, not caring who saw me. I ended up going to see my GP who sent me home to wait for an ambulance to take me to the hospital. My sister Robyn came with me. Cathy called in that day for her lunch. She didn't know what was going on and she cried when the ambulance arrived. I told her everything would be alright and sent her over to her granny's.

When I arrived at the hospital I was seen by a psychiatrist who was asking me lots of questions. I asked him, am I having a nervous breakdown? He said no, I was suffering from severe depression due to holding an awful lot in for too long.

When the doctor explained to me why I was in the state I was in it somehow made me feel a bit better. When Robyn and I left the hospital we called into Castle View to see Cathy. She had an after schools job at the time. I wanted to let her know that I was okay.

I was put on anti-depressants and referred to a local health centre to see a psychiatric nurse once a week. My first appointment with this man was very useful; he gave me therapeutic tools to use at home, one of which was writing a letter to my parents and my ex husband, stating how I felt. He advised me not to hold anything back and to be as frank as I liked, even to swear if that's what I needed to do. The main thing was to get all of my feelings out onto the paper and when I had finished writing the letter I was to burn it.

I remember that before I burnt the letter I read it to my brother Frederick who used to call in and see me from time to time. He said "Why don't you show the letter to them instead of burning it?" I explained that the purpose of writing the letter was that I could release my anger instead of keeping it inside where it was causing me pain. Besides, the people I was writing about would not have understood.

That was the beginning of my journey towards healing, my road to recovery and freedom from the emotional shackles that had lain heavy around my heart and soul for all those years. My dear friend Sister Anne gave me the phone number of a psychotherapist whose name was Samantha. She was an American woman who specialized in inner child work. I worked with her for almost a year. Anne gave me money for the sessions which were £15. Actually, Samantha charged £25 a session but she reduced my fees because I was unemployed. I will always be grateful for the support that I received from Sister Anne and Samantha. I wouldn't be here today writing this otherwise.

In therapy, Samantha worked on my inner child, the child who never felt loved, accepted or valued. She would try and bring me back to my infancy but I was unable to recall any memories. I had unconsciously shut memories out in order to protect myself. This was my defence mechanism- denial. While it had served me well in my earlier life, it was getting in the way of a healthy and happy adult life.

I was seeing Sean on and off. I knew he wasn't the man for me. He helped with the loneliness I felt inside but there was still a void, an emptiness deep inside me. The sessions with Samantha had enabled me to want to live rather than just survive. Cathy would come and stay with me, as did Sam. It was a game of going back and forth between their father and me. I was coping with things a lot better. I encouraged Cathy to go back to school. She was a bright spark with a lot of potential. I knew she'd do well in her exams. I wanted more for her than working in a cafe. I managed to persuade her to return to school and she did, thankfully. She did extremely well, achieving two A's, two B's and two C's. I was so proud of her.

I was listening to the radio one day when I heard a German producer being interviewed about a play he was putting on in a theatre in Belfast. The play was called 'A Symphony on Luther.' The production company was auditioning for people the following day. I brought Cathy along because I believed she would do well as she is artistic and talented. The producer obviously saw that for himself. She was successful in getting a part in the production. I went along to see her on the Friday night, the 22nd of June; again, I was so proud of her. She was fantastic. I remember calling into my brother Alvin's flat after the audition; he was so proud of her too.

I got myself back into music and started an English and computers class in Lower Don Street, in the Centre for the Unemployed. I felt in control of my life. I had watched Cathy study and I wanted an education for myself. I remember the first day, the nervousness I felt entering the building, meeting new people and being back in an environment that had been hostile to me as a child.

My life was beginning to improve. I was trying to make something of myself and starting to feel good- until the day my brother Frederick died.

Cathy and I were at home when the phone rang; it was Patricia's mum, Marie. (Patricia was Frederick's wife). She asked me to call over to my mother's flat. I knew something was wrong. I asked Cathy if she would like to come over with me and she did. When we arrived at the flat Marie opened the front door to let us in. She walked up the stairs, Cathy and I following behind her. My mother was standing at the top of her landing.

It was then that we were told by Marie that my brother Frederick was dead. I could hardly believe what she was saying. My mother walked into my nephew's bedroom, not saying a word. We were all in a state of shock. We went into my nephew's room behind my mother. She sat on the bed looking so pale and sobbing; her eyes were red from crying. I put my arms around her to comfort her; she was in a daze. I asked my mother would it be okay for me to hold Frederick's wake at my house but she didn't say anything. I asked again if that was okay. She looked at me and nodded her head to signal yes.

Cathy later remarked that she thought her granny should be the one to hold Frederick's wake. We went back over to the house, both of us crying; we were in a terrible state. My next door neighbour was coming up the path at the time and he asked us was everything alright. Cathy said "My uncle Frederick is dead". He was shocked at the news and offered his condolences.

That was Thursday 25/11/93, the day my brother died. It was also my son's fifteenth birthday. That same day I learned that my son's girlfriend was pregnant. She was seventeen at the time. I don't think the news hit me until much later.

The arrangements were made; my brother's remains would come to my house. I felt the wake would be better in my home as my mother was too overcome with grief. The following morning I was sitting on my own waiting for my brother's coffin to arrive. As I sat there I decided to put on REM's song 'Everybody Hurts'. I was sobbing my heart out. I could hardly bear the intensity of my feelings about the tragic loss of my brother at the age of thirty-eight, just two days before his thirty-ninth birthday. It truly was too hard to take in.

A friend of mine called to the back door. He said the hearse was outside. He walked into the living room with me and opened the front door to let the undertakers in. We needed to go back into the kitchen to allow them to get things prepared for the grieving family.

My mother and father did nothing to help me, emotionally or otherwise. The people who called at the wake brought in sandwiches and other food which I was grateful for. The undertakers knew my brother, as did a lot of people. He was well known and well liked. Patricia asked them what the cause of death was. They told us he had died of pneumonia. She told me that when she found his dead body early on Thursday morning there was an empty medication bottle beside him and that he had been screaming all through the night.

She thought he had taken an overdose. She told me they weren't on speaking terms. She had slept in the boys' room and put a pillow over her ears to help drown out the noise he was making in their bedroom. She said the noise was driving her crazy.

That was the beginning of yet more loss to come. Patricia, Frederick's wife, and my mother were at war with each other. Not long after his funeral each blamed the other for his death. My sisters, my father and Alvin were all of the same opinion. It was crazy and I wouldn't allow myself to get dragged into their madness. I felt sorry for Patricia; I knew that she loved my brother and had put up with a lot. If they weren't on speaking terms before Frederick died, I didn't see that that was anybody's business.

My mother and Patricia were as bad as each other. They were grieving the loss of a son and a husband and projected their anger and guilt onto each other. There was a stupid battle of words with insults hurled at each other because of Frederick's headstone. The words that were written on it didn't mention Patricia or their two sons. It wasn't intentional; my father paid for the headstone after much pressure from my mother and everyone was grieving. I know my father didn't set out to hurt anyone.

At Frederick's inquest, I supported Patricia. Her sister was there with her too. I wanted her to know that I didn't hold her responsible for my brother's death. We learned that the cause of death was pneumonia caused by the effects of dihydrocodeine, a drug that was given to him by his GP for pain relief. He had fallen forty feet some years before and was hospitalized for quite a while afterwards. He was lucky to be alive. He needed to use a walking stick afterwards, bless him. No one fully appreciated until the day of his inquest the agonizing pain he had lived with.

My supporting Patricia didn't go down too well with my family, especially my mother, who didn't attend the inquest or go to the graveyard. I think she must have felt that I had betrayed her. I just didn't agree with the way my family felt towards Frederick's wife, putting the blame for his death solely on her. The feud went on for over two years. Things got very nasty. As I mentioned before, Patricia and my mother were at loggerheads. Their behaviour was irrational and unhealthy; they both would have needed counselling.

I returned to the Unemployed Centre three weeks after Frederick's funeral and I found it so difficult to get back into it. I sat in the tearoom for a lot of the time. I really tried to get my life back on track but it wasn't easy.

My soulmate coming into
my life for the first time.

Six months after Frederick's death a guy from my not so distant past rang me. We had met each other at a club on the Orangeville Road. When we arrived at the club with our gear we noticed Ken's band were already on stage with their gear set up. We were double booked. We chatted with the guys in the band for a short while and they seemed really nice. They played the blues, completely different from the music we did. We didn't mind as they had their gear already set up. If fact, I was quite relieved. I fancied having a listen to them play as I love blues music. I was quite happy to let other people entertain me for a change. They asked us if we would like to play a few songs after their break. We played about four songs and after we had finished we said our goodbyes. That was that until the following week.

When we arrived back at the club the following week the barman handed me a letter from Ken, the bass player from the blues band. He had left it for him to give to us on our return the following Saturday. I opened it and read what was written in the letter. Ken was complimenting us and said he thought we were very good, especially the vocalist. (What a charmer!) The letter continued, if we knew of any gigs in and around Belfast to give him a ring. He left details of where he could be contacted. Chris, my bass player, was suspicious and he dismissed the letter. He thought that they were maybe trying to come in on our turf.

As I mentioned earlier, I hadn't seen or heard of Ken for about a year after our first meeting. I rang him about six months after we first met. I was reading an ad in the Belfast Telegraph about a blues band based in Whiteshore looking for a vocalist. I automatically assumed it was his band but he told me it wasn't. I wonder, was it just a coincidence, or fate? He let me know that he had company of the female kind with him that evening. I assured him I was thinking about work and nothing else. We politely said our goodbyes and that was it as far as I was concerned.

I was out for the evening with my fellow students from the centre for the unemployed. They had organized a party for us all to celebrate achieving our City & Guilds and they presented us with our certificates. It was a great achievement for me. We had a great night out and I managed to get through it, despite everything. My tutor gave me very positive feedback about my essays. It felt like she was talking about someone else as my self-esteem was still so low at the time. I found it hard to accept that she found me interesting and intelligent. My experiences at school and at home had been so negative. The tapes from the past were still playing in my head, replaying the same old messages: I wasn't good enough and I was stupid.

When I arrived home that evening my father told me that Ken had rung. The following day he rang again. We chatted for a while and then he asked me out on a date- I said yes. We arranged to meet on Saturday 28/05/04 at eight o'clock in Belfast city centre.

Betty had made her first communion earlier that day. She was beautiful- a picture. She looked like an angel in her lovely dress. Betty and I walked down to the chapel together. On our way there, as we were walking through Eden Drive, Sean stopped us and handed Betty a card with money in it.

When we arrived at the chapel Sam met us with his then girlfriend, the mother of my first grandchild Alannah. She was born on 13/05/94. I went down to visit my precious granddaughter on the day of her birth. My sister Robyn came too. I could hardly believe that I was now a grandmother. Alannah was absolutely beautiful with blonde hair and thankfully perfect in every way. It was such a delight when I held her in my arms for the first time.

After the ceremony in the chapel, Betty went to stay with her father. I returned home alone and was having second thoughts about going to meet Ken. In the end I decided to go. I wore a long dress with a light jacket and sandals, the same clothes I had worn earlier in the day. I was so nervous about meeting him and as I walked down Park Street I wondered about turning back but I ignored the voice in my head and kept on walking. As I turned the corner, there he was standing there, waiting on me. He looked fine. I asked him had he put weight on since I last saw him. He looked bigger than I remembered. We talked about where we should go. Ken wanted to take me for a pizza but I told him that I didn't like pizza. So we walked around to the front of the City Hall and went into a pub nearby. I learned that he was from Hillhead in England, the eldest of three children and that his father was deceased. He had attended public school and had a degree in languages. We left after a few drinks and went round to the D's Head. I was able to relax after I had had a few pints of beer. There was a band playing who were pretty good- the lead singer walked up to me from the stage and began singing to me. Ken didn't know what to make of it.

We left the pub when the music ended. On our way round to get a taxi home, he asked me could he get a hug. I said yes, so there we were, hugging each other in the middle of the street. I had asked my friend Maggie earlier that day if Ken could stay in her house as I was scared to let him stay in mine. She thought I was crazy for asking. As it turned out I felt that I was able to trust him and let him stay at mine. He slept in Betty's room.

The following morning I got up, came downstairs and walked into the living room where Ken was already sitting. We said hello to each other. I asked him if he had slept well and would he like some breakfast. He said yes and thanked me. We chatted while listening to music. He asked me if I would like to go out with him on Tuesday to Downstown as he had taken a few days off work. I replied yes, I'd like that very much. After we had finished eating I offered to walk with him to the front of the road, a short distance from my house, so he could get a taxi into town. When a black taxi stopped he got in and as the taxi drove off he waved goodbye.

I was on my own over the weekend. My youngest daughter Betty was staying with her father and returning home to me on early Tuesday evening. As I waited on Tuesday morning for Ken I felt nervous and excited. I was ready when he knocked on the door so off we went to Downstown. We had a really lovely day. The sun was shining. I had butterflies in my stomach with excitement. We stopped and had a walk around before going for lunch. I'd never been to this part of Co Down before. I loved it. We later sat and had an ice cream while looking out at the water. I felt on top of the world that day. Ken was the perfect gentleman with lovely manners, a quiet, gentle soul. I just knew he was the one.

He drove me home in time for me to be there when Betty came home. He left me to the door and we kissed each other goodbye until we saw each other the following morning. He had suggested taking Betty and me out for the day. He chose the American Folk Museum believing it would be a good place to bring a seven-year-old. I was excited telling Betty that I had met a lovely man who would be taking us both out for the day. She didn't seem that interested. The following morning Betty and I were sitting ready when Ken knocked on the front door. I opened it, invited him in and introduced them to each other.

As we set off I was aware that Betty didn't seem that happy. When we arrived at the museum Betty was walking really slowly and not really co-operating that much with me. I don't think Betty liked the fact that there was another person in my life who would be spending time with me when she had been so used to it just being us two. It was obvious she didn't seem to like Ken. I hadn't had a partner since her father and I split up. I'd had a couple of dates....nothing serious. The guy Sean I mentioned earlier had been on the scene. I was lonely, that was it.

The story continues.

A lot has happened in my life since May 1994, both good and bad. My relationship with Ken continued on and off for eleven years. At that point I decided to stop writing because I felt it was too much for me. That was then, this is February 2016 and I have resumed writing because there is so much more. I have a need to get it all down on paper. I need to finish what I started.....my life story. During our time together Ken and I were pretty messed up as a couple, emotionally and spiritually. Speaking for myself here, mentally too. After my marriage break-up and before Frederick died, I entered into psychotherapy for a year, thanks to a nun, Sister Anne, whom I had met shortly after my ex husband took himself off to America for six months. I used to see her on a weekly basis and talk about my messed up family and loveless, abusive marriage.

She was my only support at that time in my life. I was very much on my own. I am truly grateful for everything she did for me and Betty. I am the only one in my family who entered into therapy and I thank God that I did.

My dysfunctional family were unfortunately causing problems that were getting in the way of the relationship between me and Ken right from the beginning. My ex husband was also making things extremely difficult. After my brother's death, the relationship between my mother and sister-in-law went from being very cordial to catastrophic within a very short time, as I've stated earlier.

My younger sister Robyn had managed to get our sister-in- law a flat in Jamestown as she and our two nephews were living in Crossblakes at the time of Frederick's death. This was of course before the bitter fighting that occurred between them. My sister-in-law now lives in a lovely three- bedroom house, thanks to my sister Robyn. She still lives there now. She managed to get an exchange from her two- bedroom flat.

I was very much in love with Ken almost from the beginning. He, on the other hand, took a bit longer. He had quite a few relationships before me. In fact, when I rang him in 1992 about an ad in the Belfast Telegraph, he was in the company of one of his then girlfriends. Her first name was the same as mine and she came from Jamestown too.

Ken didn't have any children. That was something he decided long before he met me. I didn't want any more either. We talked about sterilisation and he opted to have a vasectomy as it's a lot easier on a man than it is for a woman. What a man! We had been together less than a year when he made the decision. It just so happened that he had only been discharged from hospital a day or so when his mum Glenda came to visit him in Whiteshore.

After leaving the Centre for the Unemployed I went for an interview at the Women's Centre. I was so nervous. Ken had faith in me and encouraged me to go for it. It was a voluntary post and I needed to start somewhere. I needn't have worried. I passed the interview with flying colours.

Ken's mum was coming over on another visit and this time I was getting to meet her. Ken was on his way up to my house with his mum. I was so nervous. No need really, as she was such a sweet, kind, lovely woman. My mother and father called over to meet her. They got on okay and Glenda seemed to hit it off with my father because his sense of wit seemed to appeal to her. After my parents left, Glenda asked me if my mother was house proud. I wondered why she asked. When I was telling Glenda about starting work, my mother asked "Who's going to do the housework if you're going to work?" I replied jokingly, "Ken will".

Glenda was a very intelligent woman who cared more about a woman's career and place in this world. Two complete opposites. My mother most definitely had OCD, (Obsessive Compulsive Disorder). It was her way of coping with her past and an alcoholic, abusive husband.

At the age of 47 I decided that I wanted to become a counsellor. Actually, it was a lot earlier than that. When Ken and I were together he always encouraged me to get back to studying. He really did believe in me, as did my art teacher in secondary school and my class tutors at the Centre for the Unemployed. The problem was that I didn't.

I enjoyed working in the centre at the beginning. I thought I would find support from the other women who worked there. Sadly, all I experienced was that the women who run the place (the ones at the top) didn't like men that much. So much so, the postman wasn't allowed in the building. He had to leave the mail in the hallway of the building. Fanatical feminism in my opinion- not them all, of course.

While working at the Women's Centre an opportunity came about that I took full advantage of. The Shanwest Women's Centre were running a counselling course for beginners. It ran one day a week. I was accepted and was over the moon. I earned myself credits for passing the course. That was the beginning for me. I had heard about another course being run by Belfast Tech, entitled Certificate in Counselling. The entry requirements for the course were three O levels, as they used to be called then. They are now known as GCSE. Failing that, you had the opportunity to write a letter outlining your reasons why you wanted to do the course. As I hadn't any of the qualifications they were asking for (I left school at the age of thirteen) I wrote a letter explaining why getting on this course was so important to me and handed the letter to the class tutor. To my amazement and absolute delight, I was accepted onto the course. I attended for three weeks but dropped out because I didn't believe I was good enough.

I did go to see my tutor after class on the fourth week and handed in my assignment. I nervously waited for the tutor's feedback and again, to my astonishment, he looked at me and said it was very good. He continued, "It's a pity you missed last week's class as it was all about self-esteem". He asked if I was coming back. I answered yes because I really wanted to but sadly didn't.

It just wasn't enough for me, Ken assuring me I had nothing to worry about, or my tutors believing in me. I didn't believe in me. The first week when the class began, we all had to introduce ourselves and say a little about what we did for a living. Thankfully, I was at the far end of the circle before I had to speak. I was absolutely petrified as I listened to each one of them saying they were teachers or from a social work background plus various other professional backgrounds. There I was, no qualifications, terrified to open my mouth and saying I worked as a volunteer in a women's centre.

I was in no way ready to start this counselling course. I was in a total mess emotionally. I needed to do more work on myself. My self-esteem and self worth were in tatters. So I left and went back to personal therapy which took fourteen more years.

I ended up leaving the office in the women's centre. I hated the politics and the bitchiness of some of the women. Plus I was bored stupid answering the phones and not much else. There was a creche at the back of the office where women who worked in the office and other women in the surrounding area would leave their children to be looked after while they worked.

I ended up child minding for a year. I absolutely hated it. It was only for a year (thank God). At that time there was what was known as the ACE Scheme. If you were unemployed for a while you were given the opportunity to join this scheme which meant you were able to work legitimately for just one year. It was utterly useless. After your year was up, you were back on benefits and got messed about for a short while before you got sorted out regarding your weekly payments and housing benefits.

I still had the music which I loved and believe me, it kept me sane. I loved Black Clouds, my three-piece band. I loved being on stage and singing. It was a wonderful escape and I felt happy and free. I got a lot of pleasure from most of the songs I sang. Of course, we had to please the audience which meant singing songs I didn't like.

My bass player at the time said to me "I don't understand because you sing those songs so well". Singing songs I didn't particularly like didn't mean that I didn't put any effort into singing them. It was just a lot easier singing songs that meant something to me. It was my job and so much more. I found it extremely therapeutic, my natural high and I loved it.

Black Clouds split up. I'm not really sure why. Maybe we just needed a change. There were no fallouts or any bad feeling.

In 1995, my guitarist with Black Clouds, James, and Ken who became our new bass player, and I decided to put a five-piece band together. We put an ad in the local paper. A guy from the same street I grew up in, who loved to watch and listen to my two older brothers play, called up to my house and began playing. We all agreed he would become the fourth member. I loved his sense of humour too. He and I got on really well. He was a fine musician.

He played a few gigs with another guy as a two-piece. All we needed now was a drummer. We put another ad in the paper and found ourselves a drummer. He was a good deal younger than us but that didn't matter as he played well enough. We got gigs in and around Belfast. I wasn't that keen on the five-piece because of the song choices. My voice was more suited to ballads, softer American and Irish folk songs. Similar to the stuff Rebecca & Co played when I was in the two-piece. I have always enjoyed the sweet beautiful voices of Joni Mitchell, Joan Baez, and Mary Black etc...

We had such a great time playing. None of us liked to practise that much. We certainly weren't doing it for the money. It was mostly because we loved the music and the craic (meaning good fun) was brilliant. We called ourselves 'Nobody's Business'. We stayed together for a year or so. Our young drummer, who was fond of the booze, had to go. Pity, he was such a nice kid and had the potential to do well. We relied on session drummers when we needed one.

In the summer of 1995, we made a recording in a little studio in Belfast. We played five songs and got them down on tape. The idea was that we would give copies to various people in the hope of getting more work. Later on, I got my tape recordings transferred onto CD format. I still have it in my music collection.

At that time I was fighting a custody battle for my youngest daughter Betty. I had applied for a divorce in 1995 and because she was only nine years old at the time, Social Services got involved to find out if she wanted to continue living with me or live permanently with him. (Her father). He had done such a good job conditioning her as well as my two older children. As they were older at the time, they weren't questioned by Social Services. My oldest daughter was living in Southeast at the time and my son had his own place.

Betty told the social worker who spoke with her that she wanted to live with her father. I have to say at this point that the social worker seemed to be very much on my ex husband's side for reasons unbeknown to me. She interviewed Betty on a number of occasions and took her out for meals to Donald's a couple of times.

I questioned the social worker about my daughter's decision to live with her father and his partner. I tried to explain to her that my children had been bought. She answered me by saying "It's my job to listen to what Betty is saying to me. Besides, I can't be seen to show any prejudice against your ex husband and his partner because they are gay".

What she didn't seem to understand, or for that matter want to, was the fact that my ex had manipulated Betty into staying with him in his usual way, lavishing her with gifts, animals, or whatever else Betty wanted.

Apparently at that time (1995) this was the first case in Northern Ireland where a gay father and his partner had fought through the courts for custody. As I've previously stated, the social worker involved in this case was very much on the side of my ex husband. I'm not sure why, although I did have my suspicions. All I knew was that she made it abundantly clear that she had no interest in my truth or what this whole saga was doing to me and my relationship with my child. She wasn't interested in my daughter's welfare. I knew I would lose, even before it got to court. I didn't stand a chance. There was no one fighting my corner. My ex-husband, his partner and their defence team made damn sure I would lose.

I was right. I lost custody of Betty. I spoke the truth to the social worker, my solicitor (who wasn't that great or at least she wasn't as good as his solicitor) and the judge and lost. My ex husband and his criminal partner, on the other hand, played the social worker and the judicial system like a fiddle and won. Thankfully, Ken was there supporting me throughout, otherwise I don't know what I would have done. Sister Anne was there for me to a certain degree. Actually, it was she who recommended the solicitor who represented me. In hindsight, I would have been better off with someone else.

Once Jeffrey had got what he wanted he showed his true colours. He wasn't interested in my daughter. He needed her to give him respectability, to say to all who knew him, including my mother, "I'm such a loving and devoted father". He fooled everyone.

As it turned out, I actually got to see more of her. Once he got what he wanted, and very shortly afterwards, he and his partner took themselves off to Africa for three weeks. I had her all to myself during that time. The poor wee darling must have wondered why he had taken off without her. When he returned, Betty went back with him. I had her for part of the week and he had her from Friday until Tuesday. I managed to make the most of my time when she was with him and really tried to make it good for Betty while she was with me. It was very difficult, though. I can only imagine the poison he brainwashed her with regarding my mothering abilities and how messed up I was because of my childhood.

He used my loveless childhood against me and God only knows what else to convince my three children that I was no good.

Yes, of course I made mistakes. My head wasn't in a good place. He knew that and made the most of that fact. I had no support ever from either one of my parents or my siblings. Betty's head wasn't in a great place either. Also, unbeknown to her, she was used like a pawn. She wasn't given or shown any love from this man who called himself a father.

I continued with Nobody's Business, my band. It really was my saving grace. Music had always kept me sane. That was something my ex husband could never work out. He always chose his moment to pick a fight with me. Of course it was always in front of our children as it was when I lived at home. My father fought with my mother in front of us mostly all of the time.

I would be in tears after getting myself ready to go out and sing because of the emotional abuse he fired at me. I would walk out, tears dried, and get into the car, the other two guys in the band not knowing what had just happened. When I arrived home from the gig with a huge smile on my face he always had a look of bewilderment on his face. His antics had failed. I was able to put all the abuse, painful memories and all the other shit behind me. Being on stage gave me the opportunity to escape into a world where I could switch off from it all. It gave me my freedom.

I moved in with Ken in the summer of 1996 shortly after my ex-husband and his lover walked into my home uninvited and unexpectedly. It was a beautiful sunny day up until that point. Betty, my youngest child, had come in through the front door. She, so I thought, was dropped off by her father. She didn't stay long. She said she wanted to go over and see her granny who lived just across the street from me.

She hadn't been away long when the next thing I knew my ex husband and his lover opened my front door walked into the living room where I had been sitting and stood in front of me. I was shocked and horrified. I jumped up from my chair and told them both to get the hell out of my house. That's when my ex husband grabbed me by the hair, trailed me out into the hall and threw me on the stairs. He had both his hands around my neck. He was shouting in my face, "You bastard, this is my fucking house, you bitch". I was terrified. I thought he was going to kill me. I managed to knee him hard in the balls. He stumbled as I pushed past him and ran as fast as I could out of the front door across the street in a terrible state, tears streaming down my face. I didn't stop until I reached the top of the stairs of my mother's flat. She was standing at the top of the stairs with a strange look on her face. I said "Call the police, he's trying to kill me". I had no sooner spoken the words when my ex husband was behind me and as he pushed me into her kitchen she calmly walked into her living room. I learned later that my ex husband's partner was in her living room.

Again, Jeffrey had his hands around my neck, trying to strangle me for a second time. Once again I kneed him really hard and luckily got away a second time. I bolted down those stairs so fast, running for my life. My top was ripped during the struggle and I must have looked like a banshee with my hair everywhere. I ran over to my next door neighbour's flat and banged on his door as hard as I could. He opened it and must have thought, what the hell is going on here? I asked him to please let me in. He took me in and as he did, my ex husband was standing there. My neighbour told him to take himself off, which he did. Mick, my neighbour, made me a cup of tea with lots of sugar in it. He sat with me, asking what had happened. I think he was shocked at my mother's actions. He saved my life that day.

I was shaking and in bits. I wanted back into my home. I didn't want to be sitting in my neighbour's flat. When Mick checked that it was safe for me to go back he walked with me into the house and said to keep the doors locked until the police arrived. I was on my own, feeling absolutely petrified. I rang Robyn, my sister, and told her what had happened. It didn't take long for the police to get there. When they arrived at my door I gave them a statement. Two of them called over to get a statement from my mother. On their return, one officer said to me "I take it you don't have a good relationship with your mother?" I said "Please don't tell me she's not going to give you a statement?" He shook his head and said "No, that's right". When they left, my sister Robyn called in to see me. I rang Ken and told him what had happened. He was in total shock, too. After our phone call Robyn came with me to the hospital.

When I arrived at the hospital I hadn't too long to wait. I was examined by a lady doctor who asked how I got the bruising to my neck and both of my arms. Robyn explained what had happened to me. My throat was sore. I was in such a terrible emotional state and I was unable to stop crying. The doctor gave me something to calm me down.

Robyn stayed with me until Ken arrived. Before he was allowed in to see me, the nurse came over and informed me that Ken was waiting outside in the corridor. She asked me a couple of times if I wanted to to see him. When she was satisfied that it was safe for me to see Ken, he was allowed in.

After about an hour I was discharged. Ken drove Robyn home and we went to Whiteshore to stay in his house. There was no way I would have been able to return to my home, despite the fact that Ken would have been with me.

The following day Ken and I returned to my house, checking to see if it was safe, which it was. Later that evening Mick's partner Anne called in to see how I was. She was shocked at what had happened. She, like everyone else, believed that my ex husband wasn't capable of doing such a thing. I told her how thankful I was that Mick had been there and taken me in, otherwise it could have ended up much worse. Ken thanked Mick personally and Anne too for helping me.

The following day, my buddy Paul (my guitarist) called up to see me with his then girlfriend. Again, they were both shocked by what had happened to me, particularly Paul. He brought up tools to fix my yard door and make it more secure so that no one could get into my house from the back.

After the attack on me I knew I could no longer stay there on my own. I was much too afraid. Ken and I spoke about this in great detail. He didn't want to give up his home in Whiteshore and I didn't want to give up my home either. All I knew was that I could no longer stay there, Betty too, although I'm not sure.

When I told my friends Paul and Maggie I needed to leave, they both strongly disagreed with my decision to give up my home. I didn't want to give it up, I really didn't. It was me who fought the housing association and Social Services when we lived in the hostel, not my ex husband. I was the one doing all the running back and forth to the housing association. We were allocated our house because of my refusal to quit. Even the nun, Sister Catherine, who ran the hostel said, "I wish they were all like you, Rebecca, this place wouldn't be long emptying".

Ken and I had never spoken about moving in together. I felt like I had no choice. Ken wasn't moving to Belfast and that was it. Once again, pressure was on me to move.

When I was seventeen, it was because I couldn't bear the fights between my brothers and my father. It was like living in a war zone, verbal, emotional and physical abuse, day in, day out. Now, in 1996, it's my ex husband's violent behaviour towards me forcing me to flee for a second time.

Word quickly got around that I needed to get out. An acquaintance of Robyn's, a woman I didn't care that much for, had asked me to do an exchange with her. She, or should I say her ex husband, who lived in a flat not that far from me, said she would give me £500 if I agreed to swap with her. I did think about it. Again, my two friends were saying don't, especially with someone like her. She tried to force an immediate yes response from me by dropping the £500 in an envelope through my front door. When I called to see her to tell her it wasn't going to happen she was raging and said, "I'm going to tell everyone your ex husband is gay". I said back to her, "I don't care! You can get a loud speaker and shout from the rooftops about my ex husband's sexuality". She wasn't expecting that response, I'm sure, as she then backed down. Some people!

I ended up giving the house to my son Sam. My head was so messed up I was not able to think rationally. I thought at least it's with someone I can trust. He of course was over the moon. His greedy cousin had his eye on it too. There was no way in hell that was ever going to happen.

At first Ken and I got on reasonably well, considering we were forced into living together. I would go up to Belfast with him most mornings and check out how my son was doing, living in what used to be my home. I would tidy up and clean the house, wash dishes etc....On other occasions I would visit Robyn and call in to see my friend Maggie.

I did decorate Ken's house from top to bottom and had the front garden looking really pretty. That kept me busy for a while. I had the music turned up loud while I worked. I prefered it that way (thankfully the neighbours didn't mind). I could not have lived in it as it was. Ken had no idea at all about cleanliness, decor or anything else for that matter. The house had a solid fuel fire in the living room and that was it. You could only get hot water. There were no radiators which meant in the winter time I froze. Ken is a warm-blooded male so the cold never bothered him in the slightest. Ken, at my request, got a new open fireplace put in along with radiators in every room. It looked like a new house by the time I had finished with it. I had made it our new home, warm and cosy.

After I was finished with the house I found myself at a loose end. I had no job or friends in Whiteshore so I decided to go out into town and see if I could get myself a job. I handed in a couple of really good references to a local charity shop. I needed something to occupy my time. I thought it would be good to get a job there. One reference was given to me by one of my class tutors and the other one was given to me by my boss at the women's centre. I never heard anything back from the woman who was working in the shop so I called in to find out if they needed me, and if not, could I have my references back. I never did get them back or a job.

Despite having no job or friends I loved living in Whiteshore. I used to go into town most days, either by myself, or if Betty was with me she and I would walk into town as it wasn't that far from where we lived. A couple of times Robyn came down with me. She loved the many second hand/charity shops that were there at the time. Our friend Maggie and her partner Joe would come down on a Saturday evening we would sit by the open fire, listening to music and enjoying a drink together.

In April 1997 I received a phone call from Robyn telling me that Alvin, our older brother, had collapsed in Cass Street early on Friday afternoon. An ambulance was called by a member of the public. It arrived at the scene fairly quickly and took him away to the Bel Hospital. I was very upset and felt slightly trapped because I was unable to get to the hospital right away. I rang Ken at work and told him what had happened. He assured me that when he got home from work he would take me to the hospital.

I had been worried sick about Alvin for some time. I remember my mother and I going to the hospital with him a year earlier and the consultant saying that if he didn't stop drinking he would have two years to live.

I remember another time going to visit him with my mother (this was before the assault on me by my ex husband), probably in late 1994 or early 1995. He was living alone on the Force Road. My mother was very concerned about his drinking, too. When he invited us both in, his flat was really messy and he looked as white as a ghost. I pleaded with him to stop drinking, saying "Mum's already lost one son, please, Alvin". I also told him he looked awful. That's when he told me to leave.

Ken and I arrived at the hospital that evening, Friday. I was uneasy about going in, partly because I didn't want to see my mother. The thought of that made me feel very nervous. I asked Ken to go in and see if she was there, which thankfully she wasn't. I was also very apprehensive about seeing Alvin. I didn't know what to expect. When we arrived at his bedside my heart broke into a million pieces. He looked so ill, very yellow with jaundice and his stomach was very badly swollen. The nurse said to me on our way in, "Don't touch your brother as you may get infected".

I had to hold back the tears while I stood by him. I said that I loved him. He spoke so low, I couldn't make out what he was saying. I remember the look he gave Ken- it wasn't a pleasant look. Afterwards we wondered what that had been about. Maybe the medication he was on? I ignored the nurse's advice and held his hand. I also kissed him goodbye on the cheek before I left. I asked the nurse on my way out, "How bad is he?" She replied, "Quite bad".

We came home from the hospital not really speaking to one another. I couldn't get Alvin out of my mind. Ken, I guess, didn't know what to say. It was very quiet; it felt like a long journey back home that night.

On Monday I went back to bed early in the afternoon. I had been sleeping a lot because of the depression and anxiety after the violent assault on me by my ex husband. It wasn't until many years later that I learned I was suffering from PTSD.

I was asleep when the sound of the phone ringing woke me up. It was after four o'clock. I lifted up the phone to see who was calling. I said hello and Robyn answered, "It's me, Rebecca, and Alvin is dead". I asked her what time he had passed away. Oh my God. She said four o'clock. I asked who was there with him at the hospital. She said our mother, Amber, our sister, and her. I said I'd be up at the hospital as soon as Ken came in from work. She said "Fine, I will see you later", and that was it.

Even though I knew he was dying, nevertheless the news of his death shocked me to the core.

It was too late to let Ken know by telephone as he had already left the office by that stage. (There were no mobile phones back then). I cried so much; my heart ached. It felt really sore, as if it were about to burst. I waited on Ken coming home. When he arrived home he took one look at me and knew the news wasn't good. I asked him to take me to the hospital to see Alvin. He agreed, but I could tell he wasn't pleased to be going out so soon after he'd just got home. That upset me deeply and I said to him, in a sarcastic tone, "Sorry that it's inconveniencing you, how the hell would you feel if it was your sister lying dead in a hospital?" We never spoke another word until we arrived at the hospital.

When we arrived at the ward I asked Ken to make sure no one else was there, meaning my mother. He went in before me, came back out and waved me in to where Alvin was. I cried while touching his face and hands, staring at the huge bump rising up from the bed sheet where his stomach lay beneath. We stayed with him for a while and again the nurse had said to me on the way in, "Do not kiss him". Again, ignoring what she had said I wasn't leaving him without a kiss goodbye. He died 28th of April 1997 from liver failure due to his alcohol consumption and hepatitis C.

He had contracted hepatitis C while sharing needles in Southeast with his heroin pals in the late 1960s and early 70s. I was aware of his conditions because I was present when my mother had the conversation with the doctor when Alvin was hospitalised in 1996.

I didn't attend Alvin's wake. It took place at my mother's flat. I felt I couldn't be a part of it because my relationship with my mother was nonexistent. My friend Maggie, who did go to the wake, said "Rebecca, you should have been there. Your poor mum's in bits". The lid of the coffin had to remain closed. I'm not sure as to why, something to do with the size maybe? I did however attend his funeral. Nothing or no one was going to keep me away from it.

He was cremated at Lawn Crematorium- that's what he wanted. I remember trying to help carry his coffin up to where it was to rest before it disappeared. I got up, walked over, put my shoulder under the coffin and had to stop. I couldn't carry the weight. Ken stepped in and carried it for me. After the cremation we all went our separate ways. Robyn was in bits, as were we all that very sad day. Later on, maybe a week afterwards, a few friends of Alvin's, my mother, father, Robyn and Amber went to a place where Alvin had loved to fish in his youth. One of his friends played a couple of Alvin's songs on his guitar while the rest threw red roses into the river. I marked his passing in my own way. He will forever be in my heart.

I continued on living in Whiteshore with Ken but our relationship became very strained. After Alvin's death I was grieving badly. Ken had no clue. I remember one evening I was sitting alone in the living room and Ken was out in the kitchen. I was playing over and over a song by the band Free, called 'Love you so'. It was written for their guitarist, Paul Kossoff, who tragically died in 1976.

The lyrics in the song spoke to me and touched me at a very deep level. I was missing my big brother. I felt broken. My protector was gone for good. I found myself reminiscing about how he used to help me when I was younger. He introduced me to the music I listen to today.

A few weeks after Alvin's passing I was given a couple of books with all the songs he had written over the years. Quite a lot of tapes with unfinished songs on them. A few art books, a brand new double tape deck, a Pioneer amplifier and a four-track recording machine that he had purchased but sadly never got the opportunity to use. I was given all these because Robyn knew I was the only one who could get his songs recorded. Mike, a friend of Ken's who was the guitarist in their band, offered to help me get them down on tape. He had his own recording studio in his house where we recorded three of Alvin's songs, and one of Frederick's.

Amber managed to get hold of his Echo guitar, his typewriter and God only knows what else. Her reasoning for claiming his guitar was that her son was learning to play, but it never happened. A while after that she got his Louden guitar which cost a lot of money. My buddy Paul asked me, "Why did you not get his guitar, you're the one who plays?"

After a few weeks I went to see Sister Anne. We talked about the wake, the funeral and what happened after. She felt that it would be a good idea for me to call and speak with my mother, saying, "It's not what you say, it's how you say it, Rebecca". She advised me to speak with her and tell her that I forgave her and me. Looking back, I don't think I needed to forgive me. Yes, she had lost two sons. Things between us were at an all-time low so I'm not sure if she was grieving me? Maybe. My heart did go out to her, nonetheless.

I remember calling to her door that day. Memories of the last time I was there at her door came flooding back. I put them to the back of my mind as best I could. When I knocked on her front door, my youngest sister Amber opened it. I could see my mother standing at the top of her stairs. Amber began walking back up the stairs and I followed behind her. When I reached the top my mother was still standing there. I looked at her and said "I forgive you, and me". Amber said, "That's good". That was that. I felt better and I guess my mother did too.

My life continued on in Whiteshore with Ken and Betty, whenever she wasn't staying with her father. I didn't see that much of my mother or Amber. Robyn and I remained quite close.

Not long before Frederick died, my mother had informed us that Jack, who we grew up believing was our uncle, was in fact our half-brother. I, along with Robyn, Frederick and Alvin, welcomed him with open arms. Amber, on the other hand, was rude and not accepting of him. I'm not sure whether it was because she was jealous of him? As she was the youngest, she got all the attention from our mother. Frederick and Jack got on great together. Frederick had such a big personality and used to say, jokingly, "You were the lucky one; you got away", meaning he wasn't reared by our parents. My mother's mother and father reared Jack as their own.

My grandfather, Jimmy Burns, a Scottish man, refused to allow Jack to go into care. He was a lovely man, small in stature who wore a cap and smoked a pipe. We didn't see that much of him. I remember him visiting us once or twice. My so-called grandmother, on the other hand, never set foot in our house. Nor were there ever any birthday or Christmas cards sent to any one of us from our grandparents.

My mother took us to see her parents a couple of times on the train (they lived in Summer Hill outside Belfast). Granda made us feel welcome but grandmother didn't. I remember Robyn and I were out playing when a dog appoached us. Robyn loved animals. She was petting the dog when all of a sudden my mother's mother banged on the window for us to come inside. When she opened the door we were made to take our shoes off and Robyn was sent over to the sink to wash her hands.

My mother only ever spoke about her mother once- it was while we were sitting chatting in her kitchen. She didn't say much. I remember saying to her, "I have never heard you talk about her to me". She very quickly changed the subject. She wasn't saying anything bad about her, her mother somehow came up in the conversation. I do know she didn't have a loving relationship with her. She seemed to get on better with her father.

My father didn't want anything to do with Jack. Apparently, my aunt, my father's sister, used to call my mother and her illegitimate son bad names when they lived with her. It was so incredibly hard for women back then who had a child out of wedlock. Growing up we heard Jack's name mentioned when my father came in drunk, which was pretty much all the time. I never really got what they were fighting about until much later.

At first Jack was very charming and kind to me. He knew I was a big Lennon fan and would make tapes for me with me sitting beside John Lennon and not Yoko on the front cover. That all changed when I started going out with Sean. Jack put a letter through my letter box one day with quotes from the Bible. He was judging me when he knew nothing about me. I believe my mother was behind it as she didn't like Sean.

I remember one day walking up Cass Street when I met Alvin. I began telling him what Jack had done. He said to me, "Take no notice of what he has to say, I'm your brother. You do what makes you happy". Bless him. I felt so much better after hearing that from him.

The 7th of June 1997 Jack had invited me, Robyn and Ken down to his flat in Headport. He seemed to accept Ken. There were no more quotes from him or the Bible about us being together. We took him up on the offer, Ken, me, Betty, Robyn and her daughter Kate. We had a lovely day despite it being so soon after Alvin's death.

When we arrived Jack took us to his flat and made us all feel very welcome. He got out his video camera and began filming us all which was a bit embarrassing, although now I am very glad as I have the recording still today. We all went to the amusements and later on to the beach. It was a nice sunny day, albeit a bit windy. Later on, before returning home, he made us all dinner.

Later on in July, our friend Paul and his girlfriend broke up. They had been together for many years. Paul's friend who had been living here with his wife was lucky enough to win a green card and they moved out to Florida. Paul was broken-hearted by the break up. His friend invited him out to Florida to live. Paul wasn't sure about it in the beginning. I encouraged him to go for it as this was a wonderful opportunity. I regretted it later- I missed my friend.

Paul asked me to go with him. I said I would go for a two-week holiday as I'd never been to Florida before. Besides, my divorce had come through. I was feeling on top of the world about that. What a great way to celebrate my freedom from that monster. I remember coming out from the courthouse with my fists in the air and saying to Ken "I think I know how Nelson Mandela felt when he gained his freedom".

For our going away party and my divorce party, we decided to go to the Fort Inn. Robyn was there, a couple of her friends, a couple of mine and Ken of course. We got up and played a few songs; that was the first time Ken had ever played a six-string bass guitar. It was magical. Everyone was in great spirits.

Paul, his ex girlfriend, me and Ken had a few drinks in our house in Whiteshore the night before we set off for Florida. Ken was fine about me going away for two weeks with our friend Paul.

Paul and I had a great time on the plane over. I got into conversation with two guys sitting not far from me. We all had a blast. In those days smoking was permitted on planes as long as you sat at the back of the aircraft. I was quite a heavy smoker, so much so that I don't think I could have managed the nine-hour flight without a smoke. We enjoyed a few drinks too- lovely memories. Paul's friends met us at the airport and drove us to where they were staying in Florida.

Altogether there were six adults staying in a small apartment. Somehow we managed it. Paul started work on the third day which left me alone for a good part of the day. I slept mostly during the day. The odd time I tried to walk down to the beach but the heat was stifling and the humidity was unbearable. I didn't particularly like that kind of intense heat. When the guys were off at the same time, which didn't happen that often, we would have brilliant music sessions. Paul's friend's wife Lucy and his sister, whose name I've forgotten, got on really well together.

Before Paul started work we went out this particular day and called into a bar. I needed something to eat. Paul, on the other hand, was more interested in having a few cool beers. There was a guy sitting playing music in the bar and when he finished for his break I asked him could we play a few songs. He was very quick to hand Paul his guitar.

We played four or five songs and enjoyed every minute of it. After we had finished, a man came out from the kitchen and said to me "Wow, for such a small woman you sure can sing". He offered us beer and free food and asked if we would come back and play. That was our only time in that bar as Paul had to work.

In the evening I would go down to the bar where Paul worked and listen to the great bands who played there at the time. It was a blues and jazz venue. Paul and I got up one evening and did a couple of songs. The atmosphere was electric. I loved the place and the food wasn't bad either.

The day I was returning home, Paul asked me to stay. I told him I couldn't. I had a daughter at home. He was really sad with me going, I could tell. His buddy was going back home to Ireland alone. When I returned home Ken seemed pleased to see me.

Paul's ex girlfriend stayed with Ken the night Paul and I left for Florida. Ken said they played music and air guitars and got pretty drunk. I was cool with that. I trusted Ken and he trusted me. Paul's ex girlfriend I learned later was raging that we went off to Florida together. Three weeks later, Paul met his new American girlfriend. Paul's ex believed I knew about this. It was just as much a shock to me as it was to everyone else. They married and have three children and are still living in Florida.

I had got the recording of Alvin's and Frederick's songs completed in time for Alvin's first anniversary. I believe mother, father and everyone else were pleased. I was sitting in Robyn's house shortly after his anniversary when Clare, Robyn's oldest daughter, was amused by what Amber had written for the back of Alvin's memory card. We were reminiscing about both our brothers. It was comforting for us both.

Saturday night May the 30th 1998 Ken and I had a drink. He went to bed before me. I had stayed behind to have something to eat. (Shortly after Alvin's death was when I began to comfort eat). The phone rang. It was my mother telling me that Clare was dead. It was after midnight. I was totally shocked, not believing what she was telling me. I asked her, "Are you sure?" She spoke as if she had been taking something which of course she hadn't. She wasn't a drinker. I asked her again and she said "Yes, I think so". I said "What do you mean?" She said Robyn had told her she was dead. She went on to say that Clare had died by suicide. I can't remember what was said after that. I ran upstairs to Ken and woke him up. I told him what had happened. He was as shocked as I was. Plus, we both had been drinking which made the experience even more surreal.

Ken got up out of bed and we both went downstairs. We talked about what we should do. I knew I needed to get up to Belfast somehow. I rang my friend Maggie who was also having a drink with her partner. There was no way her partner would have been able to drive. Luckily for me, Maggie's partner's brother Frank and his wife were there that evening. Frank wasn't drinking and offered to drive down to Whiteshore and pick us up. It seemed like an eternity waiting for them to get to us. At that early hour of the morning it would only have taken thirty minutes at the most to get to our place.

When they arrived we were all in shock at the terrible news. I was in another zone altogether. As Frank drove into the street where Robyn lived, we could see it was full of police as well as an awful lot of people. I got out of the car and began walking up the front path to their house.

There were police officers standing outside her front door. I said "I need to see my sister". The front door was open and there were two more police officers standing at the bottom of the stairs. I went into the living room, looking for my sister. There were people sitting and standing there. I then walked into her kitchen where Robyn was sitting on the floor. She just sat there unable to speak with a look of disbelief and bewilderment on her face. Her eyes were red and tears were streaming down her face. I asked her what happened. She screamed back at me "Clare's dead".

I tried to hold her but it was as if she had frozen, unable to move. I walked back out into the hall and tried to get up the stairs to see my niece. The police stopped me, saying "No one is allowed up until the investigations are complete". I couldn't believe they wouldn't let me up to see my niece and said, "Please let me up, I will believe she's dead when I see her dead". After what seemed like an eternity the police allowed Robyn and her husband up first and when they came downstairs I was allowed to go up. I remember my son coming up with me and no one else. I walked into Clare's sister's bedroom where her body lay in a black body bag on the floor. The zip was pulled down far enough so that we could see her beautiful face. There she was, dead on the floor. As I knelt down beside her, unable to stop the tears from falling, I still couldn't take it in. I was sure that if I saw her dead then it would be true. Not so.

I'm not sure how long I stayed with her before we had to leave and allow the undertakers to remove her body. I stayed a while with my broken-hearted sister and then went to my house with Ken and stayed there, unable to sleep. My son was in the back bedroom, probably unable to sleep too.

The next day, Sunday, I called up to my sister's house. There were still a lot of people there. I was able to have somewhat of a conversation with her. I learned that Clare had used a pair of track bottoms to hang herself with on the back of her sister's bedroom door. She was only fifteen years old, a very pretty kid with a quiet nature. I had been speaking with her briefly the day before when I rang Robyn. She sounded her usual cheerful self. My beautiful young niece dying by suicide was the last thing I thought would ever happen to her.

My mother and father were at the house that Sunday along with Robyn's father-in-law. Robyn's husband was distraught with grief, as were his brothers and sister. It was as if a heavy veil of grief had fallen down over us all. It was Kate, Clare's sister, who found her hanging that terrible night. She was only thirteen at the time. My heart went out to this poor child. She was completely lost.

I stayed quite some time with my sister that day. When I returned to the house I could hear Pink Floyd's music coming from the back bedroom where my son was. I lay on the mattress in the front bedroom, crying uncontrollably and trying to comprehend the waste of this beautiful young life. It just didn't make any sense- why did she want to die? She left no note. I heard stories of how she had been sniffing glue and taking drugs given to her by an older man who lived close by. Allegedly, he was a Republican who got his kicks from enticing young girls with drugs and sexually abusing them.

My youngest daughter, Betty, eleven at the time, worried me sick. She wouldn't leave the open coffin the whole time she was at the wake. I tried to get her to talk about it, how she was feeling, and get her away from the coffin. I was unsuccessful.

The morning of the funeral, Robyn refused to get out of Clare's bed. I tried in vain to talk her round but she flatly refused. A neighbour who later became good friends with Robyn succeeded where I had failed to persuade her to go to her daughter's funeral. After Clare's coffin left the house, a well known Republican woman whom Robyn and I were friends with in our childhood said to me "If there's anything I can do let me know". I passed her message on to Robyn when she finally came out of her front door. Her response, "She's a bit late".

I thought my brother Frederick's funeral was massively attended, which it was. Clare's funeral was twice that. The chapel was packed to capacity with mourners standing outside. All her friends and their families were there, her classmates and her school teachers. It seemed like the whole community were there. It was a lovely funeral service, the nicest I have ever attended.

The suicide rate at that time was quite alarming, particularly among young males. (Sadly, it still is). When the news spread about Clare's death it sent shock waves through the very heart of Belfast and beyond. The local newspapers rang Robyn's husband requesting an interview which he declined. In those days death by suicide was being reported via TV, radio and newspapers. It was just unusual to hear of a female suicide.

After the funeral was over I left the chapel with Robyn and Betty. Outside there were so many people standing and looking terribly sad and shocked. Robyn, Betty and I got into the waiting limousine that was parked a few yards from the chapel doorway. One of the undertakers opened the door of the limousine for us to get in. I noticed our sister-in-law standing outside the chapel with our two nephews who looked dazed.

Our sister-in-law never spoke with Robyn or attended the wake. They weren't on speaking terms because Robyn, Alvin, and our mother blamed her for our brother's death. They believed she could have called for an ambulance instead of listening to him cry out in pain as he lay dying in their bedroom while she stayed with her two sons in their bedroom.

I don't remember much about the burial of my niece that day, except that it seemed to be over very quickly. The graveyard was packed with mourners and I found it difficult to get close to the open grave. She was buried in the same plot as her grandmother on her father's side.

After the funeral there was a spread laid out in the local club not far from where they lived. Again, there were lots of people. Apparently Robyn had said something nasty to her son, the eldest of her children, that sparked a fight. I saw what appeared to be my son being attacked. I got up and began hitting some guy, trying to defend my son- not that he needed any help from me. As it turned out, the man was trying to calm the situation down. I completely lost it. One of Robyn's friends pulled me off whoever it was I was hitting. I had got it all wrong. My grief was so raw and explosive that I wanted to hurt somebody. I behaved like a total lunatic. On reflection, I believe I was projecting years of abuse that I had suffered from both my parents and my ex husband onto the person I was lashing out at. Up until that point in my life I had never been physically violent towards anyone. Nor have I been since.

Ken took Betty out in his car. He was concerned for her and was taking good care of her for me. Ken wasn't at the club, although he was told all about my behaviour by my so-called friend. Betty later went to stay with her father while Ken and I drove home to Whiteshore.

Our relationship suffered even further as a result of Clare's death. He didn't know what to do with me and my grief. We drifted further and further apart. I decided to leave. He asked me if I wanted to stay in his house and he would go elsewhere. I said "Of course not, this is your house".

I packed my bags and went back to the house I had given to my son. I had nowhere else to go. My son was mad as hell and deeply upset with me for screwing with his plans and making him look for somewhere else to live. It wasn't easy for me either. I felt like a total failure. I was still grieving and my head was all over the place.

One night we got into an argument, I can't remember what about; probably me needing my home back. He stormed out of the house; he'd been drinking. I went to bed and fell asleep. I was awoken from my sleep by a loud banging at my front door. I got out of bed, stood at the top of the landing and shouted "Who is it?" No answer. Again, bang bang bang at my front door. I came downstairs and nervously opened the door. I was shocked to see two policemen standing there. I said "Please, please don't tell me it's bad news, please". One of the police officers said "Your son has had an accident". Before he could finish I was in floods of tears. I said again, "Please don't tell me it's bad news". The officer continued, "Your son drove a car into a lake while under the influence of alcohol. He's been discharged and will be home shortly after his minor wounds have been dealt with at A & E". I felt so relieved and waited on him to get home. He came in wearing a splint on his arm and some cuts and bruises to his face and body. He was wearing only his jeans. He screamed in my face, "See what you done, you did this to me". At one point I thought he was going to lift his hand to me but thankfully he didn't. I took it, as I believed I deserved it. I was just so relieved he was alive. Of course what happened to him was entirely of his own making. He chose to get into a car drunk and drive. He could have lost his life that evening. Thank God he didn't.

I put in for a swap to the Housing Association as I needed out of that house and all the bad memories that went with it. I wanted to move to Wellan outside Belfast. I just thought it would be better for me and Betty to start afresh and get out of Belfast. I found a girl who was willing to exchange from Wellan to Belfast fairly quickly and thought, "This is meant to be". As it turned out, she hadn't been living there long enough. Besides, the house she lived in was absolutely filthy and would have needed a lot of work done to it. I had found out that she hadn't been living in it a year. I was prepared to move in and make a home for my daughter and me. There was no way I was risking giving up my home again only to lose it a second time.

It was the Housing Association's policy that one could not do an exchange unless they had lived in their property for over a year. The girl and her partner were desperate to get out of Wellan. Alarms bells began ringing for me. They offered me money; I can't remember how much. I wasn't moving, no matter how much money they offered. I had learned my lesson. I then decided to stay in Belfast and put in for a transfer nearer to home. There were other people who were really interested in getting into my house, including my nephew who at the time lived with my mother in her flat. There was also a girl I was friendly with at the time who practically begged me to exchange with her. She lived in an area of Belfast where I would never choose to live, ever.

Finally, the right house became available, not far from my house and just behind where Robyn lived. I decided to move and thankfully a brother of one of the guitarists I had worked with, Frank, offered to help me with the move. I was really glad of his help as I had no one else to help me. I got a van and driver and my friend Frank came with me to Whiteshore to collect my belongings. I had informed Ken that I'd be taking what belonged to me from his house to my new one. As we were leaving I left him a pouch of Golden Virgina smoking tobacco with a little note saying "I've got all my things and here is your house key- Rebecca".

We remained friends somewhat. He knew it was over, as did I. But I think he, like me, was unable to cut the ties of our unhealthy addiction to each other. He did call up after I'd moved in, maybe a couple of months later, and put up curtain rails for me.

Frank painted my hall and landing stoned; he was fond of the grass and smoked it quite regularly. I painted the rest of the house unstoned. He began visiting me quite a lot. I thought he was a true friend. I was unaware at the time just how vulnerable I was- he wasn't. He was living with a girlfriend and his son not too far away from me. He was a musician like his brother. Not as good a guitar player, but he had a nice voice. He wasn't interested in doing any music with me, nor I with him. His older brother, who had been in the three-piece band with me and the five-piece, got together with me and we tried to make a go of it as a two-piece. It didn't work out.

When all the decorating was finished I made a start on sorting out Alvin's music. There were so many tapes to get through, some that couldn't be used because the sound quality was so bad. There were other tapes with maybe two or more songs that I wanted to keep. It was so difficult listening to him trying to play what were good songs (his own) only he was to out of it, God bless him. Alvin and Frederick's friend, a fine guitar player called Tomas, now deceased, was much younger than them. He would join them quite regularly and play along with them. He later played a piece on guitar that he said Alvin had taught him which was brilliant. My buddy Paul, who himself is a fine musician, was blown away by it, as we all were.

Things between Ken and I went from bad to worse. We decided to split up again. I was at a loose end and decided to join an art class in September 1998.

I enjoyed meeting new people, some of whom were very good at art. One day (in the days when smoking was allowed inside any building) it was break time and I got speaking with two guys who were at a different class to me. It turned out one of them knew my brothers well. Gary, his name was. He was a musician who knew a friend of Alvin's whom he had played in a band with for many years. Tom Gracey. I was astounded and thought to myself, it's a small world. Belfast is quite a small place so it should have come as no surprise to me really.

We had such a laugh when we got together and found that we had a lot in common. Gary said he would let Tom know he had met me. Before long I was invited to a party at Gary's flat where I met Tom whom I hadn't seen in years. He let my father borrow his van so we could visit my brother who was shot and left for dead at the Dunn Cutts, just outside Belfast in the early 1970's. I had seen him again in a club in the early 1990's when I was in a two-piece outfit. We were playing and I noticed Tom sitting in the club with his wife. That was the last time I had seen him.

At the party Tom and I got on really well. He taught Alvin guitar when he was just fifteen years of age. Tom was a well respected guitar player. We soon became really close friends. I enjoyed his company a lot; he was extremely funny as well as a mighty fine guitarist.

Our friendship grew over the following weeks and months. Betty didn't like Tom or Frank. She just didn't seem to want to share me with anyone. I needed a friend and I found a good one in Tom. He went as a witness, along with my father and my childhood friend Maggie to the Catholic Church on the Indian Road in Belfast.

I had applied for an annulment a year before as my marriage to my first husband was invalid. He was a gay man. Although we had three children together it wasn't a marriage in the true sense of the word. We never made love. If fact what he was doing to me was relieving himself. It was truly a horrible experience. As I write this it sends chills up and down my spine and is making me feel quite nauseous. I could go into graphic detail about just how bad it was but I want to spare my children and grandchildren from the gory details as they may want to read this one day.

At my first interview regarding the annulment I was told it would cost £500 pounds for administration fees. That was in 1997. I explained that I was unemployed and there was no way I could get that kind of money. The priest replied, "Well you can provide envelopes and stamps when required". I waited over a year to find that they weren't granting me an annulment. Their reason, insufficient evidence. I was extremely upset and angry. One of my ex husband's sisters got her annulment from her first husband and didn't pay one penny. I suspect it may have been to do with the fact that her older sister worked and looked after a priest in the parish they lived in at the time. Also, I don't believe my father was a good witness. He believed what my mother believed, that my ex husband was a decent father to his children and a good man.

I remember saying to Tom that my father liked my ex husband despite the fact that he was aware that he had used violence towards me. He couldn't believe what I was telling him. He said to me that if any man lifted his finger to his daughters he would beat the hell out of them and make sure it never happened again. I know Tom and Maggie did their best for me. From that day to this, I regard myself as a non-Catholic. I never really was a practising Catholic anyway. I didn't go to Mass and certainly never believed in confession. I don't need a building to speak with my maker. I don't believe in organised religion.

On my birthday that year, the 13th of December, Tom took me out to a club where he was a regular. I had played there myself. It was also where I went to gain confidence for the talent contest that Alvin and I entered. After the band stopped playing and the people left, Tom, me and a few others stayed behind. We had a great night, Tom playing guitar while I sang. The atmosphere was one of sheer joy, a birthday I will never forget.

Christmas was approaching. I always had Betty stay with me on Christmas Eve which was lovely. The nun I knew sent presents round to my house for Betty and Tom had got her one too. It was a good Christmas.

New Year 1999 arrived and things were going well for me. Tom and his son Jack would call down. It was always fun and Betty got on really well with Jack which made things a little easier. Jack played keyboards and he and his father recorded songs they liked. Jack was a whizz kid regarding technology and made their recordings sound as if they had a five-piece band.

Ken came back into my life while Tom and I were friends. He and I would split up and get back together again. Each time Ken came back or left me Tom would say "The saga continues". It really was a crazy, messed-up relationship.

Tom, around early spring time, began complaining about his back being sore. I had a tube of muscle relief ointment that I gave him. He said that when his grandson stayed over with him he would hurt him when he was asleep, kicking him accidentally. His back continued to hurt him. I insisted, along with his daughter, that he go to see his doctor. His throat was bothering him too. It was quite hoarse although he said it didn't hurt. He went to see his doctor numerous times and was given antibiotics which didn't help him. I became quite concerned about Tom's health. He had lost a lot of weight and his back was really bothering him. He was referred to the hospital to get an x-ray done. I had myself convinced that he had cancer. On his return he rang me to say that he'd been given the all clear. I was so relieved. He told me that day on the phone that he himself thought he had cancer. I confessed that I too thought the same thing. We were both so thrilled that our fears were unfounded.

On Ken's birthday, the 6th of June, he, Tom and I went to a club just across the road from where I lived. There was a band playing and Tom was asked up to play a couple of songs. Afterwards he told me that the guitar strap was hurting his back. We had a very pleasant evening. Tom played really well despite being in pain. At the end of the night a fight broke out involving a man who lived in the same street I used to live in. He and his older brother, who lived just a few doors down from my house, got involved in some sort of altercation. I wanted out of there right away, as did we all. The night was going so well until that point.

I had booked a holiday for myself and Betty to go over and visit my buddy in Florida in July of that year for two weeks. Ken was looking after the house for me while I was away. I was a heavy smoker at that time and I was pretty anxious about not being able to smoke for eight hours or more. I got through the journey on the plane without my cigarettes with the help of a few drinks and a nap. When we arrived my buddy and his wife were there waiting for us. They took us to their beautiful apartment with a swimming pool outside. Betty made the most of it; she was never out of the pool. I had planned to take Betty to Disneyworld as it wasn't that far from where my buddy and his missus lived. The day we were meant to go I took a very bad period and couldn't move with the pain. I had suffered for years with very heavy and painful periods and extremely bad PMS.

Paul's wife drove Betty to Disneyworld while I had to stay in bed, doped with painkillers. Paul was at work all day so it wasn't a great day for me but I was glad Betty still got to go. We were there for the 4th of July celebrations and went to the bar restaurant where Paul worked. The place was packed with people which meant we had to wait hours on our food arriving. The fireworks display was magnificent and it was a great night enjoyed by all except my buddy who was working in the kitchen, trying to feed an awful lot of people. Paul took Betty and me fishing which we didn't enjoy. Betty and I loved the horse and carriage ride around St Augustine, a beautiful place, and the weather was perfect too. I loved the shops and somehow found a Native American shop. I bought a few souvenirs to bring home with me. Our holiday seemed to end pretty quickly. The journey back home wasn't as bad as the one getting there.

By the time we arrived home I was exhausted. I remember the weather being unusually hot. Betty went out to see her friends while I lay on the sofa. I couldn't sleep so I decided to take a walk down to the shops and get something in for our dinner. While out on my walk I bumped into a friend of Tom's, Gerry, a drummer. We stopped to talk as we always did any time we bumped into each other. He asked me if I had heard about Tom. I said "No, I'm only back from holiday". He went on to say that if I wanted to see Tom alive I had better get down to the hospital quick. I didn't know what had hit me; I was shocked and very upset. I asked which hospital he was in and made my way there.

On entering the ward where he was I walked right past him. I didn't recognise my friend. What I saw laying on the bed was an extremely thin, bony man with a grey complexion. I apologised, blaming it on my poor eyesight. I tried not to look shocked and did my best to behave normally but it was very difficult. He asked about my holiday and we chatted like there was nothing wrong. I stayed a while with him and told him I had to leave to get up to Betty who was going to be staying with her father that evening.

On my return home I couldn't get the image of him out of my head. I was so very upset. I just found it difficult to take it all in. I visited him quite a few times and then he was moved to another hospital. While he was in the other hospital I took a really bad chest infection- it began on the Friday. My doctor at that time put me on steroids and an antibiotic. Of course I was still smoking forty cigarettes a day. The infection took me off my feet and I was unable to get out of bed.

On the Monday, my mother was taken into hospital but I was unable to go and see her. I got a phone call on Friday afternoon, I think. It was my nephew who rang, saying "You need to get to the hospital. It's not looking good". When I arrived my eldest daughter was standing outside with my nephew and my younger sister. My daughter and I hadn't been on speaking terms since the violent attack on me by her father. She had rung me after the attack, asking what I was doing to her father and sister. I lost it and screamed down the down "Fuck off" as loud as I could. I couldn't speak for a couple of weeks after. Between the attack by my ex husband and squealing down the phone I had caused damage to my vocal cords that later resulted in my having to have two nodules surgically removed.

I heard that my younger sister had been saying that my daughter had put on a lot of weight. When I approached her I said hi and told her that she looked great. I continued, "Someone said that you'd put on weight? I think you look amazing", which she did. She was sad, of course, and worried about her granny's health. I went to investigate, trying to find out what was wrong with my mother. I got speaking with the doctor who was involved in her care and he told me just how ill she was. They needed to operate to save her life but stressed that she may not make it. It was up to me to decide whether they operated or not.

I spoke with my sisters, nephew, and daughter and we decided together that they should operate. She was so weak and so very ill but we felt she would die if they didn't. Before they let us in to see her we were told that the operation hadn't been a success and that she was on a ventilator which was the only thing keeping her alive. They informed us that it would need to be turned off after a while. We asked if they could wait until our half-brother arrived as he was coming from Summer Hill. They agreed to leave it switched on until all her family were at her bedside to say our goodbyes.

When our brother arrived he had some time alone with her. My heart went out to my father; he sat beside her bed, holding her hand and crying. The nurse said to speak to her as the hearing is the last sense to go. I took her hand and said my last goodbye and to tell Alvin and Frederick that I love and miss them. Her whole family were there, her husband, children, son-in-law and grandchildren. We all just stood by her bed and as the nurse switched the machine off my son put his hand on my shoulder. It was a very sad day. She passed away Friday the 20th of August 1999, two years after Alvin's death, seven years after Frederick had died and just over a year since her beautiful granddaughter Clare had died.

It wasn't as hard on me as it was for my two sisters, especially my youngest sister. I had said my goodbye shortly after Alvin died. Goodbye to the mother I wished I'd had.

We all came back to my house. I had made a lot of food and was planning to give my son a good send off as he was travelling to America on Sunday the 22nd of August. My son said "We can't have a party now". I replied, "We can't let all that food go to waste. We'll have something to eat and that'll be it". Only it wasn't. My youngest sister started getting nasty as she would often do when she had a drink. My son came into the living room and told us to shut up. I asked her to leave, which she wasn't happy about. After she left, my eldest daughter started on me. She was grieving and very angry with me. In those days I allowed my children and anyone else to say what they wanted and kept my mouth shut like I had done as a child and a wife. My son left for America as planned. His friend's father drove us up to the airport. His son was travelling with mine so it felt like a double loss with my son moving away, although I was happy that he was leaving Belfast and trying to make a better life for himself. When I arrived back home that Sunday from the airport to an empty house I cried. Robyn called up later in the afternoon to see me and so did my father. It was Robyn's birthday the day before, Saturday the 21st. I asked my father if he got her a card and he replied "No". I told him, "Get her a card for God's sake". He never did. Of course I asked him when Robyn was upstairs in the loo. I thought, "What kind of a father are you?" already knowing the answer to my question.

At my mother's funeral mass my friend Maggie and Robyn suggested I bring my guitar along and play the song I had written for Frederick after he died. I did. The priest stood at the hall entrance as we all entered the chapel. He asked if I wanted to sit at the altar and sing. I said "No, I'll sit with my family if that's okay". He agreed. After the funeral was over Robyn, her husband, my younger sister, my friend, my father and I went back to Robyn's house. None of us, the sisters that is, wanted to be around my father. He was like a lost sheep. We all were having a difficult day anyway, and for me, having him around was making it worse. My younger sister and I felt the least close to our father. Robyn always had more time for him than we did. Even so, she didn't want him around that day either.

Meanwhile, Tom was still in the hospital. I didn't get a chance to get to see him with being ill myself and my mother's passing. His son rang me one evening to tell me he was being moved to yet another hospital in Belfast. I thanked him for letting me know and said I would try to get to see him. I received another phone call from his son saying that his dad was asking to see me and that it was just a matter of days.

On the Friday 3rd of September I waited until Betty came home from school and told her I was ordering a taxi to take us both up to see Tom.

The taxi arrived and took us to the hospital where Tom was. I then set about looking to see where we could find him. It took no time at all. I asked at reception and was given directions to the private room where he was staying. When we entered the room, Tom was lying in the hospital bed with an oxygen mask over his nose and mouth. His two daughters were there along with his son.

As I approached his bedside he smiled at me. I gave him a kiss on his forehead and asked him how he was doing. Was he in pain? He smiled at me again, trying to pull back the sheet with his skinny, veined and wrinkled hand to show me the morphine bag. I couldn't really make out what he was saying. It was very difficult. I had to listen very closely. He kept smiling and telling me about big black flies that were on the ceiling and that Alvin was standing at the bottom of his bed.

He was asking for a Guinness and rice pudding. The nurse brought him the rice pudding but he was unable to eat it. I found the whole experience incredibly sad and extremely difficult.

His sister and her husband called in to see him as well as his ex wife. After a while I said I was going out for a smoke and Tom's ex wife came outside with me along with Betty. As we were smoking our cigarettes Tom's sister came out and said to us "What's wrong with you two, he's in there fighting for a breath and you two are out here puffing your brains out!" Her words lodged in my mind without me really knowing they had. We went back in and after a while I said goodbye to my dear friend.

On Sunday the 5th of September 1999 my friend passed away. I was heartbroken. I'd found a friend who seemed to totally get me. Loved my company and my voice. Never judged me. Made me laugh, especially when life was bringing me down. I cried so hard and missed him so much. I felt totally alone with my grief. My friend Maggie didn't quite understand, nor was she there for me. It was a horrible year. Ken and

I were still not on speaking terms and it was an extremely lonely, painful time in my life.

My mother's passing affected me too. I still grieved, even though we hadn't had a good loving relationship. I felt nothing but grief. My two male friends (my best friends) were gone. One had moved to the other side of the world and the other was dead.

I had met a man at the farewell party for Paul and his wife earlier that year. He played guitar but wasn't in a band. Later on I met him again at a bar on the Green Road. Then, towards the end of November that year, 1999, he rang me to ask if I would like to go out with him? I said yes as I was so lonely and longing for love. I'm not going to write much more about this man as he really isn't worth it. We went out for two months but he just used me. His ex wife had left him for another man and he was, as I've said, just passing time.

I got a phone call from my son on my birthday. I was delighted. He said that he wanted to be home for the Millennium. He was leaving America just before the end of December. The Millennium meant nothing to me other than make me think what Tom had said, which was that if he didn't make it he would come back and haunt us all, bless him.

Unfortunately, I was still seeing this man when my son returned home. My son didn't seem to mind. They would play a game of hurley out the back the odd time. After a while I got sick of him calling whenever he wanted and telling me we were going out on a Saturday night, then ringing me to say that we weren't. The next day, Sunday, he rang to ask me if I wanted to go out. I said no. He seemed shocked and didn't quite know what to say, except "Bye, see ya". Yes, I was lonely, but I knew he was using me and I wasn't prepared to take it any longer. I had seen a couple of wasters at that time. Men only after one thing. I wanted to love and be loved, not used.

In May 2000, the 28th to be precise, I quit smoking- it was a Monday. I knew it was likely to be the hardest thing I'd ever do. The day before, I decided not to empty the ashtray all day. I wanted to look at what I was putting into my body. Normally, I would empty the ashtrays in the solid fuel fire I had at the time. I put out my last cigarette in the overflowing ashtray and then threw the contents into the fire. Nearly thirty years of smoking, as I first began at the age of nine. I stopped and then took it up again for real at eleven. I was smoking forty a day, seventy when I had a drink.

I kept myself very busy that day. I had bought a packet of nicotine patches that came with a calendar and a pack of bright red stars. Each day I went without a cigarette I would place my star on the calendar. It was a great feeling. As the patches were pretty pricey at the time I made the seven days' supply do me two weeks. When I got to the first month without smoking it was the best feeling in the world. It was without a doubt the hardest thing to do. Seeing my friend die in the way that he did gave me the push that I needed.

I suffered very badly from physical withdrawal. For the first six weeks my mouth was covered with blisters that were sore as hell. All the poison was leaving my body and it hurt real bad. I had made up my mind that, because it was so incredibly difficult, if I ever did resume smoking I would never again try to stop. This was my third attempt. The first two times I had put on a stone in weight after just a month. This time I told myself I didn't care how much weight I put on; I was quitting for good.

I had two demons to tackle. One was to lose weight, the other was to stop smoking. I chose to lose the weight first. I succeeded in losing the weight fairly slowly and when I got to the weight I wanted to be I then tackled the cigarettes. I stayed the same weight for just six weeks after I quit smoking, and fairly soon after that I began putting the weight back on.

Of course I did care about my weight gain. I began walking a lot more and trying not to eat whatever and whenever I wanted. I also went swimming which also helped me not to put on too much weight.

My periods were becoming increasingly heavy and the PMS was quite severe. It affected my mental and physical health a lot. Before and during my period I was unable to walk, the pain was so bad. It ended up that I had only three days in the month when I would be okay regarding the PMS. My GP referred me to see a gynaecologist who tried various treatments, including Thermachoice Uterine Bailon Therapy and the Mirena coil. Sadly, they didn't work for me. My gynaecologist decided that I needed to have a hysterectomy, a full one. There was a long waiting list at that time so he prescribed medication for me to take that would shut down my ovaries. I was on this medication for a year and put on a lot of weight because of it.

I didn't care. It was such a relief not to suffer from heavy bleeding and PMS. My life was a lot better not having periods.

I have always considered myself to be a spiritual person. Organised religion doesn't appeal to me. My friend's sister gave me a book called 'The Word For Today'. It's a daily devotional written specifically for Christians. I got a lot from it. At times it felt like it was written for me. It gave meaning and understanding to a lot of what had been going on in my life. At the time, I was searching for something. I wanted a closer relationship with the God of my understanding. I also wanted a job. I volunteered to work for Women's Aid as my periods were no longer preventing me from having a life. As it turned out, I had to postpone my start date as I received an appointment to go into hospital for my hysterectomy. I was forty-four when I went in for my operation. That was in February 2001.

I was attending the hospital for haemophiliacs at the time. My GP had made a referral for me a few months earlier. This was because when I got a cut it took a long time for the bleeding to stop and also because of the blood loss after the birth of my children. Not long before I was due to go into hospital for my hysterectomy, I was told by the doctor at the haemophilia clinic that I no longer needed to go back. They were aware that I was going in to hospital for a hysterectomy but seem satisfied that I was okay and released me from their care.

Ken and I had got back together before I went into hospital; we were together for Christmas in 2000. My son was also back living with me at the time. Ken said he would take two weeks off work to look after me. At the time I thought to myself, two weeks is far too much. One week would be more than enough. For once I was glad he didn't listen to me. I remember me, Ken, my son, his girlfriend at the time and my eldest daughter and her then boyfriend going out for a Chinese in Whiteshore for Valentine's. It was a lovely evening. I was so happy having the people I loved all around me. Things would take a dramatic turn in just six days' time.

I remember so clearly, Sunday the 18th February 2001, Ken driving me down to the hospital where I was admitted on arrival. The nurse on the ward began briefing me and preparing me for theatre the following morning at eight o'clock. I was taking it all in my stride. My friend Maggie had had her hysterectomy about six months earlier and had recovered within a matter of weeks. Ken stayed some time with me on the ward and then left for home, saying he would call to see me after I'd had my operation.

Monday morning came and at eight o'clock the nurse came to see me and later the hospital anaesthetist. I was taken down to theatre and later on that evening I woke up and Ken was standing by my bedside. I was covered in a space blanket with tubes everywhere. Ken tells me that there was a doctor trying to get a needle into one of my veins. My hands and arms were black and blue. I felt really ill and couldn't bear the excruciating pain in my lower back. I asked the doctor why I was in so much pain. He said that it was because of the length of time I was in theatre. I have no memory of anything that went on that Monday. Ken explained what had happened after I had my operation. He said I was sent to the recovery room and then later on I was taken back to the ward. A little while later I needed to be rushed back down to theatre as I was bleeding internally. I had lost four pints of blood and needed to be operated on immediately to stop the bleeding.

On hearing this I insisted on a second opinion as to why the pain in my lower back was so bad. A second doctor came and examined me, confirming what the first doctor had said. I felt satisfied that what they both had said was correct. As I have said, I have no memory of being in the recovery room or of being so ill when I returned to the ward. The following day, around lunchtime, two doctors who had treated me while I was attending the haemophilia clinic came rushing into the ward and headed straight towards my bed. I could see the look of concern on their faces. They said how very sorry they were and asked me some questions. My consultant also came along a few minutes later. They were talking among themselves, then one of the doctors in the clinic said they would call back to see me later. After that they all left. I was too ill to think about what had gone wrong and why. I found the heat internally almost unbearable and I was experiencing a full blown menopause as well as being in a lot of physical pain.

I had a morphine supply attached to my body, just like Tom had. When the pain got too much I just had to press the button and morphine would be released. On Tuesday, around mid-morning when I couldn't bear the heat any longer, I slowly and very painfully walked to the bed by the window and decided that this one was mine. There were only four beds in the divided ward where I was. The bed was empty. I needed to be beside the cool air coming in from the open window. It felt like my body was burning inside. I was having difficulty sleeping too.

Before arriving for my hysterectomy, Sunday, my body was producing hormones and doing what hormones do. The next day they were all gone. My body was not only trying to adapt to this, but also to the shock from the second major operation to stop the bleeding.

When my consultant came in to see me he said "My word, you are a strong woman". I explained that I needed air; the room was too hot, as was my body. He was a lovely man who had saved my life the day before. He remarked, "I'm amazed that you were able to get out of bed at all, never mind walk across the room to this other bed". He prescribed HRT for me to take, which I did. It took nearly two years after my hysterectomy to get the correct dosage and the right type of HRT.

My children all came to visit me while I was in hospital, as did Ken, who was there every evening. My sister-in-law, nephew and father came too. Ken was such a sweetheart.

He brought me in all the things I needed and more. I was in pain too because of trapped wind. Apparently, surgery does that. The nurses were giving me all they had for wind but it wasn't taking it away. One nurse suggested getting peppermint tea. Ken brought me in all kinds of herbal teas, including green tea which I still drink to this day. I never would have tried herbal tea before, but because the pain was so bad I drank the peppermint tea in large quantities and it worked. I would have tried any kind of tea, and I did.

I was lying in bed one day when my father came along. He looked at me and asked, ''Do you know where Rebecca is?'' I looked back at him and said "You're looking at her!" I would like to think it was because he was so very vain and refused to wear his glasses. Or it may have been that he just didn't recognise me because I was looking so rough? To be honest, it made me laugh, and Ken too when I told him about it.

I had another visit from the doctors at the Haematology Clinic. They said that when I was discharged and able to attend an appointment a letter would be sent out to me. They were so nice and seemed genuinely concerned about me. A few people were trying to get me to sue them for negligence. My response was that the only thing I would be focusing on was getting better. Besides, I would never dream of trying to get money from the NHS.

I had an extremely difficult time trying to get to the toilet and being able to do what I needed to do without help. There were two trainee nurses who were simply amazing with me. They took their time and helped me in whatever way they could in the toilet and in the shower. I was so very grateful for everything they did for me. It was a different story at night-time. On more than one occasion I needed assistance during the night. This particular night I rang for help as I needed to use the bathroom. No help came. I got myself out to the toilet; it took an incredibly long time. I found my way back to my bed and rang again for help as I found it impossible to get back into my bed by myself. A member of the night staff came to my aid as I kept on ringing for help. She snapped at me when she arrived and helped me get back into bed. One another occasion I woke up extremely hot and managed to get the sheet off me but because I was menopausal I then found myself becoming very cold. I rang for assistance like before, only this time no one came to help me. I am not exaggerating when I say that it took a very long time for me to manoeuvre the sheet back over my cold, aching body.

My third day in hospital I asked the nurse to remove the morphine bag as the medication was making me itch from head to toe. I couldn't bear it. She tried to persuade me not to but failed. I was put on other medication that wasn't as strong, but at least the internal itching had stopped. The day came for my catheter to be removed. I didn't think much of it until the nurse began to remove it. I screamed with pain. Obviously I was still very tender and sore from the surgery. The day was drawing nearer for me to return home. I couldn't wait to get out of there. I had lost a stone in weight in just a week. The food was horrible, full of grease. But for Ken I would have had nothing to eat. He would bring me in something from the chippie and sometimes sandwiches.

I was released from hospital on a Sunday. It was exactly one week after I had arrived for my hysterectomy. Ken came into the ward along with my son to bring me home. It was a long slow walk to the lift and then out to the car park. Ken helped me into the car and my son sat in the back. The journey home was a painful one. I asked Ken to slow down. He hadn't been driving fast, but to me it felt as if he was. I would feel pain every time he drove over a ramp on the road. It really did hurt. We finally arrived outside my front gate and I mean that literally. There was a grass slope down to my front gate from the busy main road. Ken decided to drive along the footpath as there was no way I would have been able to walk down the steps or use the flatter way onto the footpath to get to the gate of my house. Also, there was snow on the ground.

It took a long time for me to get out of the car. Ken was very gentle and patient with me. When we finally got into the house he walked me into the living room, but I knew I needed to get to bed. The journey from the hospital to my house really took it out of me. Ken walked me up the stairs and put my pyjamas on me; there was no way I would have been able to do that by myself.

My son had done a good job looking after the house while I was in hospital. It looked as clean as the day I left it. I had taken it apart before I went into hospital as I knew I wouldn't be able to clean when I got home. When a hysterectomy goes as smoothly as it did for my friend and other women it usually takes six weeks to recover. Of course, I had no idea things were going to go so wrong for me. In retrospect, it was a good job I had given the house a thoroughly good cleaning.

When my mother went in for her hysterectomy she had me to cook and clean for her.

I had my son who was working as a chef at the time. His occupation requires long hours. I was blessed to have him there at the time, even though I didn't see that much of him. When he was there, he would cook Ken and me beautiful meals which I wasn't always able to fully enjoy because I was so ill. In the morning he would clear out the ashes from the fire (when it needed doing) and make sure it was lit before he left the house. Both of my daughters came to visit me as well, although neither of them lifted a finger to help me. When I mentioned that I needed washing done, Cathy said "I'll put it in the washing machine for you" and that was it. Betty was thirteen at the time and still living with her father. She got the vacuum cleaner out and hoovered the living room after I'd asked her. The only help I got was from Ken and my son.

Ken was a hopeless cleaner (I have OCD) so his ways of cleaning don't match up to mine. He was just incapable of seeing dust or dirt. Nevertheless, I was blessed to have him too. He would walk down to the shops and get whatever food was needed. He also helped me when I needed to turn around in bed as I was unable to do it for myself. When I needed help in the bathroom he was at hand to help me. He read to me before I went to sleep as I enjoyed it so much. No one had ever read to me before. He was an absolute angel.

He even took a sanitary towel down to my doctor's one day because we were both concerned that I was staining. There wasn't anything he wouldn't do. He completely changed his ways. He told me he had said to my son how close I had come to death. This was while I was still in hospital. He actually said "We came very close to losing her". He stopped being so wrapped up in himself and began taking responsibility for another human being, ie me. The one he loved and had taken for granted for so long.

I had a lot of time to think while trying to recover from such major surgeries. In the beginning of my recovery I would just lie and think, "When I am up on my feet I am going to go for my life". I thought to myself, "I have been given a second chance here". My higher power saved my life for a reason. My mind was made up and nothing, nor anyone, was going to stop me. It took such a long time to get back to good physical health. My emotional and spiritual health suffered too. I was all over the place. It was not easy trying to adapt but I was determined I would get 'me' back.

Ken would help me downstairs in the beginning. We went from there to taking the short walk from my back door down to the yard gate. It was a slow process. When I knew I was okay with the short walks I decided to take it a bit further. Every day I was regaining my physical strength. It felt so good to be able to get out of my bed and just walk. Ken returned to work and I really missed his support. He would keep in contact with me every day. He would even call up to see me during his lunch break. I had given him my key to let himself into the house as I was still spending a lot of time in bed.

On one occasion I came downstairs, opened the living room door and, to my surprise, saw that he had left some presents on the chair for me. His love and support inspired me to want to do better. I told him that I wanted to return to education. If I wanted to do better I needed an education. He bought me books to read and a large print dictionary. He believed in me. I was still very insecure, probably even more so because of the state of my emotional health. I doubted myself and was unsure of my abilities. Ken never gave up on me, particularly regarding my ability to get back into education and do well for myself.

After a while I was able to walk down the street by myself, albeit very slowly. Then one day I decided to go even further. I walked down to the shops, which was quite a distance from my house. I knew then that I was well on my way. I went from walking to swimming. Ken and I would go swimming in the evening and at weekends. I remember the first time I got into the water with him. As I began to swim it hurt, but I kept on going, pushing myself that bit further. In fact, after about a week, I swam a full length right down to six feet.

It was the first time since the Cool, a swimming pool where I would go to as a kid. One day I was thrown into six feet of water by a young man which terrified me. I hadn't ever dared go near the deep end of a swimming pool until now. Before long, I was able to go swimming by myself, starting with one day a week, which gradually led to four days a week.

By the time May came around Ken and I had booked a two-week holiday in Portugal. I was very excited about our first proper holiday away together. As it turned out, my son and his girlfriend at the time had booked a holiday in Portugal too, only they were leaving a week after us. I loved Portugal. Ken could speak Portuguese which meant he was able to speak to the hotel staff and others in their own language. The girl on reception was so friendly. She kept calling me 'beautiful bride'. Ken taught me a few words of Portuguese which meant I was able to order drinks and say hello. I was also able to ask for ice cream on our return from the beautiful sandy beach which we visited every day.

I was unable to sleep while we were away. I had insomnia brought about by my hysterectomy. The only time I was able to sleep was when I had a drink. As I'm not one for drinking every night it became a real problem both for myself and Ken. We tried the local drug store to see if I could get some herbal medicine which I did but it was useless. I had been taking 'bedtime tea' back home for the insomnia but I forgot to bring any with me. My mood plummeted. I wanted to go home after a week. I wouldn't let Ken sleep in the same bed as me- I insisted he sleep on the bed sofa. It must have been an absolute nightmare for Ken. When my son and his girlfriend arrived in Portugal, I made it my business to find out where they were staying. Somehow their being there made it easier for me to stay. Ken had hired a car during our stay and, as a result, we found a lovely restaurant, Cacto, the week before they arrived. When we caught up with them I invited them to join us for dinner at the restaurant, which they did.

I celebrated being off cigarettes a year while we were there and also practised the vocal exercises that I was given after my operation to have two nodules removed. I was still attending speech therapy back home and I needed to get my voice working again. It mattered so much to me.

Ken did all he could to help me while we were on holiday but I found myself becoming angry with him. The slightest thing would annoy me. I became quite negative in my thinking towards Ken in particular. I loved the holiday but at the same time I couldn't wait to get back home.

During that time in our lives he made sure to send me a beautiful bouquet of flowers every month when he got paid. Nothing he did was good enough. It felt to me like it was too little too late for us. Here he was, being and doing all that I ever wanted and it still wasn't enough. We parted ways yet again during which time I had begun my volunteer work with Women's Aid. In the beginning I loved the work. It felt good being there to support the women and their children. It gave me a purpose. I got on very well with a local woman who worked there. She would give me a lift to work which made it easier for me as it was five miles from where I lived. Sadly, she retired not long after I started. I missed her company.

I remember one day we all had to go to the head office for training. One of the speakers was talking about something. I made a comment which infuriated her. She as much as told me to shut up. I was stunned and did shut up. She publicly shamed me. No one else said a word. The room fell silent. Maybe I was in the wrong, maybe I did speak out of turn. I meant no harm, I really didn't. The way in which she dealt with it was so inappropriate. I don't remember what I said, or who she was. She totally humiliated me that day. After that I became very depressed and felt totally unsupported. A month or so after that incident I broke down. The manager took me into one of the rooms. I couldn't stop crying. She asked me why I was so upset. I couldn't answer her. I didn't know why. I said to her, "I feel so vulnerable", to which she replied "You are". She drove me home and left me at the road. I made my own way down the steps to my house. She didn't ask me if I would be alright, knowing I was going into an empty house. She drove off and that was the last I saw of her or anyone else from Women's Aid.

My son and youngest daughter had moved out. My son left for the first of his trips around world. He was heading off to Australia. My youngest daughter had moved yet again, back to live with her father. I believe the depression was triggered by the way in which I was treated at the women's refuge where I had given my all. Also, there was the empty nest syndrome and the fact that I hadn't got my HRT sorted out correctly. It was an extremely painful time emotionally. I had no support from family or friends. To be honest, I shut myself off from the world. I isolated myself, which can be a symptom of depression. I ended up behaving in a way that got me into trouble. It felt like I'd lost my soul. I was desperate and lifted the phone to ring Ken.

As I dialled Ken's number I was trembling with fear. I told him I was in trouble. He asked what had happened to me. I felt too ashamed to tell him. He said "It can't be that bad". I was sobbing during our conversation and finding it difficult to speak when he said "Come down to me". So that's what I did.

I got a taxi to the city centre and walked the short distance to the train station. I waited what seemed like a very long time until I was able to board the train to Whiteshore. When I arrived at his house he welcomed me with open arms. It took me hours before I was able to tell him what had happened. If fact, I asked him to guess what he thought it might me but he couldn't. I asked him "What is the worst thing that ever happened to you that you were terribly ashamed of?"

I finally confessed to him that I had stolen three items from a shop and the police were called. I begged the shop owners not to involve the police. Their reply was that it was their policy to get the police involved when the amount of goods stolen is over £20. The value of goods that I had stolen amounted to £22 pounds. A jar of honey, face cream, and one other item which I can't remember. The police questioned me in an office on the premises and then arrested me. After that, I was taken out of the shop by three police officers, put in the back of a police jeep and taken to a police barracks in Belfast and questioned again. They checked my purse and saw that I had more than enough money to pay for the goods. They asked me had I stolen before. I answered no. They asked me why I had taken the items. I said I didn't know. I told them that I had been suffering from depression and had never been in trouble with the police before.

I can't remember how long they kept me in the station. When they had finished questioning me they offered to drive me home. I didn't want to be left outside my house so they dropped me off opposite the shop where the offence took place. That was in January 2003.

I was in pieces. I don't know how I made it home that day. I dreaded bumping into anyone that I knew; thankfully, I didn't. Ken was my rock. He didn't judge me, he just took care of me. On the day of my court appearance he bought me a new pair of trousers and stayed by my side the whole time. The magistrate was very understanding of my mental state. I was given a conditional discharge for twelve months. I was so relieved when the whole thing was over. Ken and I left the court and shortly afterwards he treated me to lunch.

For a while afterwards I found myself tempted to steal again but I didn't. I knew I needed therapy to help me with my depression and anxiety. According to one theory, the thrill of stealing helps to elevate symptoms of clinical depression and may also coexist with obsessive compulsive disorder which I also suffer from. (As did my mother).

I found a therapist; quite a few actually. Also, what helped me was getting back into study. Ken always believed in me and gave me great encouragement.

I knew I needed to go back to learning basic numeracy and literacy skills which is what I did. I passed with flying colours. I always wondered why I had great difficulty with spelling. I knew I was intelligent and wondered if I had dyslexia? I asked the tutor if there was a way for me to find out. I explained to her that I really wanted to finish the certificate in counselling course I was on. She referred me to see an educational psychologist who confirmed that I had indeed got dyslexia, which has nothing whatsoever to do with intelligence. I asked him did he think I should go on and do the diploma in counselling. He said yes, I may find it more difficult than others, but he saw no reason why not. I felt relieved and vindicated. What I had been told at school were lies. I was not a dunce. I am not stupid. The psychologist's assessment of me confirmed that. My confidence grew from that day and kept on growing. When I successfully completed my University of Ulster Certificate in counselling in 2004 I decided to go on and do the diploma in therapeutic counselling.

I had wanted to continue studying for the diploma at the Belfast Institute of Further and Higher Education. However, due to oversubscription, I was unable to. I tried various other places including a CBT (Cognitive Behaviour Therapy) diploma course in Belfast but was unsuccessful. I felt unsure about what to do next. I thought, God has other plans for me. It seemed as though every door I knocked on at that time opened briefly and then closed again.

I decided to get in touch with one of the women who was on the same U.U. Counselling course as me which was validated by the Ulster University. She told me that there was a diploma course being run on the Force Road that had started a few weeks ago. She went on to say that she knew a few people had dropped out and gave me the name and telephone number of the centre manager. She suggested giving it a try so I did. I rang and spoke with the centre's manager who invited me down for an interview with one of the tutors who was running the course. I arrived at the centre a little nervous but determined to give it everything I had. The manager had a brief chat with me before I was introduced to the tutor.

She was very nice, a well-educated woman who asked me a lot of questions. One of the questions she asked was why I wanted to become a counsellor and what it meant to me personally. I guess she liked my answers because she said to come in the following week. To say that I was overjoyed is an understatement. I rang Ken and told him my good news. He was delighted for me and invited me to join him and his two friends for a Chinese meal. One of his friends paid particular interest in my good news. He was a lovely man who would later become a friend.

It had been a tough two years up until that point. I'd never worked so hard at anything in my life. I had said to Ken that I had visualised my graduation. He would be there, along with my confidant, Sister Anne and my children. I found the course both challenging and extremely interesting. I loved learning about all the different theories, Freud and C.G. Jung, the latter being my favourite psychoanalyst. These men were highly intelligent, their theories complex and difficult to grasp, but even so, I had a passion and a hunger to learn. I found psychology fascinating and still do. I wanted to learn about me, my family dynamic and why my early years and experiences had been a key point in my choices as a teenager and young adult.

I made it to the end of the two years and was second in the class to finish the written work. (We had to evidence our learning of all the theories in our portfolios). I was also the first in the class to get a placement at a local community centre, about eight months, maybe more, before the course ended. The second part of the course involved a role play with one of our peers as the counsellor. It had to be no less than 25 minutes and no more than 30 minutes. I felt nervous in front of my tutor. I was very aware of her presence in the room and that she was marking me on my performance. I tried my best to ignore her and did my best at my role as a counsellor. I was so relieved when that part was over. The final piece was the written exam. There were questions on our role as counsellor and also questions on the theory we used and how we incorporated that while working in our role as counsellor. My portfolio was marked off by two of my class tutors which absolutely made my day. I failed, however, on the recording of the role play because I ended in twenty-three minutes, not the twenty-five to thirty that were required to pass. I was so disappointed. Two others in the class failed too because their timing was wrong also. The tutor who marked my role play said that I got the highest marks on theory which helped a bit. This meant that I and the two other women had to resit the role play and the written exam.

We had to wait a couple of weeks and do the whole thing all over again. After repeating it again, it was agonising waiting to learn if I had passed or failed. Then finally came the phone call I was so desperately waiting for. When I received the news that I had passed I was ecstatic. I could barely take it in. I had achieved something I was told would never happen. The sheer joy I felt that day will forever be lodged in my memory. I was fifty years old when I graduated. Ken and my children were not present. Ken and I had parted ways.

My son was in Australia, I think. He was somewhere in the world on his travels, and my two daughters didn't think it, or me, important enough to attend. I felt deeply hurt by their lack of care and interest in my achievement. My confidant and another young woman whom I had got to know in 2002 while working voluntarily at a youth club were there with me. I received a card from my son congratulating me and another card from a woman I knew.

There were a lot of other requirements in order to complete the diploma. One was that you had to complete twenty sessions of personal therapy, which I welcomed. It was during this time that I did a lot of work on myself, particularly my relationship with Ken. It was beginning to fall apart yet again. My supervisor reminded me that I could do the written work on my own without Ken's help. I would always ask Ken to check the grammar and spelling before giving my work to my tutor for marking. My supervisor obviously believed in my ability to make it on my own. She was right, as I had passed all my written work and exam on my own, which felt like such an amazing achievement and something to be proud of.

While I was studying for my diploma, my father's behaviour had become quite strange and dangerous (driving on the wrong side of the road, apparently.) Unbeknown to us, he had had a few mini strokes. We found this out later from the doctors when he ended up in hospital. He was leaving bags of money sitting at the reception where he was living at the time. I also found out later that he withdrew all his savings from his bank account, which amounted to thousands of pounds. My sister Robyn and I were very concerned about this. She had said to me, "You are the oldest of the family now, you need to do something". We went and sought advice from a nearby community health centre which Social Services were a part of, as well as other professionals. I didn't find the social worker we spoke with to be of much help. All she seemed to be interested in was money.

Robyn and I decided to look for a fold where our father could live instead of returning to a high rise flat on his own. We were unsuccessful in our attempts. During his second stay in hospital, when we went to see him, the nurse had asked us to bring in his equipment for cleaning and managing his Stoma. My father had a total laryngectomy in late 1994, I think. When we left the hospital to go to his flat and get him what he needed, we noticed his flat had been ransacked. We just looked at each other and said nothing. I had my suspicions as to who the culprit might be. I'm not sure if Robyn was thinking the same as me because, as I've said, we didn't talk about it. We got what we had come for and went back to the hospital.

My father ended up being taken out of his flat by the police and Social Services against his will. A few months later he got out from hospital. He was detained at a different hospital and managed to walk out three times, despite the fact that it was supposed to be a secure ward for people suffering from dementia and Alzheimer's. He had found his way back to his flat on three occasions when he walked out. (He obviously had moments of clarity to be able to remember where he lived!)

A social worker had asked me if it was okay if she could call out and have a chat with me. This was before my father was removed from his home. I agreed, believing it would help to provide him with the appropriate care. A few months later I received a phone call from the same social worker to tell me that she, a doctor and the police were at my father's front door. She proceded to tell me what they were there for. I was in total shock.

Ken and I went to visit him when he was detained. I noticed he had no pyjamas, toiletries, nothing but the clothes he had arrived in. The hospital had provided him with a mishmash of trousers and a top. My eldest daughter, Cathy, had said to my nephew Kevin, who took everything to do with my father's money, that Ken had got my father some clothes and toiletries. My nephew wasn't getting him what he needed. However, the money Ken had spent was sent up to me and I then returned it to Ken.

It was approaching Christmas and my father seemed in good spirits. I believe he thought that he could go home whenever he wanted to. His mood changed, and for the first time in my life I had witnessed my father depressed, in fact he said to Ken and I, "I'm feeling depressed".

He was moved from the hospital and put into a care home on the outskirts of Belfast. My younger sister and I went to visit him on one occasion. Ken and I also called to see him. There was a strong smell of urine in the main entrance, and on more than one occasion he was fast asleep in the sitting room. On another visit he said to Ken and me that he was being abused. I questioned the staff about it and was told that my father had used violence on another patient. My father had bruises on his legs which he showed us. I stupidly believed the staff's version of events. He was moved again, this time to a care home not far from where I lived. He was there a year when he died. He was sitting in the day room with other patients at the time. That was Saturday February 11th 2006. He was 80 years old.

I was out for the evening for a night out with a group of women I knew when I received the call from Cathy, my eldest daughter. I and another woman were to meet up with a few other girls but then the call came. She drove me home and went on elsewhere. I went into my house alone and in shock, as one is when you learn of the death of a family member. I rang my son and waited by the living room window in the dark until he got home, which was a few hours after I had rung to tell him. When he got home I rang Dee, the taxi driver that I had become friendly with. We had got to know each other when I was doing my diploma. He was given the job of taking me to the course because of my visual impairment. He worked for an organisation which offers help to people with disabilities. He drove me and my son to the undertakers, not far from where we lived at the time. When we arrived my father's body was in a room at the back of the building. I said I wanted to see my father. One of the undertakers said "He's not ready, his mouth hasn't been shut closed yet". I didn't care. My son and I went in. I said a prayer, stayed a few moments and left.

When they were ready to release his body neither I nor my two sisters wanted to hold his wake. My nephew said that he would hold it at the flat where he had spent most of his childhood, having been reared by my parents. I disagreed because he and I hadn't been getting on. I felt he didn't give me my rightful place as the eldest of our family and I didn't like his greedy, spoilt attitude. My eldest daughter and he are on very good terms. She was and still is, in my opinion, unable or unwilling to see him for what he is. I wanted my father's body to stay at the funeral parlour and then go on to the chapel but Cathy said (under pressure, I believe) that she would hold his wake, which she did.

It was a difficult time for me. I felt excluded by my sisters, nephew and daughter. I was very much on my own during that time. At the crematorium, after my father's coffin went down, family and friends of my deceased father stood up. My sister-in-law nudged me to lead the way out of the chapel, saying "You take charge, it's not his (my nephew's) place". Afterwards, everyone went for tea/coffee in a special room for relatives and friends. It was truly bizarre as my sisters and daughters, their friends and my nephew's friends, sat at one side of the room while my sister-in-law, her two sons and I sat on the other.

Not long after my father's death, one of my sisters rang me to say that I was getting £7000. I told her I didn't want any money and told her where they could stick it. As far as I was concerned, all they cared about was my late father's money. Money my father claimed he never had when he was alive. I remember asking him to make a will years before he died as I was aware, just like my sisters and nephew, that he had money. He was a very mean man who never liked to part with his money. I remember talking with my supervisor when in therapy while studying for my diploma and her saying that money was the only thing he could control.

I felt so angry that my nephew was calling all the shots and that my sisters were only too willing to go along with whatever he said. They wanted their cut. They all made me sick to the stomach. Some time later Cathy told me that my nephew had promised her a new kitchen if she played along; she did, but he failed to deliver. As it turned out, my sisters each gave me two thousand pounds. Maybe they felt guilty that I had got nothing? I had been to see a solicitor who got details of the money my father withdrew from his bank account, which amounted to over sixty thousand pounds. Where did it all go? All I know is what I got. To this day I don't know how much my two sisters got. What I do know is that my nephew's girlfriend, who was expecting at the time, went private to have their baby. Then the following year they went off to Lapland on a family holiday. Needless to say, my relationship with my nephew was severed. I didn't and still don't want anything to do with him or his girlfriend. I was shown no respect as the eldest in my family by any of them; disgusting behaviour driven by greed. It was never about the money for me, but about how I was treated by them. There was nothing I could do about it apart from moving on with my life and continuing with my studies.

The community centre kept me on as a sessional counsellor which meant that I was self-employed for the first time in my life. It was scary for me as I was the only one keeping a roof over my head. My wages depended on how many clients I had, and if they would turn up. If a client didn't turn up for their session it meant I didn't get paid. It was what was known as DNA's (did not attend). Despite the uncertainty, I loved my work and the ethos of the centre. As soon as you walked in you were made to feel welcome, staff and clients alike. At holiday times such as Christmas, Easter and a week's closure in July, I didn't get paid. I was struggling financially, so when my youngest daughter said she could get me started as a housekeeper in a well-established hotel in Belfast I jumped at the chance. I didn't stay there long as it was getting too much for me, leaving the centre late in the afternoon and going to my other job, finishing at eleven o'clock in the evening.

I noticed an ad in the paper advertising for school counsellors and sent away for an application form. I was delighted when I was invited for an interview which lasted an hour. The first half hour was spent answering questions. The second half involved role play. I played the counsellor while one of the women who interviewed me played the client and the other the observer. After about a week I received a letter congratulating me on being successful and was allocated four schools. Two were just down the street from where I lived; one was situated on the Force Road and the other one was in South Belfast. I was really excited and nervous about working in the school in South Belfast. That old nagging feeling about me not being good enough. I was aware that it was a very prestigious school. I needn't have worried.

Before I began my work in the schools in September 2007 Paul's brother and I had booked a holiday to Florida for two weeks in October. My line manager said that it was okay as I had booked the holiday before taking up the post. I introduced myself to my key contacts and addressed the assemblies in each of my four schools. One of my key contacts was not pleased when I told her that I would be going on holiday. Nevertheless, I did what I could before leaving.

My holiday to Florida to see my friend and his family was made even better when I received a phone call while having my breakfast at Paul's restaurant. Cathy had rung to tell me her brilliant news that she was expecting a baby. I was absolutely thrilled with joy and excitement. Then, about ten minutes later, my son rang me to announce his wonderful news, that he and his partner were expecting a baby too. Their baby was due around the twentieth of June. I couldn't contain my overwhelming sense of pride and absolute joy. I shouted over to Paul, who was working behind the bar, "Paul, it's celebration time!"

sharing my good news with him. He was thrilled for me and was about to bring over a bottle of wine when I said "This kind of news deserves to be celebrated with a bottle of Champagne, buddy, not wine". He brought over a bottle of bubbly and we all celebrated my heartwarming news. Needless to say, I left his restaurant a bit tipsy. I didn't care. This was the happiest I had felt since getting my diploma and the work in the schools. Happier, even. I was going to become a granny for a second time. Only this time I would get to be involved in my grandchild's life. I was ecstatic.

The very next day I went to the shops with Paul's wife and bought two nappy bags and two sets of baby clothes. Baby suits, vests, blankets etc... I had purchased so much that Pat, Paul's wife, let me borrow one of their suitcases to put all the stuff into as there was no room in my case.

My son and his girlfriend had stayed in my house while I was on holiday. When I got home I couldn't wait to show my son and daughter what I had got for their expected babies. They seemed pleased with the gifts.

After the holiday was over I was excited and a little nervous about going back to work. It went just fine, though. I soon settled into my role as school counsellor, getting to know the reception staff and my key contacts. I loved working with the young people. I had found my niche in a job which I loved and was good at. It gave me a purpose in life. The staff, principal, and my key contact (the person whom I worked closely with in pastoral care) at the school in South Belfast treated me as a professional and with the utmost respect. The key contact said he was delighted that I was there to help with the care of the young people who attended their school. It was a joy working alongside my key contact. He was so passionate about the role he played within the school and was totally devoted to his work with young people. He was one of the nicest, most dedicated people I have ever had the pleasure to work with.

I thoroughly enjoyed my face-to-face work with the young people in all my schools. I disliked the growing amount of paperwork that came with the job, though. As time went on it became more and more ridiculous. I felt that the job had become more about the paperwork. The DE (Department of Education) were the ones who paid our wages and the organisation, in my opinion, kept coming up with new ways to keep them happy.

Meanwhile, the committee at the community centre where I worked had hired a new manager. She took over from the centre coordinator. When she came in, the ethos went out. I, along with a few other counsellors, left once we had finished working with our clients. I was extremely sad knowing that my time there was coming to an end. The centre coordinator gave me a card with a written message which read "Remember the good times!" She also handed me a small gift. She was the one who believed in me, took me on so that I could finish my diploma and gave me a job as a sessional counsellor. I will always be grateful to her. I worked there for three years, met some really lovely people and made a few friends. I left in March 2008.

I still have a present which was given to me by one of my clients and which I will treasure for the rest of my days. I remember a colleague calling to my house with a bouquet of flowers and a card from a client whom I had worked with and who had left them at the centre for me. I still have other cards that were given to me by clients. These too will be treasured. Another time, a client who I had been working with presented me with a cheque for £80. She wanted to donate this money to the centre as the counselling sessions were offered free to anyone who needed them. The centre was very grateful to my client for her generous gift. The coordinator said that it was perfectly okay to accept cards and gifts from clients. Personally, I agreed with the coordinator.

I trusted my instinct. I can honestly say that the only intention any clients of mine had when giving a card, gift, or cheque was to show that they were genuinely grateful for the help they had received. It was a local community centre, a charity helping those most in need.

I continued my work in the schools and was attending a line management meeting one afternoon, June 19th 2008. That was the day my second granddaughter was born. I was unable to pay attention and asked my line manager if I could leave early. He said no. I pleaded with him, saying "This is cruel. Please let me leave- my granddaughter has just come into the world". He gave in and told me to go, which I did. I ran out of the building and walked up the long road to a shopping centre. I wanted to get a card for my son and his partner. When I arrived at the shopping centre I went looking for a card, a gift for my granddaughter and a gift for mum. People tend to forget about the mums. I got carried away with the shopping. It was a very long walk to the street where I got my bus home, made even more difficult by the many shopping bags I was carrying.

I arrived at the bus stop and got on the first bus that would take me to the hospital. As I was making my way into the grounds of the hospital, I met my sister-in-law. She and my daughter Cathy were on their way out from visiting my son, his partner and our beautiful healthy Brianna.

My heart went out to Cathy. She was visibly upset. She unfortunately lost her baby shortly after I came home from America. She rang me one evening and told me she was staining. She was in a terrible state. I tried to calm her down, assuring her everything would be okay. I suggested we go to the hospital to get her checked out. After being examined, the nurse suggested we all go home and for Cathy to rest. The nurse went on to say that sometimes this can happen. If things weren't any better we should come back down. We arrived back at the hospital, Cathy, her partner and me. I knew she was losing her baby. I asked the nurse would it be okay for me to go in with her and she agreed. That was an extremely hard day, having to watch my daughter grieve for the loss of her baby and what would have been my third grandchild. What made it even more painful for Cathy was that my beautiful granddaughter Brianna was born on the 19th of June, the exact date that Cathy's baby was due. A cruel twist of fate indeed.

I found my way up to the ward where Jackie, my son Sam and my new granddaughter were. I can't explain in words how good it was to hold my second granddaughter Brianna in my arms. She was an absolutely beauty.

When my first granddaughter Alannah came into the world on May 13th 1994 it was such a joy. To be absolutely honest, here I was, 37 years old and not really ready to be a granny. All the same, when I went to the hospital to see her with Robyn, my sister, I fell in love with this absolutely gorgeous blonde-haired bundle of joy.

Regrettably, things didn't go how my son or I would have liked. Alannah's mum, after about two years, began making it difficult for my son to have regular contact with his baby daughter. It ended up with both of us having to go to court to see if we could gain proper access. Sadly, this made no difference. The judge's hands were tied- he couldn't force Alannah's mum to turn up when she was supposed to. It was a tough time for us, to say the least. My son and his daughter were denied the opportunity to form a bond, as were I and Alannah's two aunties. I encouraged him to keep a diary of all the times he had tried to gain access and to keep Christmas and birthday presents in the hope that one day they would be reunited so she would know that she was wanted and loved.

Around 2008 Cathy, my eldest daughter, figured out a way of getting in contact with Alannah who by this stage was 14 years of age. The idea came to her because her stepson (who was around the same age as Alannah) used Bebo to chat with his friends. Cathy tried to get in touch with Alannah using a Bebo account of her own; those were the days shortly before Facebook. Alannah ignored it. Then Cathy thought she'd get her stepson to send one which Alannah accepted. That became the beginning of a relationship that was forming between Cathy and Alannah. They got on very well. Not long after that, Alannah met her dad, Jackie, and her half sister Brianna. I couldn't wait for my turn to meet her.

When my son, his partner, Brianna and Alannah came walking up the path at the back of my house I was so excited to meet Alannah. When she walked into the hall I said "Hello Alannah, it's so good to see you. You look amazing. Is it ok for me to give you a hug?" She said yes. As I hugged her, I felt her body trembling with nerves, bless her. I had longed for this day for so long. We all had. I used to light a candle every year on her birthday, hoping that she would come back into our lives and here she was. My prayers were answered.

At one of my schools in particular, I used to wonder if she was a pupil there. It turned out she was. How strange.

From the very beginning Alannah and Cathy just clicked. Their friendship grew closer and closer. Alannah needed time to get to know her estranged family. It couldn't have been easy for this very polite, somewhat shy, grounded teenager, considering the very difficult time she had with her mum who was suffering from very serious mental health problems. Her granddad and granny reared both her and her younger sister from a very young age and, I have to say, they both did an amazing job. I felt it only right that she, her dad, his partner and her new baby sister got to know each other first. I tried to form a relationship with her but she always seemed to shy away. I'm not entirely sure why.

I would make arrangements for us to meet up and go into town at Christmas and birthdays. She seemed to enjoy our time spent together. When she did well at school I offered to take her out for lunch to celebrate, which we did. I yearned for that closeness that she and Cathy had. I guess I'm not as cool to be around as Cathy was. I was just extremely happy that she was back in our lives.

Brianna coming into the world give me a second chance at being a granny. She was and still is such a joy to be around. She and I formed a loving bond, and I have to admit that I spoiled her rotten. She can do no wrong in my eyes. Having said that, I know the importance of teaching her right from wrong. I did everything in my power to be the best granny I could be. I love her and she loves me. There's nothing in this world that can beat the feeling I have when we spend time together. My son and his partner didn't allow her to stay overnight with me or her other granny. I found that very sad and disappointing but that was how they were and I had to accept it.

My colleagues and I learned that the organisation we worked for was in danger of losing the tender from the DE. This was during the summer of 2009. We were assured that our jobs would be safe as we would be protected by TUPE (being transfered from one business to another). I was praying the tender would go elsewhere and thankfully my prayers were answered. I was looking forward to working with another counselling organisation. I saw it as the beginning of a new chapter in my career.

When September arrived we had our usual training for the first week or so. We learned who our new line managers would be and which schools we would be working in. I changed one of my schools. It was one that was given to me by the previous organisation and I really didn't enjoy working in that particular school. It caused me problems right from the beginning. Apparently there was some sort of upset by the teaching staff regarding confidentiality and the previous counsellor.

I was offered no support on my first day by either my line manager or management- it was a bit like going into a lion's den. Thankfully, there was a representative from the Department of Education there who spoke very well at the meeting which was organised by the principal of the school and teaching staff.

It was a bit chaotic in the first few months while the management and line managers tried to get things organised. The first year working for this new counselling organisation was fantastic. The paperwork was cut by half which meant I could do the work I loved with ease because there was less stress, plus we didn't have telephone counselling duties like in the previous organisation. The following year things changed. The amount of paperwork began to increase more and more. We were told that we all needed to think about working towards our BACP accreditation (British Association for Counselling and Psychotherapy). The DE were insisting that anyone working in schools needed to be accredited counsellors, which was fair enough. It was no longer good enough to just be a member of BACP.

In the summer of 2010 I began working on my accreditation. There was quite a lot of work that needed to be done, including a case study of a client you were working with (asking for their permission, which I did). Writing a piece on your continued professional development (CPD). Self-awareness (describing an experience or an activity which had contributed to my own self-awareness). My knowledge and understanding. Describing a rationale for my client work with reference to the theory/theories that informed my practice. Last but not least, I had to evidence how many client hours I worked, their issues and how long each session lasted. It cost me £230, plus I sought advice from an accredited supervisor as I needed her help (I had two sessions with her that cost £50 a session, so that was a further £100). I didn't care. As far as I was concerned, this needed to be done and I wanted to submit my work and receive my accreditation before the organisation started putting pressure on us, which they did when we returned in September of 2010. They told us that anyone who hadn't got their accreditation or was not working towards it would lose their jobs.

I found that the amount of work involved in getting the accreditation was a lot harder than my diploma. I was glad to see the back of it. It took me two months to finish. I had spent that July and August working non stop but I was very glad that I did. I posted my finished work off to BACP by registered post and was hoping it wouldn't be sent back as there were quite a few of my colleagues whose work was sent back for one reason or another. Such a relief, it really was, when I had got it finished.

My son Sam and his partner were expecting their second child in December of 2010. I was on my way up to supervision, sitting on the bus when my phone rang. It was Sam. He and Jackie were at the hospital for her five-month scan. He said that they were going to have a boy. I said "Wow, that's brilliant, a boy, fantastic. I'm sure you are both over the moon". He then told me the bad news. The scan had revealed that their baby boy had a diaphragmatic hernia. He went on to explain what that meant. The doctor told them that in the worst case scenario their baby could die at birth. The second scenario would involve surgery that would have to be carried out fairly quickly after birth. I was dumbfounded. Tears began running down my face. I didn't know what to say. I told him how sorry I was and that I was on a bus on my way to supervision and would ring him later.

When I arrived at supervision I told my supervisor what had happened. We spent the hour talking about my son, his partner and my grandson. I was unable to talk about my clients and she was aware of that. I found her support very helpful that day.

My heart went out to Sam and his partner Jackie, it really did. How awful for a woman to be five months pregnant and not knowing if the baby she's carrying will live or die. It was a long time of uncertainty and worry for us all, particularly for Sam and Jackie. I remember looking after Brianna one day while they had to go for another appointment to see the paediatrician and others who were caring for them and their baby. When they returned the look on both their faces told me they were in a lot of emotional pain. It was heartbreaking to see them so broken.

September came around so quickly. To be honest, I was glad to get back to work. It helped take my mind off Sam, Jackie and my grandson. There was nothing I could do but pray, which I did plenty of, and look after Brianna any time they needed me to.

Most of my colleagues hadn't even begun work on their accreditation. Some had made a start, a few others like me had managed to get theirs sent away, and there were some who had received theirs either before we broke up for our summer holidays or during our holidays. I always disliked addressing the assemblies each September. It was something that never got any easier, probably because I wasn't doing it on a regular basis. The school in South Belfast always seemed to be the easiest, though. I'm not sure if that's because I had such good working relationships with all who were involved in addressing the assembly.

Jackie was admitted to hospital on December 14th at eight o'clock in the morning. I had asked my then line manger if I could have the day off to look after Brianna. My line manager knew of Sam and Jackie's circumstances and the worry and stress it was causing me. She refused to allow me to take that day off, saying it wasn't immediate family. (A year later she gave the OK for a close colleague of mine to go on a foreign trip to Africa for a week! They knew each other outside of work and are both Christians with common interests).

On my way up to work in South Belfast that morning I rang Jackie to ask how she was. My heart ached for her as she began telling me what may or may not be happening that day. She was crying and I felt so helpless. I longed to be with her just to hold her hand but it never happened. I assured her that I would collect Brianna from creche and that she'd be well taken care of.

It was difficult for me to stay present with my clients that morning, to be honest. Once I got into their stories, however, I was fine. I was glad I only had three clients that day. Just before my last client came in my key contact asked me if I wouldn't mind speaking with an ex-pupil of the school. He was studying at university and wanted to know how I thought counselling helped pupils in school. He was a lovely young man. When my key contact asked me would I help him out I found it difficult to refuse him and the young man in question. I thought, "It would have to be today of all days". However, it all worked out okay. I left the school and walked down to where Brianna's creche was, quite some distance away from the school in South Belfast. I walked into the corridor, informing the staff I was there to pick up my granddaughter Brianna. Jackie had let the staff know the day before that I would be picking her up. Out she came with her small bag in her tiny hand. I took hold of her hand, kissed her on the cheek and asked if she had had a good day. She showed me a drawing she had drawn for her mummy. I asked her would she like KFC (chippies and chicken) and she said yes.

When we arrived at KFC I found us a seat very near the counter, ordered our meal and waited while keeping an eye on her. When our meal was ready I carried it over to our table. I couldn't help but notice that my one year and five-month-old granddaughter looked sad. We finished our meal and left.

I wheeled her in her pram up to the bus stop and waited until the right bus came along. We arrived at my house and I put on a dvd for her to watch as she was crazy about Peppa Pig at the time. I had tried ringing my son but his phone was switched off. I eventually received a call from him saying that his son had survived and that he weighed

8 pounds which would stand him in good stead for what was to come- the operation. I was so relieved, as were his parents.

Later on that evening, Sam called into my house to bring his wee (a Belfast saying) daughter home. He looked exhausted. It had been a long day for him and his partner. The doctor who was looking after Lorcan said that there was a window of opportunity for Lorcan to have his much-needed surgery. He couldn't survive without it. I couldn't wait to get to see my grandson. It was a few days before I or any other family member was allowed to visit. I remember feeling both anxious and excited at the thought of seeing my first grandson.

As my son and I approached the children's ICU ward where Lorcan had been since his birth on Tuesday, I wasn't sure what to expect. When my son led me to the incubator I just stood and stared at this beautiful baby boy who looked normal to me. In fact, he looked really big compared to the other babies. His chest seemed huge, probably due to his spleen and other organs having been moved up into his chest, occupying the space where his lungs should be.

I felt so many different kinds of emotions after seeing my beautiful grandson for the very first time. I was very glad and relieved that he had survived coming into this world, but fearful about the operation he needed to keep him alive. I know it was probably the most worrying time in both Sam and Jackie's lives.

Lorcan's team of doctors decided that they needed to operate quickly. They had been monitoring him closely since his birth and were well aware of just how fragile and serious his condition was. They kept Sam and Jackie informed every step of the way. They decided the operation couldn't wait any longer. It was a Friday. I remember it well. I was hoping and praying Lorcan would be okay. My son kept insisting that he wouldn't be leaving the hospital without his son.

After midday I received a phone call from my son to say that while they were preparing Lorcan for surgery he had gone into cardiac arrest and his undamaged lung had been damaged as a result. His brain was starved of oxygen for six minutes. Thankfully, he survived. As a result of this, they were unable to perform his life-saving operation until he was stronger.

About a week after that, Lorcan went a second time to the operating theatre. I, along with his parents, was extremely anxious. (Only his parents were allowed at the hospital at that stage.) What a relief when I received the phone call from Sam saying that the operation was a success.

Lorcan remained seriously ill for some time after. What a champion!! He was only a few weeks old and I felt so incredibly proud of this little fighter to have come through all that he had. Simply amazing. Not to mention the intricate skills of the surgeon who performed this life-saving surgery. Thank God for people like him. We will be eternally grateful for all that he and the other medical staff at the hospital did for Lorcan and other babies in similar situations.

Once Lorcan was allowed to go home he was in and out of hospital so many times as he had very bad reflux, too. He really did struggle physically, poor wee mite. He was also badly scarred from his surgery but he was alive, loved and cared for.

Sam and Jackie cut back on Christmas celebrations in 2010 although they did the best they could to give Brianna a good Christmas. Their main concern was taking care of their daughter and their sick infant son. I had made them dinner on Christmas Day. It wasn't the usual Christmas dinner- I just wanted to make sure they had something decent to eat.

The following day, Boxing Day, I looked after Brianna so they could both stay with Lorcan in the hospital. It must have been getting on for eleven o'clock pm when Sam returned to my house and took Brianna, who was asleep on my sofa, home to their house.

On the 28th of December 2010 I received a letter from BACP informing me that I had been successful in attaining my accreditation. I was over the moon. I will never forget December 2010. The birth of my precious grandson and all that he went through and survived, and achieving my accreditation. December certainly ended well for me and my family.

The night before New Year's Eve, my friend Maggie and her partner were coming up to my house for a drink. I had stopped the New Year's Eve celebrations a few years before as it's a sad time for me, having lost my two brothers and my two friends. One was to cancer in '99 and the other who left for America in '97. Also, Ken was out of my life too and I just didn't see the point.

The last really good New Year's Eve celebrations had been in 2008. My sister and I spent a week on holiday in Gran Canaria at Playa Del Ingles resort. It was only the second holiday we had ever had together.

On another occasion a friend of mine invited me to go camping with her just for one night in the Mourne Mountains in Co Down. While I was getting ready Robyn rang me. I told her I was going camping with a friend and taking Jack, Sam's dog with me. I invited her along. She said no to begin with as she was off the drink. She had just come off a bender (binge drinking). I said "That's okay. You don't have to drink. It'll do you good to get away". She said yes, she would like to go. When my friend arrived I said that Robyn would be joining us. She was perfectly fine about it. She had met Robyn and, like everyone else, liked her. We ended up camping at Slievemore. We got our tent up and had a lovely evening.

Our first holiday away was when we stayed at a little cottage in Portsnorth. Everyone in our family went except Alvin and our younger sister and her son. That was in 1992. This was our first holiday abroad for Robyn and me sadly it would be our last. Robyn was an active alcoholic and because of this I was a little concerned about her drinking and wondered if she would go at all. She paid her deposit and was giving me money each week to keep for her towards the holiday. She did seem to be in a better place then, despite her continuing drinking. She only drank beer on our holiday and stayed away from spirits. There was no drinking during the day either, which meant we actually had a lovely time together. To be honest, I was relieved. I took a chance going on holiday with her, knowing that she was an addict as addicts let people down due to their dependency on whatever drug they are on. But she managed to hold it together and seemed to be enjoying her holiday.

One day we took a taxi from our hotel to a huge shopping mall about six miles away and enjoyed spending a good part of the day there. On the way back to our hotel I left my purse in the taxi with €900 in it. As soon as we got into the hotel I asked the receptionist to call the taxi firm. I never did see my €900 again. Robyn took me out that night for a Chinese. I think she felt sorry for me. Luckily, I had enough money to do me until I got home.

We had paid for a boat trip the day after we arrived at our hotel. It included dinner and a fireworks display for New Year's Eve celebrations. It was a fantastic night, one we both thoroughly enjoyed. Robyn had such a great personality. She was very funny and made everyone laugh, just like Frederick, our brother. She had lost her spark after the death of her daughter, but on that holiday it came back, if only for a short while.

She instantly made friends with a lovely couple who were from Europe. They got on very well together. She also flirted with one of the male crew who was attending to everyone on the boat. I still have the photos of her and the people she made laugh that night. Lovely memories of my sister. When the night ended we got off the boat and walked the short distance to where the bus was parked and waiting to take everyone back to their hotels. The bus stopped at our hotel, which was the last stop, and on my way out of the bus, just as I put my right foot on the ground, I somehow managed to sprain my ankle. Thankfully, it happened not long before our return home.

Meanwhile, the night before New Year's Eve 2010, Robyn rang me. She was at a loose end on her own and sounding lonely. I invited her down to my house, telling her that Maggie and her partner were coming up. She said "Yes, I'll be down soon". Maggie and her partner arrived not long after Robyn had rung me. We were sitting out in my kitchen having a drink when after a few hours Robyn knocked at my door. When I opened it she had an old wooden stick in her hand and said to me "Rebecca, here's a replacement for you. Remember you said you would give me Frederick's walking stick?" I said back to her "No, I never told you I would give you his walking stick". She obviously had been drinking as she was quite drunk when she arrived. She kept going on and on about it until I finally snapped and said in a firm voice, "Stop telling lies and shut up". So she did.

I could never keep up with Maggie or Robyn when we had a drink so I said I was off to bed. Maggie wasn't too pleased. Robyn decided she would call and see a guy she was seeing who lived just down the street from me. I woke up the next morning and the kitchen was in a mess, although it could have been worse. At least the lights were all switched off and my doors locked.

It turns out they all went down to Maggie's house and continued drinking. Apparently, Maggie told Robyn's man to leave. I had never met him and had no desire to either. What I'd heard of him didn't paint a pretty picture. I noticed a massive change in my sister. She was hitting the drink hard. Some difference in her behaviour from two years earlier.

We had bought tickets in 2009 to go to see Leonard Cohen play in Belfast on Sunday July the 26th. We were both really looking forward to it. We had loved his music since we were teenagers. The tickets cost us £95 each, a lot of money, but we didn't care. It was a wonderful opportunity to be able to see this influential singer/songwriter play with his band at the Odyssey Arena. I couldn't wait and I thought Robyn felt the same way.

On Sunday the 26th, around midday, there was a knock at my front door. When I opened the door one of Robyn's friends was standing there and said that Robyn had spilt boiling water all over her foot and leg. I went out to see her- I walked up the path to her friend's car where Robyn was sitting with bandages on her foot and leg. I said "What the fuck have you done?" Her friend said she hadn't been drinking. It happened that morning and they had only just come back from the hospital. I refused to believe her. I was mad as hell with her. I had no sympathy for her whatsoever.

I was so disappointed and felt let down big time. God forgive me, I was so angry with her. They drove away and I came back into the house and thought "I'll go by myself. Who can I get to come with me at this short notice?" I rang a few people but they weren't interested. Then I rang a woman who was on the diploma course with me. She and I had become friends. Robyn said to give her ticket away. She didn't care. This woman said that she would come with me and give Robyn the money for the ticket. I'm still waiting. Needless to say that friendship ended. What kind of person does that? She had met Robyn and was supposed to be my friend- hah! Who needs friends like that? Certainly not me.

I did feel bad that Robyn had missed out on the concert as she would have loved it. I bought a dvd the night of the concert. It was of his show in London, exactly the same song set as they played in Belfast. When I got home after the concert I played the dvd from start to finish. It was definitely one of the best concerts I have ever been to in my life, without a doubt.

I invited Robyn down to my house a few weeks after the concert and we both watched it together. She loved it. I told her that I still hadn't received any money for her ticket but she wasn't bothered one bit.

I continued working with the young people in my three schools but was counting down the days until the summer break. The workload had increased so much. We had to not only do paper copies of all the referral forms etc but had to put all relevant information onto the counselling database as well. Write our own line management reports, appraisal forms and so much more. The bureaucracy was just too much, it really was. I was supposed to be working a 20-hour week but believe me it was more like a 30-hour week, only we didn't get paid for it. It became all about targets, meeting targets. This wasn't what I signed up for. I had studied hard to become a counsellor to work with people, not paper and databases. I said to my line manager at one of our meetings, "All this pressure is too much. These are young people in pain, some in crisis. It's not a conveyor belt".

My grandson Lorcan was in and out of hospital an awful lot. I got to see him when I could. His parents were worn out with all the stress. I remember one time while visiting Lorcan I sent Jackie over for a massage not far from the hospital. I had been going there myself for treatments for my feet. I rang to see if Jackie and Sam could be seen and luckily there was a space. Jackie was very reluctant to go but I insisted. When she returned I sent my son over. They needed a break. My heart went out to them both, particularly Sam, as he would stay overnight with his son and then have to go into work for hours afterwards. It was an extremely difficult period in their lives. I helped out in any way I could. I remember I would walk down to the hospital on a Saturday morning to see my grandson and stay with him for a while. He looked so helpless and pitiful, poor wee darling. I could see that he was in pain. My eldest daughter Cathy would also visit him and take him out in his pram (after seeking permission from the hospital staff). I thought it was a good idea- fresh air would do him good. A change from being stuck in a hospital cot.

Monday morning the 13th of June 2011 around eight o'clock I switched on my mobile phone and listened to a voicemail from my sister Robyn. She had left a message the previous evening. In those days I used to switch my phone off before going to bed. Her message said "Why don't you ever answer your fucking phone?" She sounded angry and I thought that she may have been drinking.

I rang her straight away and asked her how she was, was she okay? She was very upset, crying, not really saying very much except that she and her daughter Kate had had an argument. I said back to her "You two will make it up. You always do". She said "I fought the paramilitaries for her". (After the death of her eldest daughter, Clare, to suicide thirteen years earlier, some of Clare's friends believed that an alleged Republican who lived not far from their home was responsible).

Robyn blamed this person for the death of her beautiful daughter and, as a result, said whatever she liked to certain people living in the area. Robyn later moved from the house in which Clare died to a street not far from her old house. Apparently there was a neighbour living nearby who was a staunch Republican. I was told that Kate began calling this person names and making her feelings clear that she didn't like her new neighbour. She was apparently causing upset in the area too.

Clare defended her daughter and, as a result, the Restorative Justice became involved. Robyn had to go to see someone each week, I believe it was. I remember going with her once. It didn't help Robyn at all. She was told to go for counselling which she did a few times. Not long after that she was told she had 24 hours to get out of her house and the area.

I know Robyn's behaviour was wrong. She wasn't capable of being rational. She had an addiction problem as well as suffering from severe trauma after the death of her daughter to suicide. There were also unresolved issues from her past that contributed to her present behaviour. Counselling only works for people who want it. It is not something that can be forced on a person.

I helped her gather up her belongings. She didn't seem to care that she had lost her home. I went with her to the Housing Association where she had a meeting with an HA officer who explained why she was being evicted. He told her about a local hostel where she could stay. I grew angry with her because of her 'couldn't give a fuck' attitude. In hindsight, I believe she was so out of touch with her feelings. She was in denial. It was the only way she knew how to protect herself. Later on she, her husband and daughter got a flat in Dolawn and lived there for a short while before moving back to Belfast in a small cul-de-sac. The bungalow where they ended up living was for people with disabilities as her husband had acute asthma. He died from a massive asthma attack in February 2007, aged 49. Robyn was allowed to continue living at the bungalow alone. I said to her "Everything will work out fine; it always does. I'm the same with my girls, as you know. We argue, don't talk to each other for a while and then make up. You'll be fine. I have to get ready for work. Talk with you later".

I made my way to work and as I was walking down the road to my school, which wasn't that far from where I lived, I remember thinking to myself "Only two more weeks then I'm off for two months! I'm nearly there. I can do this". When I arrived at the school I did my usual and checked in with the staff at reception (who by the way were the nicest people in the school). One girl in particular went far and beyond her call of duty. Nothing was too much trouble for her. I would have been lost without her support.

I had only two clients to see that morning, or so I thought. My key contact had asked me if I could see another young person to which I replied yes, no problem. While working with the young people my phone was always switched off. When I had my break at around eleven I switched my phone on and noticed that I had five or more missed calls from my youngest daughter Betty. She had left me a voicemail. I also noticed she had sent me a few text messages.

As soon as I had finished working with my clients I rang Betty. I asked her what was wrong. She was in a terrible state and said "Mummy, Robyn rang me this morning to say she was going to kill herself and even told me what colour of scarf she would use". I asked her where she was. She told me she had driven up to Robyn's but the front door was locked and the blinds were all closed. I said "Come down to the school and I'll go up to Robyn's with you. You're not dealing with this on your own". She told me she had tried about nine times to get in contact with Kate, Robyn's daughter, but her phone was switched off. She said she had left messages on her phone. I could hear the despair, desperation and panic in her voice. I said to drive carefully. "I bet she's lying up there blocked. I'm going to give her a piece of my mind".

When Betty arrived I got into her car and she drove us up to her bungalow. I repeated what I'd said on the phone about Robyn being drunk. I was so angry that Robyn was putting my daughter through this. When we arrived outside her bungalow I banged on the door but there was no answer. I went round all the windows at the front and back and knocked on the windows, shouting "Robyn!" Still nothing. When I reached her bathroom window at the side of her bungalow an eerie feeling came over me. I decided to go over and get the key to her front door from the warden who lived across the street. I explained that I was worried about my sister. She got the key and as we walked over to her door I said "Don't you go in, I'll do it". She replied, "There's no way I'm going in there". She opened the door with the key. I walked into the hall and looked to my right where the bathroom was. The door was open. I looked in and saw my sister hanging from the shower rail.

I walked back out and nodded to Betty. She screamed and said "I need to see for myself." I pushed her away and said "She's dead. We need to call for an ambulance and the police". She was in bits, as was I. The warden rang the emergency services while we were still standing outside her door. Betty tried again to gain access and I stopped her again. I didn't want my daughter to see what I had seen. It was bad enough for her. She was the one who Robyn rang, telling her that she was going to end her life that day.

The emergency services arrived very quickly. One of the paramedic crew ran into the bungalow with a bag. The other paramedic was about to do the same when the first guy came out, nodding his head; it was too late. The police went in and did what they're supposed to do. One of the police officers came back outside asking me, Betty and the warden questions.

I was in deep shock and was finding it difficult to speak with any coherence. My head was all over the place, as was Betty's. The warden invited Betty and me over to her house and made us tea which neither one of us drank. Betty was busy on the phone to her friends telling them what happened. I believe she was able to contact Kate and let her know the devastating news about her mother. I rang my friend Maggie, my daughter Cathy and my line manager who normally didn't answer her phone. When she answered I said "Thank God you answered your phone". I told her what had happened. I guess she was shocked and dumbfounded on hearing this dreadful news about my sister. She asked me if I needed any help. She also asked me if I needed her there with me. I said "No. All I need are my children".

I rang my son Sam and Jackie answered his phone. She must have known by my voice that something terrible had happened because she said quite quickly, "I'll get him for you". He came to the phone and asked what was up. I told him what had happened and he said "Oh no, I'll be there as soon as I can".

I had rung everyone I could think of who needed to know. I felt so utterly alone. There were lots of people standing in the street, talking and crying. One of Robyn's neighbours was in a terrible state. More and more people began arriving in the street, including Cathy, my friend Maggie, her partner, a few of her children, Kate, Robyn's daughter, and my son and his partner.

I was in bits by this stage. I was aware that there were lots of people standing in the street, hardly able to take in what had happened. Everyone was in shock, crying, including me. Maggie hugged me so tight when she came over to me. I was in so much need of a hug. She was in bits as Robyn was her friend too. We stood at the bottom of Robyn's front path. The police were still inside. The undertakers had arrived about two hours after I'd found my sister's body. As they began wheeling her body out onto the path I said to Maggie, crying bitterly, "I can't watch this". She said to look away, which I did. I then said "I can hear the sound of her dead body being wheeled down the path, it is deafening". She said as she held onto me "You can handle this, at least you haven't lost a son". I asked her for a cigarette as my body was shaking. She took a cigarette out of her packet and handed it to me. I thought about taking it then changed my mind and said "No, I don't want one".

After her body had been taken away we all went down to my house. Me, Maggie, her partner and three of her children, (one of whom had only arrived home that morning from Cyprus). Also there were both of my daughters, Cathy and Betty and my son and his partner. It was one of the worst experiences of my life. I didn't know where I was or what I was doing. Somehow I felt I had to keep it together so that's what I tried to do. I don't know why.

Maggie, my son and I called down to my younger sister's flat to let her know what happened. I rang her buzzer and she answered asking "Who's there?" I said "It's me, Amber, I've got some bad news to tell you". She let us all in (which surprised me). She walked into her living room and sat down on a chair. I began telling her the awful news and when I was finished, she shook her head, saying "Nope, I don't believe it". I continued, "I know it's hard to take in but sadly it's true. I wish it wasn't". She kept saying "Our Robyn wouldn't do that". She flatly refused to believe me. Maggie tried telling her. So did my son and she still refused to believe us. I said to her "Do you really think that we would be standing here telling you something as awful as this if it wasn't true?" We saw no point staying there any longer but before I left, I wrote down my phone number and said "If you need me, call me".

Amber had stopped speaking to me. It had been months since I last spoke with her, or should I say since she last spoke to me. One Tuesday after work I had walked to my bus stop in town, got on and as it turned the corner to another bus stop Amber got on. She sat down beside me and began talking nonstop. By the time the bus arrived at her stop I was so glad and breathed a sigh of relief.

About two years earlier Robyn had told me that Amber believed she was being watched and that her computer was bugged. I didn't believe it. Then a while later Amber had called to a friend of Robyn's mother's house, asking her to accompany her to the police station to report what was going on, which she did. Robyn said that she and a friend were walking down a street and Amber started on them for gossiping about her business to everyone. I felt sorry for Amber. I thought that Robyn was being cruel, talking about her sister in that way. I had met Amber while out for a walk. She began telling me that Robyn was spreading rumours about her. I said that I didn't believe them. She threw her arms around me and thanked me for believing her, adding, "Thank God somebody believes me". She never spoke to Robyn again. In fact, she loathed her.

Amber rang me one day, not that long after I'd met her on the street. We started chatting and our mother came into the conversation. I said to her, "I used to think that it was just our dad who was strong. Now I realise that our mother must have been a very strong person". She had lost her first-born son for many years before he returned back into her life. Later, she had lost her other two sons. She didn't use alcohol to anaesthetise herself. She went through it all sober.

A day later I came home from work and switched on my answering machine. There was a message from Amber. She was seething, calling me some horrible names and saying "How dare you say that I'm not strong" and accusing me of all sorts. I listened for a minute or two and then deleted her message. She had given me proof that she wasn't in a good place. I then felt regret for not having believed Robyn. I felt very sad and sorry for my sister. The conversation we had had on the phone that day was the last until I showed up at her flat on the 13th of June 2011.

After a while, Maggie, along with Cathy, started drinking. I really wanted one too but didn't have one until much later on. Cathy stayed with me that night. When everyone had gone home Cathy asked me "Why did your brothers die so young and now Robyn? Did something happen to you all in your childhood?" The last thing I wanted to talk about was my childhood but Cathy was insistent. She was like a dog with a bone, she just wouldn't let it drop. I kept saying "I don't remember my childhood". But she kept on and on until I finally told her about the time when Frederick was high. I don't know what drugs he had taken, I just know that I was upstairs and he called me into his bedroom. He tried to get me into bed with him but I said no. He went on to say "It's okay, you'll not get pregnant". Again I said no and left his room. That was the only time anything like that happened. We never spoke of it again. I don't know if he even remembered, but I did. I remember telling Amber about it in the 1970's and she told me he did the same thing to her.

I cried so hard, having to tell my daughter what happened that day all those years ago. I believe I was about fourteen at the time. I felt so completely harassed and vulnerable. Afterwards I went to bed. I'm not sure what time Cathy went.

The following morning I woke up crying. I couldn't stop. It took me a while before I felt able to get out of bed and go downstairs. I have no memory of Cathy being there that day. I remember people knocking at my front door and I wouldn't answer it. My son, his partner and my granddaughter Brianna came to see me. Jackie and Brianna stayed with me the second night. The same thing happened the following morning. I woke up crying, unable to stop. Eventually, I made my way downstairs. Jackie and Brianna were in the kitchen. I sat at the kitchen table when Brianna, who was nearly three at the time, asked me "Granny, why are you sad?" I thought for a moment and said "Sometimes things happen that make us feel sad, sweetheart".

I rang my buddy in America to let him know as he really liked Robyn and I thought it only right to tell him. His wife answered the phone. She had met Robyn quite a few times and spent time in her company. (My buddy and his wife lived here for a short time before returning to America). They got on really well together. She was absolutely gobsmacked. She asked me what happened and I told her. She said she would let Paul know and said how sorry she was.

I had called up to see Robyn's daughter on one of the days before Robyn's body came up to her house. Kate was getting married in July and was away on her hen do on Friday, returning that Monday when she learned of her mother's death. My heart went out to her, it really did. First her sister and now her mum.

The third night my friend came up to stay with me. She's into tarot cards and that type of stuff. She brought up all sorts of stones and other spiritual stuff. I know she thought she was helping, but really it was putting my head away. Still, I was glad she was there. I hadn't heard from Maggie since that Monday.

On Wednesday morning I was up in my bathroom when I heard my back door being knocked. It knocked a second time, only louder. Then I heard my son's voice shouting "Mummy, Mummy!" I got down the stairs as fast as I could and opened the door to let him in. He looked so relieved to see me. We sat at my kitchen table and I said to him "Listen son, I'm down but I'm not out!"

The next day, Thursday, my son called up again with his partner and took me up to Kate's house. Robyn's body was being waked at her house. As we got out from his car and began walking up the path I noticed Robyn's son sitting outside along with a few other people. I went over to him and said how sorry I was. I couldn't just walk past him, I just couldn't. As I entered Kate's house I turned to my son and said "I have to go". I thought I was about to have an anxiety attack. I felt that my heart was about to burst open. I needed to get out of there. Obviously, I was deeply traumatised when I discovered my sister's body hanging. My whole body was reacting to that trauma. Of course, I hadn't realised that at the time. I just knew I had to leave and that's what I did.

Her body was due to arrive at the house around two o'clock. I said as I was getting back into my son's car, "They're all gone now, there's no one left". I felt a deep sense of loss. My feelings of loss were unbearable. I felt that my entire family were no longer here; they had all gone. Jackie started talking about her family, saying "They are all going to die". I felt really angry but didn't say anything. Inside I was thinking, "What are you talking about? This is happening to me now. You still have your family".

I called back up later that evening and somehow I found the strength to go into Kate's living room where Robyn's body lay in her coffin. She looked a lot younger. All her wrinkles were gone. She had what seemed like a kind of smile on her face. I don't know why I felt the need to take a photo of her. Maybe it was because I preferred the image of her in the coffin to the one in my head when I last saw her.

The house was full of people, inside and out. I couldn't bear it. It felt very claustrophobic to me. I found it difficult to breathe. Kate told me that people from my work had called up to the wake. I was glad I missed them. I didn't want to talk about it with anyone from work. One woman I knew at school and her friend called that evening too. Kate asked me if I wanted to call round to Robyn's bungalow and get a few of her things to remember her by. I agreed, although as I was approaching her front path I could feel the anxiety begin to rise in my chest. My heart started racing, especially as I followed behind Kate into the bungalow.

I walked as quickly as I could past her bathroom, deliberately avoiding eye contact with the bathroom door and the inside. When I got into her living room the intensity of the anxiety I felt began to subside slightly. Kate seemed very keen to offer me some of her belongings like her jewellery, cd's, glasses and a few of Alvin's paintings she had that our mother had given her after his death. I didn't want anything. I said "All I need is in my heart". She insisted I take her glasses and two Bob Dylan cds so I did. I couldn't wait to get out of there. It felt extremely difficult and eerie.

When I arrived back at my house I noticed bouquets of flowers on the front doorstep. They were from my colleagues in work and were mostly white lilies. To this day I can't stand the sight of them. I'm also allergic to them. I placed them out the back. There were also sympathy cards, loads of them, which I placed on my kitchen table. Some really unusual but lovely ones from two of my schools.

I began using the back door when leaving and entering my house. I just didn't want to talk to people. I had missed a few of my colleagues who had called when I was up in Kate's. There were a few I really didn't want to talk to at all. The ones I did, I let in when they called to the house. Neighbours also called up but I felt they just wanted information (all the gory details) which I hadn't the energy to deal with so I refused to entertain them.

Friday, the morning of Robyn's funeral, I made my way up to Kate's house. There were so many people lining the street and loads more standing inside and outside Kate's house. I met for the first time a guy whom Robyn really liked. He asked me "Are you Rebecca?" I said yes. He introduced himself and said "I think you know how much Robyn meant to me". They were really good friends but Robyn wanted more than friendship. She needed someone to love and who would love her back. She was so lonely after her husband died. Unfortunately, she wasn't lucky enough to meet that special someone.

One of Robyn's female friends began crying hysterically. She had been drinking and kept interrupting the priest who was trying to say a few prayers before the undertakers could do their job. Eventually the priest managed to calm her down and Robyn's coffin was carried out onto the street by the undertakers. Kate, her brother and a few more of Robyn's friends carried her coffin down the street. People took it in turns to act as pallbearers.

More than half way down the street my friend Maggie said "Right, it's our turn to carry her coffin". My left shoulder was very painful at the time and I said to Maggie "I don't think I can do this, my shoulder is sore". She said "Of course you can". I walked over to take over from the person who was carrying her coffin and tried to put it on my left shoulder. I just couldn't do it. It felt as though my shoulder was going to break. The pain was excruciating. I had to stop. I can't remember who came to my rescue.

I noticed an old friend of ours standing in the rain on the footpath as the funeral cortege was making its way to the chapel. Robyn and I had attended her mum's funeral a year or so before that. Our friend had grown up in the same street as us.

As I entered the chapel I noticed one of my key contacts standing there. Another one of my key contacts was going to be attending her funeral too, at least that's what my line manager had told me. I didn't see him, my line manager or any of my colleagues. I kept my head down as I continued to proceed to my seat in the chapel. Once the funeral service began the memory that stands out in my head was when the priest began talking about my sister and the many losses she suffered in her life. I believe my nephew (Robyn's son) had given the priest a list of names of all those she has lost. I wondered why he felt it necessary to do that. I'm sure he had his reasons. The priest named each one of them. Our brothers, her beautiful daughter, her husband, many of her friends and our parents. Tears began to run down my face and when Maggie noticed this she pinched my arm to get me to stop, which I did, although it wasn't easy. I guess she didn't want me to fall apart.

When we all arrived at the cemetery to lay her body to rest I began to feel very anxious. There were so many people at the graveside. I was standing right at the front along with Betty. It was all over very quickly, or so it seemed. My friend and her new boyfriend were there.

They came over to pay their respects. Betty drove me home. There was tea/coffee, a really beautiful spread laid on afterwards in a local club for Robyn's family and friends. I'm not sure why we went back to my house first. Betty parked her car behind my house as it was easier than parking at the front. We were not long in when someone knocked at the front door. Betty answered it. It was one of my neighbours. She came in, sat down and asked some very intrusive questions about my sister and said "Wasn't that her daughter who 'committed suicide' who used to live behind us?" I said as little as I could and told her that we needed to be leaving. I wish I had had the strength to tell her to mind her own business and ask her to leave. She came at the right time. She must have known we were only just back from Robyn's funeral and had seen us walking past her window, the perfect opportunity to come asking very painful and personal questions.

When Betty and I arrived at the do a short time later Maggie, her sister (a close friend of Robyn's), Maggie's partner and their families were sitting at a table all on their own. I asked "Can I squeeze in?" Maggie said "Yes, grab a chair," so I did but the atmosphere was unpleasant to say the least. I didn't feel wanted so I moved to another table. I think the reason may have been because they were there to get hammered (drunk) and didn't want to or couldn't deal with my grief.

I got speaking with a lovely woman who lived not far from Robyn. She loved Robyn. She began telling me stories of the fun times they all had together before Clare's death. I spoke with a few other people who knew Robyn well. Betty and Cathy sat with their friends. I really felt on my own and I didn't want to be there any longer so I left. I came home on my own, feeling as if no one cared about me. I took a sleeping tablet and went to bed.

The next day, Saturday, arrangements were made to go out for the evening with a woman from work. This had been arranged weeks before Robyn died. She rang to see if I still wanted to go. I said yes but warned her that if I felt the need to leave early then I would. She understood, asking me again "Are you sure you're up for it. It really doesn't matter if you're not". I didn't want to spend a night in alone. I didn't want to go out either but I thought, "I can't stay at home on my own". Later on that evening her husband called up to collect me. He dropped us off at the event. I tried to get into the music but my mind was somewhere else.

Just before the first half ended I said "I need to go". So we got up from our seats and walked out into the hall. She then proceeded to ring her husband to come and collect us. It didn't take long for him to arrive. He had parked his car across the street. On our way out of the building I noticed a guy I used to go to see every Sunday. He is a local musician who I really liked at the time. I said hello and he began chatting, telling me that he had come out for a smoke and that his daughter was one of the singers. I then said "Have to go" and ran across the road without really looking. A car just missed me. My friend wasn't so careless. I'm sure he must have thought I was on something. If only he knew.

My friend said "Rebecca, you could have been killed there. You're very lucky". Her husband said the same thing. I just needed to get away from there. I needed the safety of my own home. As we were approaching my house she asked me was there anyone in the house? I said no and told her my daughters were coming down to stay with me. She asked was I sure? As if she knew I was lying. I lied again and said "Honestly, I won't be on my own for long". She asked me if I wanted to go to her house and stay with her until they arrived. I assured her that I would be fine on my own until they got there. Why did I lie? Because I was ashamed. I didn't want her to know that although I had a family, they weren't there for me. Maggie, my so-called friend, wasn't either. I sat in my living room on my own. No one called to ask if I needed anything. I started drinking and couldn't stop crying. I drank enough to knock myself out and stay out until the morning

When I woke up on Sunday morning the pain of my grief overtook me. I know that my grief and feeling of loneliness intensified because I had been drinking the night before. I felt lost. I journeyed into a very, very dark place in my head. I understood how Robyn must have felt. I was feeling suicidal. I felt so helpless, friendless and worthless. I wanted to die. The intensity of my thoughts and feelings was getting the better of me. I wanted to pray but wasn't sure how. I even wondered was there a God? I didn't think about what it would do to my children, even though I knew what Robyn's death had done to me. Somehow, I was able to lift my phone and ask for help. I got speaking with someone from an organisation that was created by a father who had lost his son to suicide. They saved my life that day. Knowing someone was there who genuinely cared whether I lived or died was what got me through. They came out to my home immediately, a man and woman (two strangers) who spoke with me and assured me that they were there to help me and my daughter if she felt she needed help. That brought me out from the darkness and gave me hope. Thank God for those strangers who helped me at the very beginning of one of the toughest journeys of my life. I will never forget all that they did for me and my daughter. They arranged for me and Betty to go for holistic therapy which we did.

The fear I had when Robyn died was that I would be left alone to deal with this terrible tragedy on my own. I had a feeling that after her funeral was over people would move on with their lives and in a way that's exactly what they did. I, on the other hand, had to find a way of dealing with not only my sister's death but also Post-Traumatic Stress Disorder (or PTSD).

Exactly two weeks after the death of my sister Robyn I needed to get out of the house. I feared bumping into people in the street because I wasn't ready to talk to anyone about my sister. On more than one occasion people I knew would deliberately cross over to the other side of the street when they saw me approaching. That made me angry. The conflicting feelings I had about meeting people and them avoiding me were really strange, to say the least. But that's what happens when you've been traumatised.

As I was on my way back to my house my phone rang. It was my son. He began to tell me that my younger sister...before he could say any more I interrupted him and said "Please don't tell me that anything has happened to Amber". (In my mind she was already dead). She didn't attend Robyn's funeral as she was still refusing to believe that Robyn was no longer with us. My daughters, Cathy, Betty, and my niece Kate had called up to see if they could convince her but had failed in their attempts too.

Sam went on to tell me that she had painted accusations about her neighbours on their walls. Her behaviour was so erratic that her neighbours rang the police. They came out and questioned her. She was obviously not making any sense so they got a social worker out to assess her along with her own GP. As a result of that she ended up being taken away in an ambulance and was detained at a special unit for people suffering from mental health problems in a hospital on the Jazzman Road. I couldn't take in what he was telling me. He only found this out through a friend of his who had been verbally assaulted by my sister who lived in the same block of flats.

I thought, "This isn't happening" (denial) but that didn't last long. I began crying after I'd finished speaking with my son. I thought I was going to have an anxiety attack, my heart was beating so fast. I couldn't wait until I got home. I didn't feel safe.

My sister Amber was detained in hospital for one week and spent her 50th birthday there, which was so incredibly sad. I, my daughter Betty and my niece Kate called up to the hospital to see her on her birthday. I didn't go in because in Amber's mind I was responsible for her being detained. This cut me in two. Even though I knew she was behaving like this because she wasn't well it still hurt me deeply. Every time I rang the hospital to see how she was I was told by the nursing staff that Amber had left strict instructions that under no circumstances was I to be told anything other than she's doing well and that she had had a good night. Apparently, that's the law. When someone is detained it's their right to say who can access information about them, as in family or friends.

I learned later on in therapy that the trauma I suffered the day Robyn died and also trying to deal with the loss of my only living sibling because of her mental health issues had triggered other traumatic events that had happened in my life. I was suffering from extreme anxiety, fear, depression, flashbacks, insomnia, nightmares and withdrawal. I lost both my sisters, one to suicide and the other to severe mental health problems.

The support I received from the staff at the organisation for people bereaved by suicide was excellent. They were well aware of what I was trying to deal with. I ordered books on the subject of PTSD. I wanted to understand what I was feeling. I needed to learn more in order to try and help myself. All the courses I had attended about the effects of trauma on a person escaped me. I had little or no recall. Even the training I attended on helping people who are suicidal didn't help me the morning Robyn died. I honestly had no idea that my sister was actively suicidal. I understood that she was very upset. I'd seen and heard her upset many times before. I was even aware that she had tried to take her own life a couple of years earlier. I never thought of asking her that morning "Are you suicidal? Have you made any plans to end your life?" Nothing, but nothing, prepares you for a death by suicide of a loved one.

My two nephews showed me they cared. One invited me down to his flat and cooked me dinner. The other called up one night with his dad's guitar and played a few tunes. I couldn't sing and had great difficulty remembering the words of songs I once sang.

Trying to remember songs that I liked proved difficult because of the trauma. (Trauma took away my creativity). To be truthful, I wasn't enjoying the evening but I really did appreciate the fact that he had called up to see me.

The friend who came to Robyn's funeral and who grew up in the same street as us kept in touch, which helped me greatly. The people who genuinely cared were the staff as mentioned above. They made sure I got what I needed which was continuing support from people who understood only too well what I was going through. Their understanding and empathy helped me to keep it together. My son took me out on a couple of day trips with him and his family. Also, a woman whom I'd met while on a course at Quey University for 'Understanding people with addictions' took me out and bought me a bouquet of white lilies. She and her partner were recovering alcoholics. They knew of Robyn's addiction because I had shared with them and others on the course about her struggle with alcohol. In fact, one evening after I returned home from the course I rang Robyn and told her about a weekly meeting run by the couple who were recovering alcoholics. I explained that it was different from the AA fellowship. I said that if she wanted, I would go with her.

She seemed really interested and said that she would give it a try. Unfortunately, when I rang her the next day she had been drinking and said she wouldn't be going. My son used to wait for me outside with Brianna when the course ended at nine o'clock in the evening and drive me home. I told him I was very nervous on my own in Belfast at that time of the evening. I was very grateful to him.

One of my colleagues in work was very supportive. She would call for me in her car and take me out for a drive and a bite to eat. My line manager rang me a few times, asking if there was anything she could do for me. Another colleague whom I trusted and thought was my friend called a couple of times and took me out.

The first time she drove us to a lovely country park for a walk. Before we got out of the car I told her about what had happened to my sister Amber. I was very upset explaining what losing them both was doing to me. She seemed so empathic and concerned that day. I was glad of her support. I learned about six weeks after Robyn's death while out with a good few of my team mates at a pizza place that this so-called friend had told everyone that I had found my sister. This was after me telling her not to say to anyone. When I was leaving the pizza restaurant one of my colleagues who had left the restaurant and come back with a beautiful bouquet of flowers got up from his seat and hugged me. He whispered in my ear, "I found my brother, too". I was absolutely shocked at what he had said. Later on, when my so-called friend from work, the woman I trusted, called to my house and took me out for a drive I told her what this man had said. I was blaming it on my supervisor. There were only three people who knew, or so I thought. One was this woman I thought I could trust. The other was my supervisor and my line manager. I knew it wasn't my line manager. I said to my co-called friend that I would be speaking with my supervisor and give her a piece of my mind. I continued, "I cannot believe she would break confidentiality like that". That's when she turned around to me while we were sitting in her car and confessed it was not my supervisor it was she herself who had told my team mates. She apologised profusely. I never felt the same about her after that. Certainly, any personal information or worries I had I sure as hell wouldn't be telling her about.

I thought about returning to work in September, thinking that by the end of July I'd feel better. Not so. When August came around I thought I'd feel stronger and more able to return to work by the end of August. I really wanted some normality back in my life as trauma makes you feel so unsafe. It's a horrible feeling.

One Saturday in early August I called down to visit Jackie and my two beautiful grandchildren. We decided to go for a walk to the local park. As Brianna was swinging happily on a nearby swing, Jackie, Lorcan and I were sitting on a park bench when I noticed a tiny white feather fly past Jackie and Lorcan and land on my heart. I knew it meant something special. Jackie said to me "Wow Rebecca, a lot of feathers are making their way to you!" I agreed with her and put the little white feather in my purse. On the morning of Lorcan's surgery I was upstairs washing Betty's bedroom floor when I noticed two large feathers just a few inches away from her bed. I checked they hadn't been underneath the mop bucket and they hadn't. The bottom of the mop bucket was wet and the feathers I found were bone dry. It was December, one of the coldest in years. I hadn't any windows open anywhere in the house. People's pipes were bursting, it was that cold. I had kept my heating on low for over a week because I didn't want to risk any of my pipes bursting.

I was sure that the feathers were a sign that Lorcan was going to not only survive the surgery, but that he was going to be okay, which he was. I rang my son and said "Listen, you might think this sounds crazy but…" and told him what had happened. He said "No I don't think it's crazy. We've been getting our own signs". He told me what those signs were and he too knew Lorcan was going to make it- amazing stuff.

The following Tuesday Cathy rang me to say that she had bumped into Ken. She and a friend from work were out at lunchtime when they met Ken. It was the first time in over six years. He was asking how she was and Cathy began telling him about Robyn. She went on to say that he didn't look great and was visibly shaken when he learned what had happened to Robyn. I wondered why, when she had met him on the

Monday, she didn't let me know until the following day. Still, I was glad that they had bumped into each other.

I would get a bus not far from where Ken worked to take me to supervision many many times and thought to myself....strange I have never set eyes on him all this time. I knew he stood outside the building he worked in for twenty odd years to have a smoke (once the smoking ban came into place) and never once did we bump into one another. I often thought that maybe he'd moved to Scotland or somewhere else. I even thought that maybe he had died.

A few weeks after Robyn's death a man I had been seeing after my marriage break-up began calling up to see me. I wasn't into him back then and even less now. He knew that I was vulnerable, but thankfully even when I was at my lowest, I let him know in no uncertain terms that I wasn't interested. At around the same time, my neighbour next door had had a fall out with his girlfriend. He too knew of my vulnerability and tried it on with me. I thought to myself I wished I had someone who genuinely cared about me, instead of these two men who most certainly didn't.

After speaking with Cathy on the phone I decided to call Ken. I hadn't any phone numbers for him as I had got rid of any I had years ago. But I found a way. It must have been meant because I managed to get through to him at his desk! He seemed very surprised to hear my voice and I have to say it was truly amazing to hear his. We chatted for quite some time. He was genuinely sorry to learn of Robyn's passing. He asked me "Who found her?" I said I did. Again he said how sorry he was. He asked if it would be okay for him to ring me when he got home from work and I said yes.

Later on that evening he rang me at home. We spoke on the phone for hours. He said that when he bumped into Cathy he was quite surprised to see her and very saddened by what she had told him about Robyn. He went on to say that he had intended to collect a prescription from his doctor's surgery on Friday, but for some reason he went on Monday. I truly believe that Cathy and Ken were meant to meet that day. I don't believe it was a coincidence. I believe my higher power was at work in my life. He/she knew I needed someone who would be there for me. Someone who would help take care of me while I tried to get through one of the most difficult and challenging times in my life.

I received a beautiful card in the post from Ken on the Wednesday the day after our first phone call. We chatted for hours on end. He said to me on the phone on Wednesday when I thanked him for the card, "When you rang on Tuesday I thought.....the card couldn't have arrived so soon".

He asked if it would be okay if he were to call up to my house that Friday and of course I said yes. When Friday came, and it got nearer to the time when he would be knocking at my front door (the first time in over six years) I was nervous but so very glad it was him coming to see me. Since our break-up, I had gone out with a couple of men but they didn't do anything for me whatsoever. While on holiday with Robyn, there were a few men who had shown interest in me. I, on the other hand, didn't want to know. When we returned from our holiday Robyn had told my daughter Cathy about me not being interested at all. Cathy was bemused and bewildered. She was concerned that I was in my 50s and living alone. She often would say, "Mummy, if you had a partner you would be happier". I felt that I was doing just fine on my own. I had everything I needed and wanted. I had my adorable grandchildren, a job that I loved, a few friends and good health. Of course there were times when I grew lonely. Deep down I guess I did wish I could find that special someone to grow old with. I believed that I had evolved as a woman. I wasn't prepared to go out with just any man just because I was in my 50s. If I couldn't be with my soul mate I would contine to live on my own. It was that simple.

The trouble was, the men I went out with weren't Ken. A colleague of mine would ask me on occasion when we were on a night out "Are you still in love with Ken?" Of course I denied it and said no. But she knew different. I behaved in the same manner when out with her. I just wasn't interested in the few men who had approached me.

When the door knocked that Friday evening I really felt nervous. I opened the door and Ken was standing there with a bunch of flowers in his hand. I invited him in and asked how he was. He said it was good to see me and gave me a hug. I was in need of a hug from him. We spent the entire evening talking mostly about Robyn. I remember crying and feeling that I was unable to stop. Ken just held me. He was so gentle, understanding and very much present with me in my pain. This was what I needed and thankfully at last able to receive from this man whom I had always loved and who had always loved me. He stayed over that Friday night and in the morning we talked some more. We had a lot of catching up to do. I was very raw, having just lost my sister a little over a month before. We were chatting away and listening to music, glad to be with each other again, despite the awful circumstances that had brought us back together.

He never left my side from that Friday onwards. He came back into my life on the 9th August 2011 and we were both so happy being back in each other's lives again. I remember Ken saying to me "I hope I'm not getting in the way of your grieving". I replied, "No, your love is helping me to heal".

We spent a lot of time together enjoying each other's company. We talked about him moving in with me as he was spending more time at my house than at his. He was very excited about the move. I was less so. Of course I wanted his company and companionship. He is my soul mate who by God's grace had come back into my life. I felt nervous and excited at the same time. I had got so used to making it on my own and standing on my own two feet. I was content living on my own- that was until the loss of my beloved sister to suicide. That old saying is so very true.. You find out who your friends are when you are faced with the many difficult challenges that life throws at you. I found out that I hadn't got what I thought I had regarding friends, family etc.....

I introduced him to my two beautiful grandchildren, Brianna and Lorcan. I was nervous that Brianna wouldn't take to him. I was wrong. She took to him straight away.

Later on he met Alannah too. My son's partner Jackie also seemed to get on well with Ken. All was good. Cathy and Betty seemed happy that we were back together again.

I had planned to go on a walk in the Mournes with the Suicide Awareness group to help raise much needed funds and help bring about awareness of suicide. The Saturday morning had arrived and I said to Ken, "I can't go on the walk, I'm just not ready". He said back to me "Don't worry about it. I'll go in your place", which he did and helped raise over £100 pounds. I remember telling my line manager at the time. She was very impressed, saying "I like this Ken".

I had arranged a get-together in my house, inviting my two nephews, Cathy, Betty and Ken of course one Saturday evening. It was a great night. I had made a lot of food. The craic was really good. It was the first time since Robyn's death that I felt happy having the people I loved around me. Everyone there seemed to have a good time. My son couldn't make it, unfortunately, as he was working and his partner Jackie had no one to look after the kids. I invited Robyn's daughter Kate, but she didn't come.

The last time I was with my daughters and my two nephews was at Kate's wedding. I found it a very difficult day. I don't like attending weddings at the best of times but I wasn't going to let my niece down.

I found it a sad day- very sad in fact. One of Kate's in-laws said to me "I think it's terrible that Kate's mother isn't here, how selfish of her". I chose to walk away from her as her very judgmental comments made me very upset to say the least. I thought, "How wrong of you to judge my sister when you never ever had to walk in her shoes". That get-together wasn't a happy one for me at all. When the evening disco started I said my goodbyes to Kate, her new husband, Cathy, Betty and everyone else. I couldn't wait to get out of there and get home where I would feel safe.

Kate's wedding was on a Saturday (my friend Maggie and her sister, Robyn's friend, didn't turn up for Kate's wedding. They rang me while we all sat on the bus waiting to be driven to the reception. They both had been on the drink.) I felt let down by my friend and sad for Kate as I believe she felt that her mum's friend had let her down too, especially when her mum's friend had said that she would be there for Kate as her mum couldn't.

That wasn't the first time my friend Maggie had let me down after Robyn's death. I was out one day at a local shop and as I approached the check-out, I saw my friend Maggie, her partner, Robyn's friend and her partner standing with a load of booze. As they stood there at the check-out waiting to pay for their items I remember being surpised when I saw them there. My friend said hi, I said hi back. I hadn't seen or heard from her since Robyn's funeral. She seemed surprised to bump into me at that moment, maybe a little embarrassed too. She then turned to me and said, "We're heading off to Bunryan for the weekend, do you want to come?" I was flabbergasted by what she had asked me. While I was searching for something to say back to her she said, "Hurry up, we're heading there now". I said "No, you're fine, I don't fancy going at such short notice". She answered me by saying, "Right, no problem see you later". I knew that their getting away meant non stop drinking which I didn't want. I guess that's why I didn't get an invite earlier as they didn't want me there ruining their drinking binge. I was deeply hurt and felt totally let down by my so-called friend. I understood that her way of dealing with her own personal losses and the death of my sister, who was also her friend, involved drinking lots of alcohol. It still didn't make it easy for me. She rang me a few weeks after their trip away and said "Listen, I know that you probably think that I haven't been there for you, but she was my friend too and I'm finding it hard. I said "I understand. This is an extremely difficult time for us all".

Betty had ordered me a taxi and came out with me, telling the taxi driver "That's my mummy, you make sure you take care of her and get her home safely" Which he did.

Kate got married just before Ken came back into my life. Her wedding took place six weeks after Robyn's death. My niece Kate looked so beautiful on her wedding day. It went very well, considering, although I'm sure Kate was feeling sadness that her parents and her only sister could not be there.

I knew I wouldn't be able to return to work in September. I was still feeling very raw. PTSD takes time to deal with. I felt that my line manager was pushing me somewhat for a return date. I hadn't got the answer she wanted. I really wanted to get back to my schools but I just wasn't ready. When July ended I knew I wouldn't be ready to return in September but was hoping by the end of August things would change; they didn't, or should I say I hadn't. My line manager called out to see me about my returning to work in October. Again, I said I hoped that would be the case but was unable to give her any guarantees that I could.

Ken was going over to Scotland in November to look after his sister's animals for a couple of days and asked me if I would like to come with him. I jumped at the chance. The part of Scotland where she lives is so beautiful. The scenery is absolutely breathtaking with the stunning landscapes, mountains and the many surrounding lochs. We both felt that being surrounded by nature would do me good mentally and physically, which it most certainly did. I decided to let my line manager know that I wouldn't be returning to work until after Christmas. For the first time in a long time I put my needs before anyone else's. It felt right for me to take a break from everything. I made the right decision. The whole experience from getting onto the boat in Belfast, then the two hour drive to Gourock once we'd arrived in Scotland, to boarding another ferry over to Argyll was amazing. I loved every minute of it. Ken's sister was leaving the following morning with her husband for a short break away which meant we had the bungalow to ourselves.

Ken drove me to some of the most amazing places over the next two days. We explored as much of this beautiful country as we could. I fell in love with the place. I thought that Donegal had the nicest scenery (which it does) but this place takes Mother Nature to another level altogether. I really enjoyed the drive up into the mountains with the music blasting. Absolute heaven.

We called into the the sheltered housing to see his mum while we were there. She had had to leave her home (which was the bungalow we were staying in, now his younger sister's and her husband's home). Catherine, Ken's younger sister, had lived with their mum up until the point where she could no longer care for her.

When Ken and I first visited her in her new home not far away from her old one I was shocked at her deterioration. Ken spoke to his mum about our plans to marry. (We had decided to get married in July 2013 before going over to Scotland.) She smiled at us both and said to me "You'll make a lovely bride". I don't believe she recognised me but I could tell she was so happy for us both. When we left, I burst into tears. I apologised to Ken, saying "I don't know why I'm feeling so sad. I'm supposed to be supporting you". I continued, "I guess it's just such a shock to see her unable to do anything for herself".

The last time I had seen her, Ken and I were staying with her in their first cottage in Scotland after moving there from England. She was taking care of us both, making meals etc. That was in the autumn of 2001. It really was a shock seeing her that way. Ken did warn me about his mum's deterioration. Nevertheless, it was still very sad to see.

About three weeks after we arrived home Catherine, Ken's sister rang asking him, "Are you sitting down?" She continued, "I've received a letter and other correspondence from a producer who helps investigate missing families and helps in bringing them together. He's from a television show in New Zealand called 'Missing Pieces'. Catherine continued, "They're making inquiries about mum. We've got an older sister and her name is Paige".

Ken was in complete shock trying to take in all that Catherine was telling him. He was overjoyed with this news right from the beginning. All these years he and his two younger sisters grew up believing that Ken was the eldest in their family. Now they were about to embark on an amazing journey of discovery.

They had a whole other family living in both New Zealand and Australia. Ken could hardly contain his excitement. Catherine was less enthusiastic to begin with. His other sister was curious in finding out more about her 'elder sister'.

As time moved on they found out more information. Ken agreed to go over to Northeast to do a TV interview which would then be shown to his half sister in New Zealand. After that, they first communicated with each other on the phone then later via Skype. It was an exciting time for all involved.

2011 was our first Christmas together after too many years apart. Still, we both believe that it took the time it took in order for us to get it together. We both did a lot of growing in the years we spent apart.

It was my first Christmas without Robyn. Ken and I had called up to Kate's house on Christmas morning with Christmas presents for her and her four children. My heart went out to her. She was spending Christmas with her own family, in-laws and friends.

Christmas would have been even more difficult for me if Ken hadn't been there although he was somewhat distracted by the news of his newly-found family, which wasn't surprising. My son invited us both up to his house for dinner, which was lovely. I had my soul mate, and all of my children and grandchildren were there which helped a great deal. We left for home shortly after we had had our dinner as I wasn't great being around people in those early days after Robyn's death, even those I love.

A new year, 2012, and a new beginning. I was making plans for my return to work. My supervisor suggested I go back on a 'phased return', working in the office and not with clients. I didn't like the idea of working in the office. I didn't study to become a receptionist. I said to my line manager that I would prefer to go back to my schools. She didn't object at all; quite the contrary. She knew that I was needed more in the schools than in the office. She was only too happy for me to get back into the schools.

She had arranged a day and time with me to come out to my house and work it all out. When she arrived at my house, laden with paperwork, I thought to myself "What's this all about?" She told me that some of the paperwork had changed and that there were some new forms that I would need. She left me parts of the new forms and said she would get me the other parts at our next 'training away day'. My head was beginning to spin at the sight of all this paperwork. We agreed I wouldn't be carrying out any initial assessments with any young person for fear that there may be any suicidal ideation issues. She went on to say that she would do her best to keep those clients away from me. A promise she couldn't keep and shouldn't have made. My assistant team leader would be doing all assessments in my schools and I would continue on with the clients once she'd finished carrying out the assessments.

As we continued talking about my return to work she announced that two of my schools were no longer mine. I was shocked when she said that. I asked her why this decision had been made. Her reply, "I have a huge jigsaw to put together. You weren't at work so I had no other choice but to allocate your two schools to someone new". (The two schools she had given to another new counsellor were just down the street from me.) I still had my school in Belfast. The only reason for that was simply because my key contact and the vice principal went to the office of the counselling organisation telling the CEO that they only wanted me working at their school. My line manager continued to talk to me about other schools she was thinking about sending me to. I could go to schools were I was needed like a run-around. I said to her "You can't do that, I don't drive. I would have to rely on public transport. I'm also visually impaired which would make it too difficult". I could feel the anxiety in my body working its way up to my chest and throat. I said to her, "I'm feeling extremely anxious here". Her reply, "You're making me feel intimated." I burst out crying, saying "You know that I wouldn't hurt you for the world".

She got up from the chair in my living room and said "Let's talk about this another day. I'll see what I can do". After she left I just sat and cried. My anxiety levels were sky high. I thought "Why is she punishing me?" That's what it felt like. I was also shocked when she said she felt intimated! I was in a state of confusion over the news that two of my schools were no longer mine to work in. She pointed out to me that the schools don't belong to anyone, which is fair enough. But to make such drastic changes to someone who was suffering from PTSD wasn't the way to go about things. My interests were most certainly not her concern. She handled the whole thing really badly. In my opinion, she wasn't much of a therapist. She should have known that these drastic changes would have added to my PTSD. Either she did know and didn't care, or else she was incompetent, or both as a line manager and as a counsellor. Either way, I found her lack of empathy towards me and my situation very unpleasant.

On another visit to my home my line manager told me the names of the other two schools I would be working in. She said that one of the schools would be really good for me to work in. That turned out to be a lie- more on that later. The other school was at the very top of the Ring Road. This was a school that my so-called friend worked in. I was allowed to get a taxi to and from the schools (which they paid for) as they were quite a distance from my home. I sometimes would walk down the Ring Road after work just to clear my head and walk to the bus stop in the city centre to get my bus home. I did the same at the other school in White Road for the same reasons.

I found it tough going to these new schools. I had to start from the very beginning. The staff at the school in Ring Road had to get used to working with me and me with them. They seemed to have had a very good working relationship with the previous counsellor. My key contact at the school in Belfast was so stuck up. She was a doctor of some sort. I found working with her extremely difficult. Can't say the same about the staff who worked at reception at the front of the school. I would have been lost without their help. My key contact gave me the impression that I was bothering her any time I needed to speak with her, especially if it had anything to do with child protection issues. She would question my concerns as if the issues I brought to her attention were not valid. I always went with my gut. I didn't care for her attitude towards me. I may have just been a counsellor in her eyes but I knew my job and did it well.

My key contact hadn't provided me with an appropriate room to see my clients in. I was sent along with my clients to an art classroom. Totally inappropriate. The room was dirty, not much privacy and there were paintings strewn all around the tables. The smell from the paint was very unpleasant too. I spoke with her about it and her reply was, "The only other appropriate room in the school is already in use".

When working with clients we had to have a door with a window in it for child protection purposes. I was getting nowhere with this woman so I spoke to my line manager about it. She had a meeting with her and I was at last given an appropriate room to work in. I must say, the best thing about working at this school were the young people. It was a privilege to be able to work with them, it really was. These young people were some of the nicest people I'd ever worked with, absolutely wonderful. When they came in to see me a lot of them were broken but boy, they had such big hearts. I truly loved these kids.

The other school was less chaotic to work in. I had a good room. The staff on reception were lovely and we worked well together. One young person whom I had been seeing said she had spoken with her friend about counselling. She went on to say that her friend had issues and needed to speak about them. She asked if I would see her and that she didn't want to see the other school counsellor. I told her that that was fine by me. When the young person in question made it known to the reception staff that she didn't want to see my colleague she obviously got to hear about it. She said to me later "Ha, I've been told that a young person at my school asked for you specifically. Imagine!" She continued, "Once I got 'over myself' I was fine about it."

I had been back working in the schools a few months and to be honest, I wasn't enjoying it. I loved the young people but found that once again the amount of paperwork was ridiculous. I just found it so stressful. I was still trying to deal with the loss of my sister on top of everything else. It was a very tough time for me indeed.

My line manager was so busy as our team was growing so much that I was assigned to my assistant line manager, which I was very happy about. She was much more supportive towards me. Line management meetings with her were a lot better.

One day at the school in Belfast I had two clients to see. Once I had finished I checked with reception to see if there were any more young people to be seen and I was told no. I packed up, left the room and on my way out of the school I asked again, "No one else for me to see?" Again I was told no. So I left the school and decided to walk into the city centre and get my bus home. While I was on the bus I received a phone call from my assistant line manager telling me there was a young person who needed to see the school counsellor. I explained that I was on a bus on my way home. She said, "You can get off the bus and get a taxi back up to the school". I replied, "I'm unable to get off the bus where I am now. There's no taxi depot nearby. Why can't you send the other counsellor who works in the school?" She said, "Are you telling me that you're not going to return to the school?" I replied, "That's exactly what I'm telling you". I was mad as hell. I had left the school a good hour before receiving the phone call from my assistant team leader. I really didn't care what they did to me. I'd had enough. I did find it strange, however, that my line manager didn't ring me again that day or the day after. In hindsight, she was probably waiting until I'd calmed down and in between times she would decide what action to take.

The good old reliable Rebecca who went far and beyond the call of duty was gone. I could tell my assistant team leader was shocked by my response. Before Robyn died and my two schools were taken away from me I would had said "Yes, no problem". As far as I was concerned it was their problem. This wouldn't have happened if my team leader hadn't made the drastic decision to mess me about. She knew how difficult my key contact was in that school. She didn't care one iota about that or my feelings.

The third day after the incident she sent me an email telling me that she wanted to see me. I had calmed down by that stage. When I arrived at the room where the meeting took place I could tell she wasn't amused. We sat down, her on one seat, me on the other. Then it began. She spoke to me like I was a child, scolding me for not doing what was asked of me. She went on, "You only saw two clients that day. It's in your contract that you see three". She continued, "Do you understand that I needed to have this conversation with you?" She then tried to lay a guilt trip on me by saying that the young person was in a really bad way.

There was no point trying to get my point across when she wasn't in the mood for understanding where I was coming from. Besides, I hadn't the energy to get into a disagreement with her. If I had returned to the school I would not have been paid for the time it would have taken me to get back across town, which would have been at least three hours. Also, I wasn't the only counsellor working for that organisation. There were counsellors, including me, who would on occasion only have seen one client. Sometimes that happened. When it did, we would then go home. That's how it was.

In my next line management meeting with my assistant team leader she said, "Rebecca, that's not like you at all. Are you upset over your schools being taken away from you?" I said "Yes I am. Wouldn't you be?" She said she would do all she could for me regarding getting my schools back. When I asked her "Who are 'they', the people responsible for making the decision to take my schools away?" She told me who they were. My line manager and her right hand woman. Neither of them had a clue about how wrong a decision they had made in light of my circumstances. Useless pair, in my opinion.

My assistant team leader stayed true to her word. At our next meeting she told me that I had got one of my old schools back and was working on getting me the other one back. She asked me, "Rebecca is this what you want? Would this make you feel better?" She told me about the meeting she had had with the two people involved in my situation and that she feared me leaving. She continued, "I said to them that if we don't do something Rebecca will walk". At least she cared enough about me to fight my corner and she most certainly did.

On the last meeting of the year with my line manager she informed me that I had my two schools back. I was overjoyed. I really was. I said "Thank you, can I give you a hug?" She looked at me, shook her head and said no!

I was counting down the days until the end of June when I would be off. It had been a very difficult return back to work, one that needn't have been so difficult but it was nearly over. I had made it and was looking forward to returning to my old schools in September.

Ken and I decided to take a two-week holiday in Cyprus in July of that year. It was wonderful to get away in the sunshine, although it was extremely hot. Nevertheless, we made the most of it.

Ken and his newly found sister communicated quite regularly via Skype. In the beginning, I would sit with him and his sister's husband Danny would sit with her. I found it very difficult, the fact that Ken had found a whole new family and I'd lost mine. I stopped going in with Ken. I don't think he minded as he was just so blown away with it all. For me, it was a constant reminder of what I'd lost. Then Ken announced that Paige was coming over to visit her mum for the first time ever in October. His two sisters, one in particular, were a bit hesitant to offer Paige a place to stay. As it turned out, Ken's younger sister offered to let her stay with her and her husband for the weekend. It was an exciting and emotional time, maybe a little strange too for Ken's two sisters, not quite knowing what to expect. Ken on the other hand just couldn't wait to meet his older sister. He had invited her to stay with us for a week after her weekend in Scotland. He'd done this without consulting me about it. I was livid. I felt that he had totally dismissed my feelings and had shown no respect for me and what I needed or wanted. After all, it was my home. I know there was no malice intended; he just got carried away and let his emotions run away with him. All the same, I wasn't looking forward to her visit. I'd never met her. I had only spoken with her on the phone and Skype. I thought, "I'm not strong enough to wear a mask of joy for a week" when all I felt inside was a deep sense of loss for my two sisters. His joy just reminded me of my pain.

Ken went over to Scotland that weekend to meet his older sister for the first time. They all bonded well. Paige went with her siblings to meet her mother for the first time. It was a joyous occasion for all, particularly Paige and her mum.

As Ken's car drove up outside my front door I found myself becoming very anxious. I desperately wanted to do my best for Ken and his sister. I found her very pleasant and really likeable, which helped with my anxiety.

When Ken and I got back together I asked him to let his family and friends know about Robyn. I thought it would help me when we went to visit them or them us. I was still feeling lethargic as grieving takes up so much of one's energy. I just couldn't do the 'all's well with me' act. Paige stayed a full week with us. It took its toll on me, it really did. I found it hard, hiding my feelings. There were times when I probably made her feel unwelcome. I just found it emotionally draining. I didn't intend to make her stay uncomfortable and thankfully I think she enjoyed most of it. This is why Ken and I should have had a conversation around her staying with us. Lessons learned. I had returned to work which made it a bit easier for me while Paige was staying with us. Paige returned home after her week's stay with us. Before she left she met my son and his family. We ate out on a Friday night at the restaurant where my son was head chef at the time. That was a lovely night out. I was really happy for Ken that he'd met his sister. He was a happy man.

In late December 2012 Ken and I decided to go out for our Sunday lunch in Lisburn just outside Belfast. When we arrived back home, Ken received a phone call from his younger sister telling him that their mum had taken a turn for the worse. My heart went out to him. He was in shock, as one is on hearing that kind of news. He felt powerless to do anything other than wait for another phone call from his sister who was with her, thankfully. Their mum had been moved into a care home a few months previously as her condition had deteriorated. It was an agonising wait for him that day. He received the dreaded phone call not too long afterwards and was told that his mum had passed away peacefully. She died on the 30th of December, aged eighty.

Arrangements were made by his family regarding her funeral. His older sister was very lucky to have met her just a few months before. Maybe it was meant. Ken and I travelled over to Scotland for her funeral in January. My line manager said it was okay for me to take that day off. The funeral service was really lovely. Ken and his middle sister each paid great homage to their mum at the reading. They did her proud. Their older sister was unable to make it as she was in New Zealand. It must have been difficult for her to have lost her mum twice. It was also a difficult time for Ken, coming from his background and culture where they don't talk about their feelings. I could see and understand what he was going through, whereas he was oblivious to what he was feeling. I had total empathy for him in his sadness and all the other rollercoaster ride of emotions one goes through when we lose someone we love.

When Ken and I first made our wedding plans we were inviting my children, grandchildren and my son's partner Jackie. I had intended getting a blessing from my key contact in Belfast who was a reverend. Ken's family were also invited. We had made plans to hire a blues band to play at our reception. However, I was still in a dark place regarding my sisters and the PTSD. I couldn't bear the thought of Ken's sister there when none of my siblings were going to be. So I cancelled the invitations, not explaining my reasons to my children. Betty was in Australia and Cathy seemed okay about it. However, my son was absolutely furious, to say the least. He rang me one Saturday night. It was about nine o'clock in the evening and he gave me dog's abuse saying, "What the hell is going on with you? We received an invitation to your wedding and then you uninvited us!" I tried to explain why but just couldn't take his angry outburst any longer and put the phone down.

After our conversation I had a rethink and invited them all to our wedding, still not explaining why I had changed. My mind. I spoke with Ken about it. He sent Sam a message saying something like "If you both just want to come Alannah could look after Brianna and Lorcan for you". Sam went ballistic and sent me a text telling me were I could stick my wedding. I was totally confused as to why Ken had said what he said. He explained, "I thought I was doing them a favour". Then it was my turn to go crazy. I said to Ken, "In the morning you may call up to their house and explain what you meant. This is getting seriously crazy". He agreed and when he woke up the next morning he drove up to my son's house and had a chat with him. Thankfully, it got sorted. My son admired Ken's courage for calling to his home to speak with him man-to-man.

No doubt things were far from well with the way my head was. I was making decisions based on my emotional state. My son, I presume, must have thought thought"How dysfunctional is this?" He had his own concerns regarding his son and the stress of starting his own business. Nevertheless, I was in a lot of emotional pain and also having to deal with problems at work, along with the PTSD. It was an extremely painful time in my life. I was trying to deal with it albeit in a way that must have seemed unreasonable to those I loved. But unless you are going through it yourself you couldn't possibly comprehend what hell it was being in my shoes.

Ever since the arrival of my grandchildren Brianna and Lorcan into the world, the need for me to be involved in their lives was, and still is, so important to me. I was denied the opportunity to form a bond with Alannah. Thankfully, history wasn't repeating itself with these two.

Before Ken came back into my life, every Saturday I would walk from my house down to get Brianna. I remember pushing her in her pram up a steep hill and from there managing to get us both to my house for lunch. Afterwards, if the weather was good, I would take her to a local park. She loved it there. When spending time with her at my house I would sing to her and put music on, which she also enjoyed. She would move her small body to the rhythm of the music and I would dance along with her. I absolutely loved spending my Saturdays with her. She was such great fun to be around. She made me so very happy with her beautiful smiling face. The way she would talk with me made me laugh. When she went into a mood that was funny too, although I never let her know.

Later, when Ken came back into my life, he and I would call up to their house every Saturday in his car and take them out somewhere or simply spend quality time with them at home, although it was a few years before we were able to take Lorcan out with us too. When we were, it was even more terrific. Ken formed a bond with Lorcan almost instantly. It's totally understandable as he's the most beautiful boy in the world, a precious gift from God. We are very blessed to have such a special boy in our lives, as are his parents, his sisters, aunts and surrounding family. It's a privilege to have him in our lives.

In 2013, by the time May arrived, as usual I was ready for a break from school. I was excited about our forthcoming wedding on the 20th of July that year. Everything was coming together regarding our plans.

We had booked a week in Paris and one in Rome for our honeymoon. I had never been to Rome before (neither had Ken) and thought it would be the perfect place to fly on to from Paris.

Towards the end of May, on a Saturday evening, my niece Kate called to our house to tell me that Amber had broken into her home while she, her husband and their children were out for the day. She continued, "Amber told me that people were chasing her and that she was in danger". She went on to tell Kate that she had been to the police station in the early hours of the morning to make a complaint. Kate thought I needed to be aware of what was going on with Amber and to get her help from her CPN (Community Psychiatric Nurse) or GP. I immediately felt my anxiety levels beginning to rise at an alarming rate. Kate continued, "If anything were to happen to her when she's out on the streets in the early hours of the morning we'd never forgive ourselves. If she were to die, you, being the only sibling left, would have to pay for her funeral". Kate's predictions and assumptions about me being responsible for paying for her funeral if she were to die only added to my anxiety.

The first place I rang was the hospital where she had been detained in 2011. I wasn't sure who to ring as I'd never had to do this before. I was hoping they could advise me as to what to do and who to see. They were pretty hopeless. I spent an entire week pleading with her GP, CPN team and her social worker. My fear was that she was a danger to herself, leaving her home in the early hours of the morning. She was extremely vulnerable. The system here regarding mental health stinks. All I was told, time and time again was that they can't detain a person unless the person themselves are aware they are at risk. In other words, see their doctors, CPN team and social worker. The trouble with that is, Amber didn't realise she was ill, so how the hell is that supposed to work?

I got a phone call from a social worker on the Thursday evening telling me that Amber had been out again in the early hours at the police station. It was then that the police contacted social services. Again I asked, "What are you going to do? I've already lost one sister to suicide. I can't lose another. You need to do something to keep her safe". On Friday, around lunch time, the social worker rang me to say that they were going to have Amber detained. Finally, after nearly a week of constant phone calls, they did what they should have done long before. I was so relieved. I knew she would now be safe.

The following morning I said to Ken "I need to get away for the weekend. All this stress has left me feeling totally burned out". He agreed and off we went. I thought that getting away would be all I needed. I would be refreshed and relaxed enough to start back to work on Monday morning. It was great to escape for a couple of days, away from all the stress and worry.

When I rang the hospital to enquire after my sister I was told the same as before. She'd had a restful night and was in good spirits. It broke my heart that I wasn't able to see her and that she didn't want anything to do with me. I actually tried to explain this to whichever nurse answered the phone. She told me that that was one of the areas they would be working on with Amber. It didn't work. Still to this day we don't have a relationship.

Monday morning came along and I walked the short distance to my school where I had only two young people to see. It was fine. I got through the morning with no problems arising. I went home and added what I needed onto the database. The following day, Tuesday, I was working in my Belfast school. I hadn't any clients to see that day as there were exams going on. All I had to do was get myself there in case there were any 'drop- ins' (a young person who needed counselling could just call in without an appointment). That morning, on my way down town on the bus, I could feel my eyes beginning to well up with tears. I struggled really hard not to burst out crying. It was very challenging indeed. When the bus eventually stopped in town I couldn't wait to get off. As soon as I did, I rang Ken. He could barely make out what I was saying. He said "I'll be there as fast as I can". Thankfully, he didn't work that far from where I was. He was with me in about ten minutes. He must have run the whole way. I had crashed- that's what it felt like. (I remember a few of my colleagues and my supervisor warning me about 'burnout' and wondering what they were talking about, never believing it would happen to me!) Although, in my case, it was what had happened to my sisters that had been the major cause. I was stopped in my tracks, unable to move. I couldn't stop crying. My body couldn't take any more. It was my body that forced me to listen.

Ken took me up to see my doctor. He'd made an emergency appointment. My doctor said I was suffering from extreme stress. He wrote me out a sick line for two weeks and advised complete rest. Ken rang my work. My assistant team leader answered the call. He told her that I was in a terrible state over my sister and that there was no way I'd be able to go to work. She was lovely on the phone and said for me to take good care of myself. It felt like Robyn all over again. I knew I wouldn't be able to return to work any time soon. One week led into another and before I knew it, the end of June was approaching.

My friend, the one who had blabbed my business to my team mates, had invited me to lunch. She wanted to meet up before the school term ended. She told me that everyone in our team had given money towards a wedding gift for me, which was really very kind of them. We agreed to meet after my supervision. She said she would collect me from there and take us both out to lunch. As soon as I got into her car she said "Well hi, good to see you. You can tell me all that's been happening, but only if you want!" I had learned my lesson. There was no way I was going to tell her my business so she could then repeat it to her buddy, our line manager, and whoever else. I lied about why I was unable to return to work.

We went and had our lunch where she handed me a card with a gift token inside for M&S. I thanked her and asked her to pass on my appreciation to the others. People in Ken's work were very generous regarding the amount of gifts we received. One of our dear friends gave us a cheque for £1000 that helped a great deal towards our honeymoon. What an exceptional gift from an exceptional person. He was to be Ken's best man but took a stroke four days before our wedding. Luckily, Ken's brother-in-law stepped in.

My big day was drawing near. I had my wedding dress, shoes, handbag, jewellery etc. I had also appointments booked with a hairdresser and a make-up artist. Everything was in place and going exactly to plan. Ken and I had made an appointment to have our teeth whitened the day before our wedding. He had all his business in order too. He was staying in my daughter Cathy's house the night before so that we would not see each other in advance of the ceremony- tradition and all that.

I had asked a friend of mine of recent years if she would be my matron of honor at my wedding. She was delighted to be asked and pulled out all the stops to help me, including staying with me the night before my big day. I decided not to ask my old school friend because I didn't feel she would be able to as she had suffered a stroke in late 2011. Besides, we hadn't really remained good friends because of reasons I've stated earlier in the book. I did invite her and her sister to my get-together a week before my wedding but they chose not to come.

The night before my wedding I was nervous and really excited. This time I knew what I was getting; a good man. My soul mate. I was 56 years old and Ken was 55. In our six years apart he hadn't had a relationship with any other woman. I hadn't had a relationship with any other man. I had gone out with a few, but as I've already stated they weren't Ken. I found it difficult to sleep the night before. Ken rang me while I was in bed to wish me a good night's sleep and continued, "Soon to be my bride- I love you". He too was nervous but really excited about our big day. We said good night and as I put down the phone I felt like the luckiest woman on the planet.

The next morning my friend and I got up and had some breakfast. While she was upstairs getting showered my hairdresser arrived. As I had had my shower first, my hairdresser was able to do my hair. She had no sooner finished when the girl who was doing my make-up arrived. It was all go, go, go. I was upstairs getting ready when the front door knocked. It was Alannah and Cathy. Cathy handed me a wedding gift. She looked rough, as if she'd been drinking a lot the night before. She was her usual bubbly self. Alannah looked really lovely. How nice to have my first born grandchild attend our wedding.

The summer of 2013 had been absolutely brillant, and so it was on the day of our wedding. When I arrived at the Castle (the venue where we had decided to get married and have our reception) with my matron of honor, Mary, I was nervous but not overly so. Ken and I met in a room the staff at the castle had set aside for us. We would go from there before entering into the main room where the wedding ceremony would take place. Ken's best man was with him and Mary with me. When it was time to enter into the main room, I can honestly say that I had never felt happier. Ken's face beamed with happiness too.

It was so good to have my children there (two anyway, as Betty was still in Australia.) My three grandchildren being there too, on one of the happiest days of my life, was so wonderful. It was a day I will never ever forget. The wedding ceremony was relatively quick. Once we had made our vows to each other that was pretty much it. Afterwards we all went outside as the dinner wasn't being served until a short while later. That meant we had the opportunity for some photos to be taken. Alannah, who is absolutely amazing at photography, took photographs of me and Ken on our own, and also of all our guests. Ken's friend Kenny, his wife and goddaughter were outside in the beautiful grounds of the castle, waiting to see us. We had a really lovely dinner which everyone enjoyed. The atmosphere couldn't have been better. The two younger grandkids seemed to enjoy themselves too. Alas, it was soon nearly over (well, that part of our day anyhow.) When we left, Ken drove us to Downstown. We retraced our steps, beginning with sitting at the harbour and eating ice cream. We then took a stroll and sat on the same bench we had sat on over twenty years earlier. We called into one of the oldest pubs in the North of Ireland. I had a pint, Ken sipped on an orange juice. Again, just as we had done all those years ago. The sun was beating down on us- such a perfect day. When we arrived home we had a drink outside with two of our next door neighbours. They, along with two other neighbours, had bought us wine and champagne as wedding gifts for us both. It was nice to sit outside in the evening sunshine, sharing our happiness with two of our neighbours. We didn't stay out too long as we had an early start the following morning.

We were both up around four thirty getting ready for our flight from Belfast to Paris. I was so excited to be returning to my favourite city. The fact that I was going to be in the company of my new husband made it even better. When we arrived at our hotel we were greeted by a very friendly concierge. Then when we entered our room we found a welcoming note and an ice bucket with a bottle of lovely white wine in it. What a warm welcome and an amazing start in this wonderful city.

On Monday morning we walked the short distance from our hotel to Pere Lachaise Cemetery to visit the grave of Jim Morrison. It was fascinating to see where he was laid to rest. We spent a few hours visiting graves of other famous people who are buried there too. Ken spoke French to the hotel staff who seemed to appreciate it. They all were so friendly and professional. The breakfast in the morning was delicious and fresh every time.

We didn't waste a single minute of our time while we were there- sadly it flew in. We explored so much of this magnificent city with its fine buildings, architecture, restaurants and the Musee d'Orsay. We booked ourselves on a romantic cruise along the river Seine. We sat at the front of the boat, having the best view and enjoyed a beautiful fine dining experience. There were red rose petals on our table and champagne on ice, absolutely superb. Seeing the city light up at night with its magnificent buildings on either side was truly amazing.

The bus tour around the city was very impressive and educational. We got to see all the famous landmarks like the Eiffel Tower, Notre-Dame, Arc de Triomphe, the Louvre, Moulin Rouge, Louvre Pyramid and much much more. Best of all for me was when we visited the Pont des Arts pedestrian bridge. I put a lock on the bridge along with the thousands of others. The gesture is said to represent a couple's commitment to each other. I was thrilled to pieces to have had an opportunity to celebrate our love and commitment to each other in this very romantic, special way.

I am a huge fan of Van Gogh and, as such, Ken made sure to take me to the bedroom he slept in. At number 2, Place Lamartine in Aries, Bouches-du-Rhone, known as the yellow house. The journey there was amazing in itself. We needed to get two trains. One of the trains we travelled in was very state of the art. I noticed a two-decker train pass by and to my absolute astonishment, a three-decker train too. I had never seen any trains like these before in my life. I loved the journey. It really made our day even more special.

I had been to see Van Gogh's room on my first visit to Paris but I wanted to see it a second time. Good job I had already seen it as it was closed that day. The first time I was able to get in and made my way up the very steep steps to his bedroom. As I touched the wall in his bedroom with my hand, I could feel the energy. It was an amazing experience.

We had a beautiful day there, despite the house being closed. There was a cafe named after Vincent where we enjoyed a bite to eat and a much-needed cold drink. The little village of Auvers-sur-Oise is stunningly beautiful. We took our time exploring it. We went to Cimetiere d'Auvers to visit Van Gogh's grave. I hadn't seen it on my first visit. Before we arrived there, we found ourselves at the church he painted in Auvers. It was a very surreal experience for me. On our way to his grave we passed the wheatfield he had painted. It totally blew me away to have walked where he had once walked, imagining him painting the church and wheatfield.

Ken and I loved every minute that we stayed in Paris and went out every day we were there. Sadly, the time had come for us to leave, although we were both excited about our next adventure- Rome! We said our goodbyes to the staff at the hotel. They had booked us a taxi to take us to the airport early in the morning. The rain was pouring down. How lucky were we! We arrived at the airport and thankfully, we didn't have a long wait. We boarded the plane to Rome and off we went. When we arrived we both noticed right away the difference in the temperature. It was hot, very hot.

We took a train to the area where we were staying in Rome, which was easy enough. When we arrived we began walking along the street, feeling somewhat lost. We stopped a few people for directions to our hotel but they didn't speak any English. We were feeling the heat and were weary from the flight and train journey, and also frustration because of the language barrier. We stopped and asked a group of young people for directions. They very kindly took the time to explain where we were in relation to the hotel. We had struck lucky. We were literally just a few hundred yards away from our hotel. Hooray!

We arrived outside the hotel, suitcases in hand and very happy to have found it. When we arrived at reception we very quickly realised that the staff weren't as friendly as they had been in our hotel in Paris. We went up to our room, which was nice enough, put our things away and set out to explore Rome. We got a train into town and found a small but really nice place to eat. It was very reasonably priced and the food was very nice. Our first night was extremely uncomfortable. Our room was like an oven, it was so hot. The next morning we took a stroll down to the local shops where we bought a small fan and kettle. We had asked the staff at reception for a kettle and fan but they informed us that they didn't provide them.

We were getting dressed to go out for the evening and because the room was that hot, Ken's teeshirt was soaking wet in a matter of minutes. I said "Right, that's it". We went down to reception. I asked to speak with the manager. The guy at the desk said he was the manager. "What's the problem?" I said "Look at my husband, he's soaking wet. The air conditioning is obviously not working. Do something about it". He gave us a set of keys to a new room which did seem better to begin with. At least we were out of the room where the air conditioning wasn't working at all. The fan and kettle were a godsend. I needed my tea, Ken his coffee. After a day or two the air conditioning wasn't that great in our new room. Thankfully we had the fan. The small things that really matter, eh! The breakfast wasn't that great either. Still, we made the most of Rome. I think we were spoiled in our hotel in Paris!

We used the trains frequently to find our way around Rome, which was a brilliant way to explore this amazing city, starting with our first ever visit to the Colosseum. It was fascinating to look at, imagining the events that took place there over the centuries. We also explored the many other buildings and statues in the area. We visited many beautiful churches with their marble floors, paintings, statues etc.

We visited the Roman Forum and the Vatican, which are truly incredible. Pope Francis wasn't in residence at the time of our visit, not that Ken or I cared that much. We had planned to visit the Sistine Chapel but there must have been at least three hundred people queuing in the hot sun to get in. I just wouldn't have been able to stand for hours so we gave up on that idea.

We went on a bus tour while we were in Rome as it really is the best way to see any large city. The architecture is incredibly beautiful-spectacular, in fact. There were so many magnificent buildings we got to see on the tour. It was the perfect opportunity to take as many photographs as I could for our wedding and honeymoon albums. Precious memories of our perfect day and wonderful honeymoon captured forever on camera.

Alas, this trip was at an end too. We packed up our belongings and headed to the airport. Before we left, we dumped the little kettle and fan in a nearby industrial bin. I had bought so many things while in Paris and Rome that there simply wasn't any room in our suitcases for anything else. We sat forty minutes before the plane finally got off the ground. Not sure why. When we arrived in London, the rush to catch our connecting plane to Belfast left me feeling completely out of breath. Thankfully we made it in time. On the flight to Belfast I couldn't stop itching. I noticed huge insect bites on both my ankles. It felt like I had been bitten by mosquitoes, the itching was so bad. It seemed to take a long time to get to our final destination, which of course only takes around 30 minutes.

When we arrived at Belfast Airport it felt so good to be back on home ground. It had been an amazing two weeks. We were both very fortunate to have had an opportunity like this. I was just glad to be going home where I could have a look at our photos and presents and get into a hot bath before retiring to my own bed for a good night's sleep. Our friend Mary was waiting for us in the airport car park.

We waited like everyone else for our luggage. Every case had been picked up by their owners. Ours, on the other hand, were nowhere in sight. We waited for a little while longer and nothing. When it became obvious that our cases weren't on the carousel we approached the airport reception desk. The man whom we spoke with assured us that everything would be alright. He said that our luggage was still at London Airport and that it would be delivered straight to our door the following evening. I was disappointed but relieved we would be getting it back, albeit a lot later than we had anticipated. We rang our friend to let her know what was happening. She was perfectly fine about it. When we arrived outside to where she had parked Ken offered to pay for the parking ticket but she insisted that it was ok. She stated "I've taken care of things; it's so good to see you both".

Mary drove us home and in doing so, learned a little about our adventures. I said jokingly, "You'll have to wait until later before you get your present". She just laughed, repeating, "I'm so happy for you both". Sure enough, our luggage arrived the following evening, which was great.

The bites on my ankles, in particular, were quite bad. The skin had ballooned up. It was like a thin bubble of skin on both ankles where the bite was just underneath them. They looked worse than they actually were. Thankfully the itching had stopped. I had never had this happen to me before. Maybe it was because I was older and still menopausal? My doctor said it was nothing to worry about but warned me not to burst the skin but just let it happen naturally. It took many months before they finally did burst and even longer for the scars to disappear.

On January the 23rd 2014 I posted my letter of resignation to the counselling organisation I had worked for for over three years. I felt relief and, at the same time, a sense of sadness. I knew I couldn't continue to work under such stressful conditions. My line manager had been putting me under pressure from September of 2013 up until January 2014. She kept asking me when I was coming back and why my GP was was so unwilling to cooperate with them when they rang or wrote for information. As far as he was concerned, it was none of their business. He was not amused when I told him that my line manager had said to me that he was being dishonest. He had written on all my sick lines 'hospital investigations'. She sent me a letter to sign, giving them permission to check my medical records. Counselling organisation behaving in this manner: bloody disgrace. My GP said, "How am I being dishonest? I've written the cause of your absence from work". He was bemused by her attitude. As I've stated already, with a line manger like her and the pressures from this organisation, getting out when I did was the best decision for me. But, it was another loss. A loss of a job which I worked really hard to get and one in which I loved.

I made up my mind there and then that I would never again work for any counselling organisation where they expect much more from you than face-to-face counselling, the reason why I got into this type of work in the first place. So much more is expected of a counsellor. They expect one to jump through hoops! Not any more. I decided to start up my own private practice. I went to various workshops on how best to achieve this. I continued with my CPD (Continued Professional Development) and my BACP accreditation. That was my focus from here on in.

The day my world came crashing down.

The day my world came crashing down was Tuesday, the 11th of March 2014. I was at home when I received a phone call from my son asking me had I seen the newspaper. I replied, "No. The only time I get the paper is when you're in it'. He continued, "I received a call from Kevin" (his cousin). He told me that there was an article in a well-known newspaper about his so-called father. The man he hasn't had a relationship with in over twenty years. He went on to tell me what the article was about. As he proceeded to tell me he became really angry. He said that the article (which was a full-page article) included pictures of his father detailing information about an alleged sexual assault on two young males by him a few years earlier. I was absolutely stunned and shocked, hearing about this from my son.

I was totally unaware of what was written in the paper about my ex husband. I had no knowledge of his conduct with any boy. How could I? When the marriage broke up in 1992 I had no idea what he did, except for the time when he tried to strangle me in 1996.

I was a naive seventeen-year-old virgin when I married my first husband. I was desperate to get out of an abusive home but not so desperate that I would have knowingly entered into a relationship, let alone marriage, with a paedophile/sociopath. He charmed me when I first met him. That's what these kind of people do. I was just a kid from a broken home, trying to make a better life for myself. My mother met this person when she worked in a hotel in Belfast in the early 70's. I wasn't aware of anything going on when my children were younger. I honestly wasn't. If I had suspected any sexual abuse from my ex husband towards any of my children I would have done something about it. When he was mentally and physically abusive towards them, I stepped in and took it for them, as a mother does.

My son felt so much shame about his father's sexuality (it was a big thing back then for a young person growing up in Belfast). I said to him at the time, "I know it's difficult for you. He's gay, not a paedophile", trying to reassure him. My son continued shouting at me down the phone with absolute venom in his voice, accusing me of not being there for him or his family. I said "I'm so sorry, son. I'm in complete shock here". He was so angry with his so-called father. Of course, he wasn't there, so I got it instead. I said to him, "You have a selective memory. I was and have been there for you and your family. If I didn't call up to see my grandchildren every Saturday I wouldn't get to see them at all". That's when I'd had enough and put the phone down.

I immediately walked over to the shops to buy the paper, quaking as I made my way over to my local supermarket. It was like hearing about my niece's death by suicide. I knew it had happened, I just needed to see for myself. I couldn't wait to get back home and read this article for myself. I nervously turned the pages, looking for the article, and there it was. I was horrified at what I read, and seeing the pictures of this man made me sick to my stomach. I couldn't believe what I had just read. I didn't know what to do. I remember feeling ashamed to ring Ken. It took me a while before I was able to lift the phone. Before I did, I rang the newspaper to ask about the article. The woman I spoke with asked if I had been affected by the article and did I know this man? I said yes, I knew him, but didn't say in what capacity. She told me all I needed to know. I felt ill and deeply sad for the young people in question. I immediately thought, "Oh my God, I have worked with so many adults and young people over the years who had been so badly affected by these monsters". The mental, physical and emotional pain they cause to innocent people- I never ever thought I would be connected in any way to such a person. It filled me with disgust and utter contempt for this vile excuse for a human being.

I rang Ken, hardly able to speak. Eventually I told him about the phone call from my son. He was in shock too and assured me that he'd be home as soon as he could. My youngest daughter Betty had rung me a couple of weeks before, saying "My daddy told me that there was going to be something bad written about him and that it is all lies". I asked her what she meant. As she continued the conversation with me she dismissed what she'd said at the beginning of our conversation and went on to talk about other things. Betty made it sound as if it was no big deal. I didn't pay much heed as I wasn't interested in learning or hearing anything about her father. I was more interested in learning about how she was doing as she was due her first baby in June.

I waited anxiously on Ken arriving home. I was still feeling a deep sense of shame, guilt, and uncertainty about where to go and what to do next. My head was completely melted. When Ken got home I showed him the paper and wondered what on earth he thought while reading it. He didn't seem that surprised, saying, "He's a monster. I hope he gets what he deserves". All that afternoon I was in bits. My son sent me a text, apologising. His head was all over the place, as was Cathy's. Betty, God help her, refused to read the article. She had been so brainwashed by this sociopath whom she'd thought of as a loving 'dad'. It ripped our already broken family to pieces. My children were suffering mentally, emotionally and spiritually. I too was in bits. I really wasn't sure how in God's name we would all get through this living nightmare.

I began making plans to get as far away from Belfast as I could. I had thought about moving when Robyn died. Everywhere I went there were memories. My siblings were all gone. My only living sibling passed me by on the street as if we were strangers. It was just too painful.

The shame was back for real. I was so afraid that neighbours and people who knew me would stop and ask me questions. The man who saved my life in 1996, and his partner Marie, would often stop and ask about my ex husband not long after he tried to kill me. I could never understand why. He fooled everyone into believing he was a great guy. Even the Judiciary when he won custody of my beautiful daughter Betty.

My eldest daughter took to alcohol, food, and drugs when she found out. I was worried sick about her. Cathy had written him a letter a few months before the truth came out about him. It took him over a week to reply. They hadn't had a relatonship in nearly ten years. When she confronted him about the allegations he turned on her. Their relationship was severed for a second time. I remember saying to her, when he allowed her back into his life, "If he hurts you again I will go crazy". Cathy was falling apart right before my eyes. Betty was in complete denial and my son had his new business to help take his mind off this insane time in all of our lives.

On Wednesday the 16th of April I wasn't feeling very well. I had been in bed most of the day. Betty had paid (or at least I think it was her who paid) for a private scan and I said I would go with her. She called for me around tea time. I went out to her car with her. She drove us over to where the private clinic was. It was a 3D scan in colour of my fourth grandchild. I must say I'd never seen anything like it; it was amazing. When she dropped me home I went straight to bed.

The following day I felt no better. In fact, I was feeling quite ill. I found it difficult getting out of bed. It was a struggle getting out to the loo. On Good Friday my condition grew worse. When Ken came home from work I said "I think I need an ambulance". He didn't hesitate and rang for one right away. He was asked questions by the paramedics about my condition. Ken spoke very calmly, answering their questions until they arrived at the house around twenty minutes later. Ken let the two paramedics in when they knocked at the front door. They made their way up to the back bedroom and began carrying out tests, taking my temperature, oxygen levels, and asking me lots of questions. They worked on me for about 20 minutes, saying "We're taking you to the hospital. Don't worry about having to lie on a trolley, you're going to be seen right away". At that time it was all over the news that patients were having to wait on trolleys for hours before they could be seen by a doctor. Sadly, it's 2017, and things still haven't improved- quite the opposite.

I was able to walk out to the ambulance with the help of the two paramedics. Ken was walking with me too. I got into the ambulance and more tests were done on me. I can't really remember what they were. I do remember one of the paramedics telling me to slow down my breathing. He feared me hyperventilating and helped me to slow down. When the ambulance set off, Ken stayed with me until we arrived at the hospital. I was wheeled straight into A&E where I was put into a cubicle. I had more tests carried out and yet more questions were asked by a lovely female doctor. I was then sent for an x-ray and wheeled back out to the corridor of A&E and waited there for twenty or more minutes. The doctor came over to me and said, "Rebecca you have pneumonia. We are admitting you".

Not long after that I was taken to a ward where there were only four beds. Poor Ken, I could tell he was concerned about me. I was concerned about how he would get back home. He reassured me that he'd be fine and told me to take it easy and that he loved me. As he left the ward I began to cry. The nurse who was looking after me asked what was wrong, was there anything she could get me? I asked for a sleeping tablet which she got for me and helped me out to the toilet. Thank God I was in the hands of someone who cared about me.

When I woke the next morning I felt very weak and very down too. Ken rang to ask about me. He and my daughter Cathy called to visit me. Cathy had bought me a beautiful bouquet of flowers and a box chocolates. Good job they got there when they did as the nurse explained that I was being transferred to another hospital at eleven that morning. The ward I was in was only short term. I was the only person there. I wasn't overjoyed about being transferred but there was nothing I could do about it. I was being moved and that was it.

Ken accompanied me in the ambulance to the other hospital. Cathy left to go home. She was visibly upset at seeing me so ill. She said that she would call to see me soon. When I arrived at the hospital I was taken to my bed which was just off a main corridor. There were four beds altogether. I felt as weak as I tried to get into the bed from the wheelchair. I was helped along by two of the nursing staff. They put me on an intravenous drip and assessed me, making sure that I had all I needed and that I was comfortable. Ken stayed with me until after lunch was over and went home afterwards.

That evening Jackie, my son's partner, called to see me, as did Ken. The woman in the next bed to me was unable to do anything for herself. My heart went out to her. She would shout out in an angry voice from time to time if anyone tried to speak with her or help her in any way. She called the nurses and other people who were looking after her terrible names. She was hard to make out at times. That was until she began hurling sectarian abuse at those who were trying to do their job. It did annoy me, I'll be honest. It brought back unpleasant memories of the last time I was in this hospital having my appendix removed when I was a child. Back then I didn't understand completely what was going on but I soon figured it out, though. I know this poor woman was obviously very ill. I had no idea what had happened to her. All I knew was that she was bedridden and most likely in a lot of pain. Nonetheless, I did wonder why she called everyone a 'Fucking Fenian Bastard'!

The following day was Easter Sunday the 20th, Betty's 27th birthday. She came to visit me with her huge bump, my soon-to-be born ganddaughter. I had Ken bring all her birthday gifts up to the hospital that day so I could give them to her. My son Sam and Brianna, my beautiful granddaughter, called to see me too. Sam had brought me in a beautiful bouquet of flowers and Brianna presented me with a cute little girl on a bike with a plant in it. One of the women across from me shouted to my son "You can't bring flowers in here". He replied, "Right you are". We carried on with our conversation and when everyone was leaving, Ken took the flowers and plant carrier home with him. Ken visited every day without fail, bless him. I asked him to keep the house clean while I was in hospital, which he did. He would bring me in sandwiches or fish and chips as the food wasn't that great.

My two friends came to visit on different occasions and Cathy called to see me. On this particular day she was in an extremely anxious state, crying and saying how difficult she had found the drive over and parking her car in the parking lot as she'd never been to this hospital before. I decided to ask Ken to pull the curtain around my bed so we could have a little privacy. Cathy was in a really bad emotional state. She seemed unable to stop crying. The fallout between her and her so-called father was taking its toll on her. I tried to calm her down. My heart was breaking, seeing my daughter in such a dreadful emotional state. I advised her to seek professional help as soon as possible and she said she would.

When she left I burst into tears. Ken was so loving, kind and supportive. I don't know how I would have coped if he hadn't been there. One of the nurses happened to call in to administer other medication I needed every day. When she saw me in floods of tears she asked if there was anything she could do for me. She continued, "Shall I get you one of your anti-depressant pills?" I politely refused. After Ken and Cathy left, I stayed in my bed with the curtain still around my bed. The woman who had said to my son that flowers weren't allowed in the ward came over to my bed and pulled the curtain back, saying "That's not doing you any good, isolating yourself like that". I was too weak and depressed to tell her to 'go away and mind her own bloody business'. The nurses would always ask me when they came around with the meditation trolley, would I like an anti-depressant. My answer was always the same, "No". My doctor had prescribed them for me before I took sick. I tried them but they didn't seem to agree with me so I stopped taking them. They were on the list of medications that the paramedics asked my husband to get for them that Friday night when they came out to my home.

I was taken for another chest x-ray on the Tuesday. Any time I saw the consultant who was looking after me I pestered him about going home. I felt so down while I was in hospital. I didn't like being around strangers, two of whom I didn't like at all. The woman who was facing me was great craic. She and I really hit it off. She had a brilliant sense of humour. Listening to her tell some of her life stories had me in stitches. I was really sad to learn that she was being discharged on Wednesday but at the same time happy for her as she was going home. She, like me, hated being in hospital.

The next day, Thursday, when my consultant came to see me I asked again, "When can I go home?" He said, "I think it'll be okay for you to go home after lunch". I rang Ken to tell him the good news. He said he would be there to bring me home. I was so happy to be getting out of there. I said my goodbyes to two of the nurses who had been so kind to me while I was there. They took really good care of me and the other patients on the ward. I could hardly wait until lunchtime. I had my bag packed and I was ready to go by twelve o'clock. When Ken arrived I was so happy to see him. We had to wait a while for my prescription before I was allowed to leave the hospital. We were out of there by two o'clock.

The walk from the ward to the lift was a slow one. It was the same getting from the lift out to Ken's car. But I didn't care. I was going home. Once we arrived at the back door and walked into the kitchen I noticed a few pieces of fluff on the floor. I bent down to pick them up and Ken said, "Leave it. I'll help you upstairs; you need to get to bed, love". Typical of me- weak as a kitten and my bloody OCD takes over. I had no choice but to listen to Ken's advice. I felt very tired and knew that I needed to get to bed. For the first couple of weeks that I was home I did nothing but sleep. Ken looked after me, making meals, tidying up, getting the laundry done etc. No one else offered to help us, as usual. Ken did his best. I tried to recover, although I was doing things around the house that I shouldn't have been doing.

Our move to the country-
our first home together.

Ken and I had applied to the Housing Association for a transfer before I became ill. On Thursday the 1st of May 2014 we received a letter from them offering us a bungalow on the outskirts of Belfast. We decided to go and have a look at the property. Our friend Rose, who lived in Killinchy at the time, drove us all down to see it. It was lovely although quite small, a detached bungalow which sat on a couple of acres of land that I liked- total privacy. There were a few neighbours scattered around the area. We called at the house nearest the bungalow to introduce ourselves. The lady who came out to speak with us seemed very friendly.

The problem was that the Housing Association were demanding that we move in on Monday. They let us have the keys to view the property on Friday so we could have a look around the inside. We literally had an hour to get from Downview to view the bungalow and then get back to them before their office closed at four o'clock. It was a mad rush. We barely had time to check the inside. The road in and out of Downview is bad for traffic at the best of times, but on Fridays it's a nightmare. Ken and I were dismayed at the way this was handled by the Housing Association in Downview. We made them aware of my health condition but it didn't seem to matter. I tried to explain that even a healthy person would find it difficult packing up a three-bedroom house in two days. They still refused, saying the bungalow was lying empty too long and that if we weren't going to take it they had another family who would. I was too weak to be put under this pressure. Ken and I discussed it and we both agreed it couldn't be done. Also, Ken felt that it may have been a bit too isolated and that I may get lonely with no one around to talk to all day every day. So we informed them early on Monday morning that we wouldn't be taking the bungalow.

We decided to pack a few boxes of stuff that we weren't using, just in case we got another letter from the Housing Association. We knew we were going to move- we just didn't know when or where that would be.

I had to return to personal therapy as I felt I really needed to. Ever since that awful day in March my head had been in a spin. I was wondering about all sorts of things. I thought about my childhood, why in the name of good God was I so stupid as to marry such a bad person. My children were suffering too. My daughter Betty, who was due her first baby soon, was still living in her father's boyfriend's flat, still in denial. It was just a mess. Cathy was off the rails. My son was burying himself in work so as to escape from the reality that his father is a sociopath. I wasn't feeling great, emotionally or physically. Betty told me that Social Services were out to see her because someone had told them she was living where she was living. She was so upset, saying "This is the worst day of my life. If I find out who it was I'll never speak with them again". She just wasn't able to see that maybe her soon-to-be-born baby was at risk. I was angry at times with Betty. In my head I could understand because of my training. It didn't make it any easier though as her continuing to live there with her boyfriend meant that none of her family were able to visit. Social Services did nothing about it. She still continued on living there rent free. That was the incentive or motive, whichever way you want to look at it; her father having complete control.

Betty's baby was due on the 10th of June. I went with her to the hospital. She was examined by a doctor who told us that Betty's baby wasn't ready to come into the world just yet. Betty was given another appointment for Friday the 13th, Robyn's third anniversary. Again, nothing was happening. My heart went out to Betty. All she wanted was for her baby to be born. The doctor told us that if she didn't go into labour by herself they would take her in the following Friday the 20th of June. I was praying she would be able to go into labour by herself but that didn't happen. Ken and I drove down to the flat where she was staying- we stopped at the top of an entry just across from the flat at around seven thirty. Betty came out with her boyfriend. When they were settled, off we went to the hospital. It was only a short distance which meant that we arrived at the hospital in plenty of time. I was so excited about my new granddaughter coming into the world. Betty was a little anxious and excited at the same time.

When we arrived, Betty was taken to a ward where all expectant mothers stay before the birth of their babies. I stayed with Betty for a while and made sure she was in good hands, which she was. I called down to see her later on that evening. She was in good spirits, just waiting and wondering when she was going to give birth. Thankfully, her father stayed away, or at least I didn't have the misfortune to bump into him. I'm not sure if Betty had asked him to stay away, knowing I was going to be there. An added pressure on Betty, no doubt.

I set my alarm clock for seven thirty when I got home as I wanted to be with Betty first thing on Saturday morning. I got up and was in the middle of getting ready when Cathy rang me, saying "God love our Betty.

I bet she's really nervous. I feel sorry for her, down there all by herself". I said "I'm cutting this conversation short as it's keeping me back". I asked Cathy, "When are you going down to see your wee sis?" I made my way down to the hospital to the ward and there she was, bless her.

I arrived there just before nine o'clock. Betty's boyfriend got there after nine. In the afternoon, at around one o'clock, Betty was taken to another room where she was being examined and monitored, both her and the baby. By two o'clock she said she could feel a lot of pressure. I asked the midwife if Betty could have an epidural to help relieve the pain. She agreed and went to get the anaesthetist to administer the pain relief drug to my daughter.

I excused myself any time Betty was being examined so as to allow my daughter her dignity. Her boyfriend stayed with her, which I know she was glad about. Around six or seven o'clock Betty was complaining about the pain. I could see that she was still hurting. I asked the midwife why she was in so much pain. She explained to us that sometimes an epidural doesn't work. Betty was taking the gas and air to help her. I was in complete empathy with her, knowing what she was going through and what lay ahead of her. At around 9.30 the doctor who came to see her decided that Betty needed to be moved to the theatre to have a c-section. God love her. It wasn't for the want of trying to bring her baby into this world the natural way. I had to stay in the room where Betty had been all afternoon. Her boyfriend was allowed to go with her, thankfully. He came out at around eleven o'clock holding his beautiful baby daughter in his arms and wearing a huge smile on his face. I couldn't wait to hold my precious granddaughter in my arms. She was so gorgeous, the spitting image of her father. She was born at 10:30pm on the 21st of June 2014, weighing 7lb 2 and a half ounces. Betty was exhausted. It had been a very long day for her but she was absolutely fine. I wasn't allowed in to see her, which was understandable. I was really tired but so very happy. I rang Ken and told him our great news. He drove down to the hospital to get me and Betty's boyfriend and drove us both home.

The following day I felt surplus to requirements, to be honest. I had a gut feeling that I was going to be pushed out of this wonderful experience of being able to see my granddaughter and daughter whenever I wanted and needed to. I rang Betty to ask her would it be okay for Ken and I to visit? She replied, "My dad's coming this morning with his boyfriend and my boyfriend's parents are coming down too". She continued, "Would you mind coming in the afternoon?" I felt like I did when Betty first told me she was pregnant- fearful. I feared her father would take over, just like he did when Betty came into the world. Although he waited until all the hard work was done, like walking them up and down the bedroom floors when all my children were teething. Changing towel nappies in the 70's, finding out about nursery places for Sam and Betty. Cathy didn't go to nursery or creche. Walking them to and from school, Sport days etc....

My first visit seeing my daughter and granddaughter.

My son Sam rang me to ask about the situation regarding visiting his sister and brand new niece on Sunday morning. I said that I had spoken with Betty and that it was okay for us to visit on Sunday afternoon. I suggested, "We'll go down together- why should we let "him" stop us from going to visit?" He agreed with me and said he would call down to my house to collect me and Ken after he'd picked up Cathy, in time for the afternoon visiting times.

It did feel a little scary for me, anyhow, and I was hoping we wouldn't bump into him and his partner. Thankfully, that didn't happen. Betty was as pleased to see us as we were to see her and her baby daughter who was now given her name- Kyla. I brought down presents for Betty as I had for Jackie when Brianna was born. We all bought presents for the new arrival in our family. It was such a happy occasion. Brianna was delighted that she had a new cousin, Sam and Cathy were over the moon to meet their new niece, we were all very happy to see them both. Betty was obviously sore after her c-section and seemed anxious to leave the hospital as soon as possible. I encouraged her to stay in until she got the okay to leave.

It was a bittersweet time for me. I was feeling sad, knowing that my daughter would be returning with her baby to her father's partner's flat. I thought it was an absolute disgrace that Social Services were perfectly okay about it. There was nothing I could do. I was in fear of losing my daughter and granddaughter if I had interfered. I had to accept things as they were.

As I've stated before, none of us were able to visit Betty and Kyla when they left the hospital. That hurt me a great deal. I thought "I'm her mum, why doesn't she want to come and stay with me?" Of course I already knew the reason why. He had perfect control, as he always had. I didn't stand a chance, nor did my daughter. The conditioning was done when she was a child, just like with her two older siblings.

My mothering instinct took over as I and a friend called down to see Betty and my new granddaughter on the 27th, six days after Kyla was born. I got to feed her for the first time and it felt great, it really did, although in the back of my mind I was aware that her father and his boyfriend may have been watching us go into the flats. I found out later from Cathy that we had to pass their father's flat to get to see Betty and Kyla's. At the time I did wonder if he was watching us as Betty would have needed to inform him that I was coming down.

Very soon after that visit I knew deep down that I was not going to be as involved in my granddaughter's life as I would have liked to have been. Betty brought Kyla up to visit Ken and me on Sunday, the 6th of July. Betty and her boyfriend were having difficulties in their relationship before Kyla was born. That afternoon Betty asked us if we would look after Kyla for a while as she had something to sort out with her man. She said she was going to drive down to see him. I pleaded with her to let Ken drive her to wherever she intended going as she was advised not to drive until six weeks after her c-section. She paid no heed to me whatsoever and ran out of the door. I was very concerned about her physical and emotional wellbeing. She was not in a good place.

Ken and I enjoyed looking after Kyla. She was such a pleasant baby. I fed her, changed her and made sure she was okay. It was going on eleven o'clock before Betty returned. Ken drove them both down to the flat. Betty said that she had got things sorted with her guy although I wasn't so sure.

The following Saturday night, Betty let her father look after Kyla (she was still very much in denial, made easier by Social Services' lack of care or interest in the welfare of my granddaughter). On Sunday evening, it was Kyla's other granny who would be looking after her. I thought, "I wonder when I will get a look-in?" When Betty called up to see me with Kyla a few days later I asked her when I was going to get some time with Kyla. I told her how I felt excluded and she said "Mum, you haven't been well". Which was true. A good excuse for her. I was more than willing to have Kyla stay over when I was feeling fine but her father and her boyfriend's mother were given first choice. I was in the background- not really that important. Certainly not valued enough or given my place. History was repeating itself and I knew it. That didn't make it any easier for me to deal with it- quite the opposite.

Things were beginning to happen quicker than I would have liked regarding our move out of Belfast. We needed appropriate time so we could pack up our belongings and not be rushed as we had been with the previous offer. We received an offer for a two-bedroom bungalow in Finn Town but this time we had to wait until the previous tenant's belongings were removed from the premises. Also, there was work to be carried out on the bungalow, which suited us fine. On Saturday the 28th of June 2014 Ken, Kyla, and I drove down from Belfast to see if we would be interested in taking this property. We happened to be looking after Kyla that day.

It was a beautiful sunny day. My darling Kyla was sleeping in her baby seat in the back of our car when we arrived in the street where the bungalow was. Ken stayed in the car with Kyla while I got out to have a closer look to see if there was anyone in. I knocked on the door a few times and realised no one was. As I made my way down the path, a couple of men came walking towards me. I said to them "Myself and my husband have been allocated this bungalow. Is there any chance I could get inside to have a look around?" One of the men was so nice and said "Yes, no problem at all. Come in and have a look. We're relatives clearing out our aunt's belongings". The bungalow had that 'old' smell with carpets on the floors that looked very worn. Some of her furniture was still there. Their relative was quite old and suffering from dementia, bless her. I asked if I could have a look out in the back garden. Again the young man obliged me. It looked fine. The grass seemed as if it had just been cut. There were a few bushes and an old dilapidated garden shed. I thanked the men for allowing me in. As I walked down the path to the car I knew that this was the place for us. Ken was very pleased, despite the fact that he only seen it from the outside.

After that, it was all systems go. My least favourite thing to do in this world is pack! Ken and I were over the moon to have been allocated a bungalow in such a lovely village. It was perfect for us. I didn't want our neighbours in Belfast to know right away that we were moving. We tried to keep it from them for as long as possible. I was just making sure no one would hassle us for the house. I don't really think that would have happened. I just didn't want to risk a repeat of the time I was allocated my house in 1980 when a woman called to the front door, asking "Who's getting this house." Besides, I couldn't be bothered with nosey questions.

On the 3rd of July a senior housing officer called out to see me to sign the tenancy over. It was a pretty scary thing for me to do. I had lived there for sixteen years. Moving out of Belfast for a second time; only this time it was 'us', my husband and I moving into our first home together. The housing officer reassured me, saying "Don't worry, you're not going to end up homeless. If it doesn't suit you, you can always stay". That was very reassuring indeed. Change isn't easy. It was a big deal for me, even though I knew moving to Finn Town was going to be much better for us. I was leaving my home town and a few friends behind. I knew deep down my time here had come to an end. A brand new chapter was about to begin for us both.

My children understood that I needed to leave all the painful memories behind. It is only forty minutes at the most from our old place to our new one. They all had cars so it wasn't a problem for them to come and visit me. (Although they didn't visit that often anyway, despite the fact that I was only living a short distance away from them in Belfast). I felt sad about that and was very much aware that my neighbours' children and grandchildren would visit them on a regular basis.

A therapist I had seen a few years before said that I should never compare my life to the lives of others. My old school friend, Maggie, would often ask me "Why doesn't Sam let Brianna stay over with you?" I gave her the same answer my son Sam gave me when I asked him that question. He said that it would only cause friction between him and Jackie. He continued, "Her sister and nephew are trouble. There's no way I would let Brianna stay with them. I can't say yes to you and no to Jackie". I accepted his explanation. The last thing I wanted to do was come between my son and his partner.

Ken and I celebrated our first wedding anniversary on Sunday the 20th of July at the castle where we had taken our vows the year before. We had a fantastic day together. The sun was shining, just as it had the year before- another perfect day.

On Thursday the 24th of July we finally got the keys to our new home. We were both so excited. We were packed and ready to go. On the 29th we moved in. My friend and her then boyfriend helped us out a great deal. Ken's friend in work also helped us out, as did Cathy. We had booked a van which took two runs from Belfast to Finnish Town to bring all our big furniture down.

Ken had been driving up and down non stop the day after we received the keys. He brought whatever smaller stuff he could fit into his car and left it at the bungalow. It was tough going but he didn't mind one bit.

I was still weak from the pneumonia so it was difficult for me but thankfully we had help. We began the move around nine o'clock on Tuesday morning and didn't get finished until around six. We had great bother getting our sofa inside the living room. It sat in our new front garden until our friend got home from work that evening. The neighbours must have wondered who the hell was moving in to their quiet neighbourhood! Our friend needed to remove the pane of glass from the living room window in order to get the sofa inside. The kitchen units were in a poor state. When I tried putting cutlery and stuff into the drawers, they fell on to the floor but we got there in the end.

The first few days Ken and I were busy moving things into upboards and drawers etc. From the 24th until the day we moved, Ken and I spent five days cleaning all the floors with bleach and disinfectant, washing everything in the bungalow and opening windows, letting air circulate around the place as the smell of 'old' still lingered.

To begin with we didn't really notice that there were quite a few repairs that needed attention. We were that busy getting things sorted as one does when just moving into a new home. The Housing Association was supposed to have had all repairs done for us before we moved in. There was a leak in the hot press, windows that didn't close properly, the boiler out the back needed repairing. I will say this, though, they came out right away and did what needed to be done.

Next on our list was the decorating. We didn't know a soul down here so I asked my next door neighbour if she could recommend a painter and decorator. She later slipped a note through the letter box with a man's name on it. When I saw her the following day, she asked did I receive the note. She told me that Jack was a decorator. She knew him through working with his mother who was in need of daily care. She went on to say that he was very witty. I contacted him that day and explained who had given me his contact number. He asked what I needed doing. He said he would call out to see me and give me a price for the work.

He called out that evening to see me and again I explained what I wanted done (which was every room in the bungalow). He asked me to put the kettle on for a cup of tea and then asked about my colour scheme. When I showed him the colours for each room he said "Oh, so you like bold colours". I made him his tea and asked him how much he would charge me and how long would it take him. He replied "£800. The work shouldn't take more than a week". I agreed for him to begin work on the Monday.

I was waiting on Jack all that day. Ken had come home from work at six. He was only in the door when Jack appeared at the front door in his overalls. In he came with a brush in hand. I said to him "I need this work done during the day starting at nine in the morning, preferably earlier". He said "I have another job to do during the day and I can only start here after six". I explained, "That's no good to me. Sorry. You've wasted your time. You forgot to mention that on Friday!" He said "Fine" and left. Back to the drawing board, so to speak.

I saw an ad in the local paper advertising painting and decorating who offered a guarantee and free quote. So I made a phone call and spoke with a man named Fred. Again I went over what I needed done and asked him when he could call out and discuss it. He said: "I'll be with you in fifteen minutes". He did indeed call out. The problem was that a few days after he and his son began work in our home I had to sack them. Their work was truly appalling. Fred began arguing with me, pointing his pen in my face and calling me a 'BLOW-IN!' Meaning, outsiders- not from the area. Laughable really.

I ended up getting someone else in to finish the job properly. The smell of the paint, not to mention the fumes, affected my chest. I ended up having to go on a course of antibiotics. In between times, Ken and I were busy sourcing floor covering, blinds, new bedroom furniture etc....Hard work, especially when I wasn't feeling great but we got there in the end.

Sam, Jackie, and our grandchildren came to see us in our new home. Betty and Kyla also came down to visit us. On Sunday 31st of August Sam and his family called down to see us again. We went out to a nearby restaurant situated near Ford Lough. I was delighted to have my family with me for the afternoon. I began to feel a little unwell while we were out having our lunch. There's a beautiful forest near where we live and I wanted to show Sam and Jackie where we sometimes take Brianna and Lorcan on a Saturday when they come down to stay with us for the day. Before we were able to go, I needed to call into the bungalow and take a few puffs of my inhalers. The kids love the forest, as do I. I don't think Sam and Jackie were too taken with it. As Sam said to me, "This isn't really my thing". Still, they got to have a walk with us and the kids in nature and saw for themselves how their children love it.

Later on, when they returned home, my chest felt really tight and I was struggling to breathe. Poor Ken wasn't too sure what to do for the best. Around 10/10.30 Ken rang for an ambulance. When the paramedics came in to see me they examined me and said they didn't think it was anything too serious but because of the pneumonia and subsequent chest infections, they felt it best to take me to hospital. Ken followed in his car behind the ambulance. I was eventually seen by a doctor who told me that I had yet another chest infection. I was given a few antibiotics to keep me going until Monday. We got home at three thirty in the morning, both of us exhausted from the waiting around. It felt great being home and it was such a relief for me that I didn't need to be admitted. Ken took four days off to look after me. He collected my medication, cooked our meals and made sure everything was okay.

On the 8th of September I rang Cathy's doctor as I was going out of my mind worrying about her. She had fallen into the wrong company, drinking and taking drugs. I didn't know what else to do. I rang her doctor again the following day. This time he rang me back. I explained to him that she wasn't coping well with the news regarding her so-called father and that I didn't want her to become just another statistic. He was very understanding and said he would speak with her. I also searched for the therapist she had been seeing about a year before. She got on very well with him. I found his number and rang him but he was obviously working as the answering machine came on. I left a voice mail and before long he called me. He explained that he no longer worked in Belfast and recommended someone else. After a phone call from Cathy during which she told me she was amazed she was still alive, considering her abuse of alcohol and drugs, I said to her "Cathy, please stop. I can't bury you. I couldn't bear to lose another person whom I love". Thankfully, she listened and stopped socialising with the people who were not good for her to be around. My prayers had been answered. I had never prayed as much in my life. I had masses said for her in Rome, America and here. I lit candles and never left the chapel just down the street from where I live. On the 12th of September, Cathy, Betty and Kyla called down to see me. It was so good to see my children and granddaughter, especially Cathy. I knew her crazy days killing herself were at an end.

Ken and I had booked a holiday some months before we left Belfast. We were off to Portugal on the 14th of August for ten days. My doctor (whom I changed to a local doctor) made sure I had a supply of antibiotics, just in case. I packed my nebulizer as a precautionary measure. I wanted to make sure we would enjoy this well-earned break, which we did. As it turned out, I didn't need my nebulizer nor the antibiotics. The hot climate obviously did my lungs the world of good.

When we returned from our holidays I felt like a new person. We continued to collect Brianna and Lorcan on Saturdays which made my day. My grandchildren are my tonic. They make me feel extremely happy and alive. Betty and her boyfriend called down to see us on Sunday and I made us all dinner. The following evening I was to keep Kyla overnight but Betty texted to say that the health visitor was coming out to see Kyla on Monday morning. I was disappointed but I totally understood. I did get to keep her overnight, however, on the 8th of October which made my day.

Betty had been busy for weeks making plans and getting Kyla's christening organized for Sunday the 26th of October. She invited Ken and me to the party afterwards along with her sister Cathy and brother Sam to a club in Belfast. She asked me if I would look after Kyla after the party so that she and her boyfriend could carry on celebrating without having to worry about Kyla. At the time I went along with what Betty wanted. I even asked her if there was anything she needed. I got the stuff in that she said she needed and then it hit me. I thought no, I will not allow myself to be used. If I'm not good enough to be invited to my granddaughter's christening, I am not showing up at the party for people to sit and gossip, asking "What kind of a mother is she when she didn't bother going to her granddaughter's christening!"

I felt deeply hurt that she had invited her father, his partner and her boyfriend's parents. Betty's cousin Kate was the only one who was asked. She was invited by Betty to be Kyla's godparent. Sam and Cathy weren't invited either to Kyla's christening. Cathy was hurt that Betty had asked her cousin to be Kyla's godmother. The only family on

Betty's side that attended the after party was Kate, her cousin. Such a sad state of affairs.

She rang me the day before and I said I was upset. She said back to me, "What's wrong with you now?" I tried to explain but she was in no mood for listening and put the phone down. I cried like a baby, feeling so hurt and rejected, not to mention disrespected. In the very beginning, when she announced that she was pregnant, I knew deep in my soul that I would eventually end up getting hurt by both her and her controlling, manipulating father and sadly I was right. We didn't speak to each other until March the following year. Cathy said to me a couple of times, "You should get in touch with Betty. Even my friends said you should". They didn't live my life or have a clue what it felt like to be rejected by your youngest daughter.

I had made up my mind I wasn't ever going to let Betty hurt me again. She got in touch on the 27th of March 2015 via text, accusing me of being a bad mum, saying "How can you just stop being involved in your daughter and granddaughter's lives?" I replied, "You chose to shut me out of your lives".

I reminded her about the 13th of June 2011 when she rang me about Robyn, asking her "If I didn't love you why would I have gone with you that terrible day, why did I prevent you from entering your aunt's bungalow and why did I fight the courts for custody?" We exchanged a few more texts and she said she was going to let her counsellor see my replies. I said "Go right on ahead. I didn't do anything other than love you. I feared you would shut me out of Kyla's life and that's exactly what you did. Don't you get it?" I asked her to sit down with me and talk it over like two adults. She reluctantly agreed, but not until after Mother's Day. My son Sam and Brianna were the only ones I saw on Mother's Day that year.

She called down to see me on Friday the 3rd of April 2015 in my bungalow. We had a long and honest heart-to-heart. I admired her willingness to engage with me and I told her so. I tried to explain where I was coming from as her mum and Kyla's grandmother. I asked if she could put herself in my shoes and see how I felt, being excluded from such an important day in both their lives. I'm not sure she was able to do that. The main thing was that we had had a dialogue and were back in each other's lives again. Betty left my home feeling happier and of course I was chuffed that I had them both back in my life. I can't find the words to explain just how good it felt. Betty and Kyla came down for an overnight stay on the 8th of April. A few days later Brianna, Lorcan, Betty, and Kyla all enjoyed a family day out with me and Ken. We went to a country park near where we live. The swans and ducks come right up beside you, looking for food. It was a great family day out for us all.

Cathy, Betty, Kyla and I would go out regularly to Sam's restaurant and stuff our faces. The food is to my liking as I am quite a fussy eater. We went to other eating establishments and enjoyed family time together. Things were going well despite the fact that Betty was still in denial regarding her father. Thankfully, Cathy seemed to be coping better, which helped me a great deal.

My health was not good. I was taking chest infections on a regular basis and having to take antibiotics. This meant that I wasn't able to have Kyla stay with me as much as I would have liked. However, whenever I could I did as I loved having her stay with me. On Friday the 15th of May Betty brought Kyla down to stay with me. I was looking after her overnight and planning to have Brianna and Lorcan come down as well on the Saturday. I felt the old familiar tightness in my chest and tried to ignore what my body was telling me, but when it came to lunch time I knew I just couldn't do it. I rang Ken who was at work and told him that I was feeling ill. He suggested getting in touch with Kyla's grandmother and asking if it would be okay to bring Kyla up to her earlier than planned. She was totally fine about it. I also let Jackie know that I was sick and wouldn't be able to get Brianna and Lorcan. Ken and I drove Kyla up to her other granny. She told me to go home and get to bed which is exactly what I did.

On Monday morning I got an emergency appointment to see my doctor. It had got so bad that I needed a neighbour to collect my prescription as I was finding it difficult to breathe. My doctor put me on another course of antibiotics along with a course of steroids. It actually took another course of antibiotics and steroids (that was two in three weeks) before I began to feel better. Sam, Jackie and the kids came down to see me on Sunday the 31st of May. That cheered me up so much. It was lovely to see them and to know that they cared.

On June the 9th Betty and Kyla called down to see me and I was able to get Lorcan on Saturday. Brianna was sick, poor darling, so it was just us three. It was good to have the one-on-one time with my precious grandson.

June the 21th was Kyla's first birthday. Betty decided to have a party for her at her other granny's house. Ken and I collected Brianna and Lorcan to take with us. We also called at Cathy's house on the way. I hadn't seen Cathy in a while. She said to me "Mum, you've put on a lot of weight". I explained that I'd been on so many courses of steroids and antibiotics because of the many chest infections. I was forced to rest as a result, which of course doesn't help with weight loss.

I was beginning to feel well enough (or so I thought) to take Kyla overnight five days later. Ken brought Brianna and Lorcan down the following day. It was too much for me looking after the three of them, especially when I had Kyla from early afternoon the day before. It took me three days to recover. But, as usual, I didn't listen to what my body was telling me. I love my grandchildren so much that I didn't care about me. To be honest, I was aware that it was too much for Ken as well but I told myself that I only see them once a week. One overnight stay and a few hours the next day, we can manage. If I wasn't able to get Kyla on a Friday night, I would have her stay over a night during the week. It did make it easier having the three of them on a Saturday.

I had seen my doctor on Thursday the 3rd of September as my chest was giving me bother. She prescribed another course of steroids and antibiotics for me to take. I asked her advice because I was worried I might not be able to get away on our holiday to Spain on Saturday the 5th. She reassured me, saying I would be alright with my medication and to bring my nebulizer along with me in case I would need it. I trust my doctor 100%. Even though I wasn't feeling good physically, I knew everything would be okay.

I had arranged with Betty to have lunch with her and Kyla the previous week.They both came down the day before we went away. We had lunch at a local restaurant not far from me. Kyla was in terrific form. She had everyone in the place smiling and laughing. It was so good to see them both. I came home a happy woman.

Cathy's 40th birthday

Ken and I had a lovely holiday in Fuengirola, Southern Spain, and as it turned out, I didn't need to use my nebulizer. The course of steroids and antibiotics, not to mention the beautiful weather, helped me to enjoy our time away.

Cathy, Betty, Kyla and I enjoyed a beautiful lunch at Sam's restaurant after our return home from Spain. Ken and I were getting Brianna and Lorcan the following day. It was absolutely wonderful to see them all and to spend some quality family time together.

Cathy's 40th birthday was approaching, so as a special treat I thought it would be a good idea to take her away for a couple of days to the Hilton hotel in Mount Patrick. I asked her if that was something she would like. She seemed delighted with the idea. I made a reservation for Monday the 28th of September, checking out on the Wednesday. I then received a call from Cathy telling me that she was going away to Blackpool instead with her friends on Friday the 25th. I was disappointed and hurt. I cancelled the provisional booking· and thankfully I hadn't lost any money. I guess she'd rather spend a few days away with her friends than with me. A lot more fun to be had, I would imagine.

She began her birthday celebrations that Friday. Cathy had asked if Ken and I would like to go to her brother's restaurant with her and her boss on Thursday evening. I said of course, count us in. I had intended paying for her meal and drinks as one of her birthday treats from me. I didn't realise that she had asked my nephew and his girlfriend to come along as well. I thought "Okay, it's her birthday, I'll let bygones be bygones. All the same, if she had told me from the beginning that they were coming I wouldn't have said yes. We could have gone out for lunch or dinner on our own somewhere else on a different day.

Just before her 40th, she left to go to the south of Ireland for the weekend and then booked herself on a holiday to the Costa del Sol for five days. Ken's birthday gift to Cathy was a massage and dinner afterwards at a lovely hotel and spa not far from where we live. (He also paid for me to have a spa treatment too). Later on we went out for a few drinks at a local bar. We were both delighted to have Cathy stay over with us. Her birthday celebrations went on for a month. That's how she likes it. She's like a child in a grown-up body.

I began to feel unwell again and needed to see my doctor. I rang the surgery and an appointment was made for that morning. When I arrived at the surgery, my doctor examined me and prescribed Clarithromycin 500 mg and another course of Prednisone (steroids). I had taken another bad chest infection. My emotional and physical health had suffered badly since finding out about my ex husband. My children were struggling too (although they never spoke to me about it, especially Sam and Betty). The terrible revelation about their father in 2014 had deeply affected our relationship with each other. When they all found out they took it out on me. As I've said before, they couldn't or wouldn't say anything to him.

The following evening Ken rang for a doctor. When the out-of-hours doctor came out and examined me he said that my doctor had prescribed the right medication for my condition. In fact he said, "You're on the Rolls Royce of antibiotics. It's going to take a couple of weeks before you begin to feel well. Even after you've finished taking the antibiotics you'll still not feel great. I recommend that you get plenty of rest". I was in bed for three days. The antibiotic had quite severe side effects. I was unable to sleep properly, which didn't help much. All the same, my breathing became a lot easier.

Betty and Kyla called down to see me on Thursday. We went out for a bite to eat at a sandwich bar just down the street. It was good to get out of the house for a while. Betty told me that Social Services had called out to see her father. I think it was late July, beginning of August. She told me that she had received a phone call from her father as she was driving into town one day. He told her that she needed to come home as Social Services wanted to speak with her. She went on to tell me that her father was trying to tell her what to say to them.

Cathy knew about this before I did. Betty had confided in Cathy and begged her not to tell me. One Sunday evening Cathy rang me, very upset, saying she couldn't tell me the reason why. She had given her word not to tell me. She said, "This is too much for me". She told me that Betty and Kyla had stayed with her on the Saturday night. I knew right away what was wrong. I asked to speak with Betty. I asked her outright what was going on. She told me she now knew the truth about her father. Poor darling. Her poor heart was shattered. Once again, she felt she couldn't get support from her mum because that's what she was told from an early age, that I didn't want to know. I tried to assure her that I did and would be there for them both.

Cathy felt for her and knew she needed to tell me. She continued "My heart goes out to her. She's just beginning to grieve. I'm still hurting but I've had a while to get my head around it. God help her. She has a baby to think of. I'm worried about her".

Social Services said that while Betty and Kyla were living in her father's boyfriend's flat Betty needed to keep Kyla away from him, otherwise they would take Kyla away from her. Betty said that someone who knew her father had gone down to where he lives and started shouting about the crimes he'd been accused of. Then after that, Social Services finally got their act together and did what they should have done when they first visited her father.

The thing that baffled me was that Betty's boyfriend and his parents now knew the truth. What kind of man would allow his baby daughter to be around such a person? I had offered to let her stay with us but she declined my offer. Betty was now on the emergency housing list. I couldn't wait until my daughter and granddaughter were as far away from there as possible.

Ken and I collected Brianna and Lorcan on Saturday as usual. Again, it was great to spend time with my grandchildren.The following Saturday we got all three of them, Brianna, Lorcan and Kyla. Such great fun we had with them all, although by the time they all went home I was fit for nothing. I kept Kyla over on Friday nights whenever I was able to. Ken would call for Brianna and Lorcan on Saturday and drive them down so we could all enjoy a family day together.

Christmas was drawing near so we decided to take all three grandchildren to visit Santa's grotto. Brianna enjoyed the experience but Lorca and Kyla weren't that bothered. We made sure to give them a good day and that's exactly what they got. Ken and I loved having them and spending time with all three as they are such good fun and great company.

My 59th birthday was approaching and Betty and Kyla called down to take me out. Betty invited me to lunch at a hotel nearby. It was my birthday treat from her and Kyla. She was fined £50 for parking on the street outside the hotel. I felt bad about it and gave her the £50 to pay the fine later on. My friend Mary had invited me and Ken over for a meal to her house on the Saturday evening. It was the first time we had seen her in her new home. All her grown-up children were there which made the evening very enjoyable.

Sam invited me for a birthday lunch on Sunday the following day, my birthday. Ken, Jackie, Brianna, and Lorcan all came along which made the day extra special. A cake was brought out with lit candles on it. I was absolutely thrilled to bits. This was the first time in my life I had celebrated my birthday three days in a row. Wonderful memories of my 59th birthday.

Cathy and I had a fall out in early December. She talked about taking me out for lunch then changed her mind. The usual with Cathy. Whenever it's my birthday or Mother's Day she tells me where we're going and what we'll be doing. It's never "Where would you like to go, or what would you like to do?"

Jackie gave me my birthday presents from Cathy as we were leaving the restaurant on my birthday. Cathy texted me later on to ask if I liked my presents. I texted her back to say "Yes, they're lovely, thank you". I don't like it when there's a fall out with my children. I understand that they were conditioned at an early age but it still causes me emotional pain when I get hurt by them.

An example of this was when Cathy put a post up on Facebook saying that she had bought jewellery online which she thought was very reasonable, only to discover the opposite. She believed she was getting quality jewellery for much less than she would have paid at a reputable jeweller. I wondered at the time who would be getting this imitation jewellery! I had a feeling it would be me and I was right. She had put the two bracelets into an Argento bag that had been used before. That hurt. I didn't say anything to her. I know that I allowed her to treat me this way. I was still terrified that if I upset the apple cart, so to speak, she would continue not to speak to me.

The weekend beginning Friday the 18th of December, Cathy and I met up for lunch in town at my son's restaurant. That evening, Betty and Kyla stayed over at ours. The following day, Brianna and Lorcan joined us. We went to Jumping Jacks where the kids had a fantastic time which always makes me feel on top of the world. On Sunday we called up to see Sam, Jackie and the kids to leave them their Christmas boxes. Not forgetting Alannah's too.

On Christmas Eve, Cathy made Ken and I a lovely lunch. Afterwards, we set off to visit our friend in Cushen Place. It had been a while since our last visit. The drive down is so lovely. The views as we approach our friend's house are spectacular. It reminds me of parts of the Donegal landscape- stunning.

Betty, her boyfriend and Kyla were coming down to spend Christmas Eve and Christmas morning with us before heading up to Belfast to have dinner with her boyfriend's mum. I must say it was lovely for Ken and I to have our family stay with us on Christmas Eve. I made breakfast for us all while Betty got herself and Kyla ready. They both looked amazing. It was so exciting to watch Kyla's presents being opened. The poor wee dote had no clue what was going on. It felt more like Christmas having my family with me. I kept Kyla overnight four days later and as usual we had all three on the Saturday. We took them out to Jumping Jacks and KFC afterwards.

Early in January, I met Betty and Kyla in Belfast where we all enjoyed lunch together. A few days later Cathy invited us up for dinner which was really nice. She's such a good cook although living on her own has made her lose the motivation to cook. In fact, she tries to tell me and everyone else that she can't cook! All was going well with myself and my children. It can be hard work trying to keep it all going smoothly when I'm the only one in therapy. Kyla had a sleepover with us the following evening.

Betty, Kyla and I had lunch together a second time in Belfast. Then on Saturday Ken picked up all three grandchildren and drove them down to our bungalow to spend time with us.

Saturday is our special day when we get to spend time with our precious Brianna, Lorcan and Kyla. They bring us so much love and joy. It's always difficult for them and us when it's time to go home. They give us so much love. It keeps us going until we see them the following Saturday.

Ken and I decided to get away for a couple of days to Sligo. I suffer from SAD (Seasonal Affective Disorder) and I like to get away in January/February time. The weather is as bad down there as it is here but getting away seems to work for me.

I had been in a lot of pain recently. The winter months are hard on my lung conditions and my arthritis. I have suffered from back, neck, thighs, and knee pain for some years now. I had been wearing orthotics in my shoes for a lot of years because of the pain in my neck and back. I was told by a doctor whom I used to be a patient of, in 1999 that I needed to wear orthotics in my shoes. As a result, I've been wearing them ever since. In late January I had an appointment to see my GP. I was in a lot of physical pain. My whole body was hurting from my arms to my legs, eyes, fingers, hands, knees, everywhere. She examined me and said, "You have Fibromyalgia". She proscribed co-coda mol painkillers for me. It took a while to sink in, but at the same time, I now had a proper diagnosis. I had been in pain for years and it took until that day to find out what the real reason was.

Not long after receiving my diagnosis, Betty called with Kyla. We were going to have a look at her new home which had been allocated to her. (Betty asked her boyfriend's mother to see the house before me. Again, that hurt me.) When Betty and I arrived I liked the look of this two-bedroom house right away. We couldn't get inside as Betty hadn't been given the keys yet. There were repairs to be carried out before they could move into their new home. My prayers had been answered yet again. The first offer she got was for a two-bedroom flat. It was in a rough area which Betty rightly turned down. To be offered such a lovely house in a nice area was something truly wonderful for my daughter and granddaughter. This was a great opportunity for Betty. A brand new chapter in her life, away from the pain of living in Belfast with all its sad memories. I was thrilled for them both.

I continued looking after Kyla overnight whenever I could. Ken continued to collect Brianna and Lorcan every Saturday or, when it really was too much to have all three, alternative Saturdays.

Making plans to get away to New Zealand and Thailand

I decided to pay for a holiday for Ken in February to visit his sister and family in New Zealand. I had been putting money away to start up my own private practice but because of my poor health that unfortunately didn't happen. (I had got my own website and 50 flyers to put up in Finn Town and Belfast.) So I thought, "I'll spend the money on a holiday for Ken". I couldn't have made it without him during my darkest days when I wasn't at my best, physically or emotionally. He had never been to New Zealand before and I knew he desperately wanted to go out to visit his family. So I bought his ticket for him to go and see them for three weeks on November the 1st.

I received my first appointment to see a psychologist in the middle of February. I had been waiting over a year to be seen. I had gone private and was horrified at one therapist's approach and techniques so I left. Another woman I'd seen made me think yes, I like how she works. But sadly she let me down. My head was not in a good place since finding out about my ex husband. That and losing both my sisters, not to mention the PTSD. I was finding trust particularly difficult. I felt people were letting me down, either by dying or by leaving my life for other reasons. I was so glad to be in treatment at last and I found I was able to engage with the psychologist.

Yet more disappointment around Mother's Day.

Cathy kept asking me what I wanted for Mother's Day and mentioned going to her brother's restaurant on the Saturday before. I said I would like to go to our favourite Indian in Belfast on Friday so she agreed that that was fine. Next thing I know, she doesn't want to go. Changing her mind yet again. As it turned out it was left for me to make the arrangements. But because she had left things to the last minute, everywhere was booked up. I managed to get us (Cathy, Betty, Kyla, and me) a table at a hotel near me. I was receiving mixed messages from Cathy by text. When I was at a training event in Belfast on Tuesday, she rang me sounding stressed out about the dinner on Sunday. A few days later I said to Ken "I'm not going through this nonsense again. Let's take ourselves off". I needed some head space.

I was so hurt by Cathy's behaviour that I didn't stop to think about Betty and Kyla. They were supposed to be staying overnight with us after we had all had our meal. I told Betty what had happened. I thought she understood. I'd just had enough and I really couldn't take any more. I was beginning to detest Mother's Day. I texted Cathy and told her I was cancelling. She asked why. I received my Mother's Day presents from Cathy seven weeks later.

In April, Ken booked a three-week holiday for my 60th birthday to Thailand in December. To say I was chuffed is an understatement.

I had always wanted to visit Thailand as it's such a spiritual place with the Buddhist monks and the many beautiful temples. All of my children had been and spoke about what an amazing country it is. He booked a guided tour in the North of Thailand, visiting Bangkok first. Exciting times ahead.

Brianna's Special Day.

Brianna was making her first Holy Communion in May. I could hardly believe it. My Brianna was growing up so fast. Ken and I were delighted to be joining her on her very special day. We arrived at the chapel not far from where they live. As we entered the chapel, Ken spotted Sam, Jackie, Brianna and Lorcan right away. We made our way over to them to say hello. I couldn't get over how beautiful Brianna was in her white gown, flower crown, veil, bag and shoes. She was an absolute picture. Brianna showed me her Argento charm bracelet her dad had bought for her. I had bought her a first Holy Communion bracelet in a jeweller's in town which I put on her other arm. Lorcan was dressed beautifully as well.

I thought it would be a good idea if Ken and I took Lorcan outside with us. That way, Brianna, Sam and Jackie could all enjoy the ceremony without disruption. Lorcan finds it difficult to sit in peace for too long, much like any child. I suggested to Sam and Jackie that Ken and I take Lorcan out to the park. They agreed. Brianna was okay about us leaving. She was so wrapped up in her big day. I hugged and kissed her before leaving, telling her that I loved her and would see her back at her house. Sam told us that the service would probably last for an hour and that there was tea/lemonade and sandwiches laid on for the families afterwards in the chapel hall. He said they would meet us back at their house. I asked, "How will we get in?" He answered, "One of my chefs is there preparing food. Just let yourselves in".

Lorcan, Ken and I drove to a park in Lismore where Lorcan loves to play. He had an absolute whale of a time; that was until the rain came on. He always cries when he's taken away from what he loves doing. We put Lorcan into the car to take him back home and he soon settled down. When we arrived there we let ourselves in. I walked out into the kitchen to make me and Ken a cup of tea and coffee. I introduced myself to the chef and Ken said, "I'll try and not get in your way. I just need a cuppa". The young chef didn't introduce himself. He was up to his eyeballs making what looked like Thai curry and sandwiches, and had other pots on the stove. When I had made our tea and coffee Ken, Lorcan and I sat in the living room, waiting on the others returning. When they all arrived back at the house Brianna barely knew we were there, she was so full of joy and excitement. I asked her for a hug and kiss and then she was off out with her friends. Sam came into the living room and asked Ken if he would like a beer. I wasn't asked if I would like a drink. Jackie, Lorcan and Alannah all sat on one of the sofas while Ken and I sat on the other. There was no conversation going on between us and them. It was as if we were invisible.

Sam came in, set a tray of sandwiches down on the coffee table and said "I'm away out to the shops. See you later". That was it. To say that I felt extremely unwelcome is a complete understatement. I felt that they didn't want Ken and me there; they all made it blatantly obvious. Alannah- I don't think she even said hello, although to be honest, she very seldom did lift her head to to say hello when Ken and I came to visit. There was no offering of a plate or napkin for a sandwich or a cup of a place tea- nothing. I thought to myself "I'm not hanging around here where I'm made to feel like a spare part". They couldn't have made it more obvious that we weren't welcome. I said to Ken "Shall we go?" He nodded yes and that was the end of that.

Cathy told me when she rang me later that she, Betty, my nephew and others were invited to the evening party. She said that there was going to be all sorts of gorgeous grub there, including some of her favourites from Sam's restaurant. She couldn't wait to go.

That sickened me to my stomach. I felt like I had been stabbed in the heart. As I said to Ken, we wouldn't have gone anyway as we live too far away. But it would have been nice to have received an invitation.

That was really the beginning of me and my son's downfall regarding our relationship. I was noticing a change in his behaviour towards me. Not only from learning about his so-called father's behaviour, but also from when he and his business partner opened up their restaurant two years earlier. Particularly when his partner pulled out and he was running his business independently. His ego was growing as well as throwing all of himself into his work. His priorities changed completely. I was so far down his list of priorities. Whenever he introduced me to anyone in or outside his restaurant he did so by introducing me as his 'Ma'. He had never called me that before.

Three weeks after Brianna's big day Sam sent me a text. It began with "Hello there, how are you doing?" Sam using that kind of language incensed me. I thought, 'Whatever happened to 'hi mum'? I spoke to my psychologist about how I was treated at Sam's house on Brianna's special day. I also spoke to him about how he addresses me at the beginning of a text. That's when he can be bothered to send me a text.

My psychologist, Paddy, listened very intently to how my son's behaviour was affecting me and said, "Yes, it's quite impersonal". I replied, "It's how you would address a stranger in the street, 'hello there'! I went on to tell him my response when all three of my children treat me badly. He said that I am off the 'Drama triangle'. (Created by the psychotherapist Stephen Karpman.) Paddy went on to say that I don't regard myself as a victim but sadly, they do. The triangle is a model of dysfunctional social interaction. A person can either be a rescuer, persecutor or victim. I used to be a rescuer before I got into psychology. I also viewed myself as a victim in the early days before I entered into personal therapy.

On Robyn's 5th anniversary my son sent me a very abusive text. This was after he texted me a day or so before. I answered his first text saying that I didn't like the way he addressed me at the beginning of his texts. It felt very impersonal. Whatever happened to 'Hi mum'? I went on to say that I hoped he was keeping well. Love, mum. Or words to that effect. The language he used in the text on my sister's anniversary deeply upset me. He said I was being childish and that it was my own fault I had left Belfast and was lonely. He continued, "You had three ablebodied children so you were lucky. I don't know how I turned out as well as I did, having two parents like you and him".

I almost lost my breath. I felt as if I was taking a panic attack or a heart attack. My heart was broken into tiny pieces. How could he be so cruel, attacking me in this way, especially on a day like today? I just cried for hours. Cathy sent me a text saying "Thinking of you today". That helped a bit. I will never forget that day for as long as I live, although I have forgiven him. I felt as if he had taken a knife and pushed it right through my heart and soul. I was in shock that he could treat his mother in such a harsh and cruel manner. I was broken by his hateful words towards me. I just couldn't understand why he had completely turned his back on me.

Ken, Betty, Kyla and I were all invited to Brianna's eighth birthday party at Vertigo, an amusement centre in Belfast. Betty called to ours to get a lift to Brianna's birthday venue as she had no idea where the place was. When we arrived Brianna, her mum, dad, and all her friends were in a private room where the party was taking place. I walked up to Brianna who was sitting at the top table with her dad and wished her a happy birthday. I gave her a hug and kiss and her birthday present. Her father never made any attempt to acknowledge me nor I him. It was slightly awkward for me but thankfully, Brianna was too busy enjoying her day to notice. After a short while the poor darling began throwing up all over the floor. Her dad ran to her rescue to help his daughter. Before she sat back down I sat her down on my knee and cuddled her for a while.

I suggested to Ken that it might be a good idea to take Lorcan to a play area just outside the party room. Ken thought it was a good idea as it was better fun for Lorcan who loves playing on the big slides. It also meant that Ken and I were able to get away from an unpleasant atmosphere between me and my son.

Jackie came over a short time later to get Lorcan and off they all went, leaving us behind. The fall out between my son and me didn't spoil things for Brianna and that's all that mattered to me.

I had taken another chest infection in August and started taking a course of antibiotics. The first course didn't take it away so my doctor put me on a different antibiotic which didn't seem to shift it either. My chest had improved but I still didn't feel right. It took another couple of weeks before it finally went. I needed my chest to be completely clear before I could get the vaccine for my trip to Thailand and also the flu vaccine. I had to cancel both vaccines a couple of times. I began to feel anxious. I was beginning to think will this chest infection ever go away; it went on that long. Thankfully it did.

In early October I received a text from my son. I was stunned and at the same time so happy. He didn't apologise for his last text to me but his message was lovely all the same. I could hardly read it for tears rolling down my face. He said that Jackie had told him I wasn't well and as I was the only parent he had had in over twenty years (his words) he wished only the best for me. I sent a reply thanking him for the text and suggested we get together to talk about things face-to-face. I explained what his message meant to me and that I had never stopped loving him. We texted each other back and forth a few times and it made me the happiest woman alive.

I put an ad in the local grocery shop for a cleaner as I just wasn't able to do any housework because of the chronic pain and respiratory problems. I found it extremely difficult to admit that I could no longer do the things I once did with ease.

I began to feel unwell again and Ken took me to our local hospital. This was a few days after I had seen my doctor. She prescribed a course of Doxycycline for me to take but I just wasn't feeling good, even after a few days on my medication. When I arrived at the hospital I had my bloods taken and a chest x-ray which revealed that I had two bacterial infections going on at the one time. The doctor who examined me gave me another week's antibiotics to take and said it would take two to three weeks for it to clear. I felt so weak and breathless; it was a horrible feeling. It meant more rest, the thing I hate the most, but I was looking forward to my holiday in Thailand and I knew I had to take care of myself.

Late in October Cathy texted me to thank me for her birthday presents that I had given to Jackie a few weeks before to give to her. I was over the moon to hear from her, just like I was with Sam a few weeks before. I replied to her message saying I was glad she liked them and asked how she was keeping. She texted back saying she was doing really well and going to India for six weeks for yoga training and a spiritual retreat. I invited her for lunch and suggested we have a chat face-to-face just like I did her brother. She said maybe after her return from India. I wished her well and said I would keep in touch via What's App.

Halloween party just before Ken sets off for New Zealand

On the last Saturday in October I organised a party at our bungalow for Brianna, Lorcan and Kyla for Halloween. I had been doing this for years. It was an opportunity for us to have fun with our grandchildren, playing games, face painting and generally just making the most of our time spent together. I felt a tinge of sadness as Cathy had been down with us the year before with Kyla. Unfortunately, Kyla wasn't well that day and Cathy and I were still not on speaking terms.

I made sure Kyla would get her party bag. I asked Ken would he mind bringing it up for her and of course he said yes. Ken drove up to Betty's house after he dropped off Brianna and Lorcan at their house. Bless him. It involved a lot of driving that day for him but he didn't mind one bit.

In the early hours of Tuesday morning, November the 1st, Ken left for his long journey to see his family. His first flight was from Belfast to Manchester then from Manchester to Dubai and then on to New Zealand. I really didn't envy his journey. I wouldn't have been able to travel for all those hours at all. I was very happy for him and at the same time, welcomed the opportunity to have the place all to myself. Time for me.

I was perfectly fine on my own, enjoying my own company and doing what I wanted, when I wanted. I met Betty and Kyla in Belfast for a meal where her boyfriend works. Betty and Kyla called down to see me at the bungalow too. Sam, Jackie, Brianna and Lorcan called down as well. Then on another occasion, Sam and I went out for a beautiful meal at a lovely restaurant not far from where I live. I got out and about quite a bit. Trips to Belfast and elsewhere. That was until I took another chest infection. I was becoming really concerned as to whether or not I would be well enough for my much-anticipated trip to Thailand. I also needed to go back to using the nebulizer every day. On another visit to my GP she informed me that I have bronchiectasis as well as COPD and chronic asthma. I thought I just had asthma!

Ken kept in touch most days while he was away via What's App. Cathy and I also were in touch the same way. My main concern was getting better. All I kept telling myself was "Even if I have to crawl up the steps of the aircraft I will. I'm going to Thailand, no matter what!"

Ken returned home on Wednesday the 23rd of November at nine thirty in the evening. I couldn't get over how well he looked considering his incredibly long journey home. It was great to see him home safe and sound. He was also very happy to be home. We sat and talked for hours about his travels. The second weekend he was there he, his sister and nephew travelled to Australia to visit his brother. What a wonderful experience for him. I was so happy for him.

Thailand for my 60th Birthday

Wednesday the 30th of November had finally arrived. I was ecstatic and couldn't wait to leave for Thailand. Ken drove us both to the Belfast City Airport where we boarded a flight to London. We then boarded another flight from London to Dubai and from there to Thailand. Thankfully, my chest was okay on all three flights. I had a bag of medication with me just in case. I preferred the break-up of flights as I didn't fancy a long flight from London straight to Thailand.

By the time we reached Bangkok I was fit for nothing. I just wanted to get to our hotel and get to bed. The car journey from the airport to our hotel took over an hour. The hotel was beautiful. Once we were settled into our room I couldn't wait to get out to experience an authentic Thai curry. We met our tour guide, Tony, who was so friendly and warm. He showed us where to go for a meal not far from our hotel. He took us to a street restaurant where they cooked the food outside. The aroma of spices coming from the many kitchens that lined each side of the street was like nothing I'd ever experienced before. I couldn't wait to taste the food cooked by these amazing people.

My first taste of proper Thai food was simply delicious. Ken had never tried food like this before either. We were not disappointed. Such an amazing first night. The atmosphere was electric with men and women driving up and down the street on scooters while we sat eating our food. I loved it. The place was buzzing with people of all ages going about their business. All the eateries were packed with local people as well as tourists soaking up the Zen-like vibe.

We stayed in Bangkok for four nights. During the day we visited the principal landmarks such as the Wat Trimitr temple with its precious gold Buddha. Wat Po, home of the stunning reclining Buddha, the Grand Palace -Thailand's most sacred monument- and the spectacular Temple of the Emerald Buddha. We also took a boat to the floating market of Damnoen Saduak. Later on we went to visit the tallest Buddhist pagoda.

Day five, we travelled by bus to Kanchanaburi- River Kwai. We took a train ride across the famous bridge to Wang Po Station. Ken and I thoroughly enjoyed the hour's journey. It was absolutely fascinating. We went on from there to see the ruins of Ayutthaya, the ancient capital of Siam.

Altogether, we stayed in seven hotels visiting various temples, monasteries and the seated Buddha, driving through the rural countryside to Chiang Rai via Phayao. We also got to see the legendary 'Golden Triangle' where the borders of Thailand, Burma and Laos meet. My favourite by far was our visit to Wat Ron Khun (White Temple) in Chiang Rai. I have never seen anything so spectacularly amazing and beautiful in my life. It was magical, a place my granddaughter Brianna would absolutely fall in love with, just like I did. It was designed by Chalermchai Kositpipat, a famous Thai visual artist. A truly creative genius in my opinion. We flew to Phuket on the 13th, my 60th birthday. By that stage I was really looking forward to just chilling for the last week of our holiday. Although visiting all the above was exciting, educational, and the experience of a lifetime, it was hard going nonetheless. We were constantly on the move. Having the chance to stay in one place for a week and going to the beautiful beach each day was just the ticket.

Ken and I stayed at the Andaman Seaview hotel and I have to say the hotel staff just couldn't do enough for us. We were given a beautiful room with a dining area and small kitchen. It was spotlessly clean, which matters a great deal to me.

When we first arrived one of the front desk staff carried our suitcases to our room and when Ken offered him a tip, he politely refused. We were in our room about thirty minutes when there was a knock at the door. Ken opened it and there stood a chef with two other members of staff. The chef had a huge piece of cake on a plate with a lit candle on it. One of the female staff handed me a very unusual bouquet made from pink paper, green leaves and bamboo- very unique and beautiful. Such a special gift that I will never forget. I was totally overwhelmed by their thoughtfulness and the time they spent preparing this wonderful birthday gift for me. I can honestly say that no one had ever done anything like this for me before. Their humility touched me at a very deep level.

Ken and I went out the following day to the Andaman beach just across the street from us. It was lovely just to be able to walk along the beach and simply admire the scenery. We discovered another beach a few miles from our hotel called 'Kata' beach. It was even more spectacular. I was able to have a swim in its warm blue inviting water.

We were told about this beach by a couple who owned a small grocery store just down the street from our hotel. We had called in on the first night we arrived at our hotel. We gathered a few groceries in a basket and when got to the checkout we realised we hadn't enough money to pay for all the items. We asked if it was okay to leave a couple of the items back. The gentleman at the checkout said "No, it's okay. You can pay us tomorrow". Ken and I looked at each other, hardly believing our ears. We asked "Are you sure? What time do you open in the morning? We will call in first thing and pay what we owe". The owners of this little store never even asked us what hotel we were staying in. The gentleman said to us "I know you'll be here, it's okay".

Again, I've never had that happen to me before. Quite the opposite. I called into a shop just down the street from where I live one day and took a bottle of water from the fridge. When I got to the checkout and put my hand in my bag I realised I hadn't my purse with me. The man serving me asked where I lived. I replied, "Just down the street". He said "Oh right." Meaning put the water back, which I did. Okay, I was a stranger to him. Just goes to show you the difference between cultures.

Sadly, our time in Phuket was coming to an end. We left on December the 21st, four days before Christmas. I shall always remember the many beautiful Thai people we met during our stay there. I have never come across such humble, good-natured people. I hope one day to return.

Ken and I arrived back home safe and sound with one suitcase missing. It just happened to be the suitcase my nebulizer was in. We did get it back on Christmas Eve, thankfully.

I had invited all my children and grandchildren to our bungalow for a bite to eat and to give them all their Christmas presents on Christmas Eve. Sam, Jackie, Brianna and Lorcan arrived first (at the right time.) Cathy, Betty, Kyla and Betty's boyfriend came about 30 minutes later. It was one of the happiest Christmas Eves I've had in a long time. Having all my children and grandchildren (all except Alannah) there was just the best feeling in the world.

Betty had invited me and Ken to her new house for our Christmas dinner that year. Betty then informed me later that she was invited to her boyfriend's mum's for Christmas dinner. By this stage I half expected to be let down by either one of my children. That's not to say that I didn't feel hurt, but as I've said many times before, I let things go just so I could hold on to my family. It was a high price to pay, my own self respect and worth, but I believed they came first even though they thought the opposite was true.

My son rang me the night before Christmas Eve. He sounded angry. I asked him what was wrong. He said that Cathy had been texting him non stop about who was going to make me and Ken our Christmas dinner as Betty had let us down. He continued "I'm up to my eyes here and she's busting my head". I said, "I don't want anyone to feel that they're under any pressure to make me a Christmas dinner. I'm perfectly able to make my own". He seemed to calm down after that. I then said, "I'm looking forward to seeing you all tomorrow evening. I'll see you all then", and that was that.

This is what Cathy does when Christmas or Mother's Day is approaching. She prefers to pass the buck and it gets on Sam's and Betty's nerves. It doesn't exactly make me feel great either.

As Sam and Jackie were leaving Jackie turned to me and said "You put on such a lovely spread for us all this evening. Why don't you come for dinner tomorrow?" I replied "Thank you Jackie but Ken and I are just going to stay put". Sam then said "Listen, just come up for Christmas dinner". I said "Honestly son, we'll be okay here". Then Sam and Jackie said "Come up to ours", to which I replied "Thank you, we will. What time do you want us up for?" Sam said about 2.30. We said our goodbyes to them. After a little while the others left too. It did feel good having them visit us.

Ken and I had a lovely Christmas breakfast together and watched some TV before heading up to Sam's for our dinner. It was lovely to see the kids on Christmas Day excited and happy. Our meal was divine as always. Ken and I washed up. Sam lay on the sofa after dinner. As soon as we were done we left for home. Brilliant day had by all.

A few days after Christmas Day I began to fell unwell again. This meant yet another trip to see my doctor who prescribed more antibiotics for me. Despite my feeling unwell Ken and I decided to pay our dear friend a visit on New Year's Eve. I found the journey on the way down unpleasant because of the car fumes coming from the other vehicles passing by us. When I am unwell due to my chest I'm quite sensitive to fumes coming from traffic, tobacco, etc. But we made it and, as always, it was great to see our friend in such good spirits. His ex wife was there with him when we arrived. I like her a lot; lovely woman. When we arrived home a few hours later, I made us both some dinner. After that, Ken and I sent Happy New Year text messages to our families and friends. We enjoyed a few drinks together while watching Jools Holland's Annual Hootenanny. That's how we like to spend our New Year's Eve.

Appointment at the Pain Clinic

January the 16th, my appointment to attend the pain clinic after waiting nearly a year. The doctor prescribed Fentanyl patches for me to use and said to stop taking the Tramadol I had been using for about eight or nine months. My GP started me off on 50mg which were about as much use as taking Smarties sweets. She then increased the dosage from 50mg to 100, then 150 and finally 200mg. I had taken very little of the 200mg as I was afraid of becoming addicted to this drug. I only ever used the 200mg when I really couldn't bear the pain. They didn't take away the pain, they just made me feel drowsy.

After a few days on the Fentanyl patches I noticed my anxiety levels soar. I began at level five and shot right up to a hundred in a matter of minutes. This went on for a couple of days. I couldn't bear what was happening to me and Ken couldn't be around me. We were nearly headed for the divorce courts, it got that bad.

The problem was that I should have come off the Tramadol gradually. The doctor at the pain clinic didn't instruct me to do that. My GP didn't either. As it turned out, according to the doctor at the clinic, I was suffering from withdrawal symptoms from the Tramadol. He prescribed another medication for me to take in tablet form this time but it didn't agree with me either. Back to taking Cocodamol and thyme herbal tea that Cathy suggested I take. It seemed to work for a while and then the pain came back with a vengeance. Soon after all that palaver, I took another chest infection which of course meant yet more antibiotics.

In February this year I learned that one of my key contacts in Belfast where I had worked had passed away. I couldn't believe it when I was told about his death. He died in December last year at Christmas time. I felt so sad and utterly shocked at his passing. We got on so well together. I had a lot of respect for this wonderful man. I sent a sympathy card to the school and to his wife and family. I felt sad that I didn't find out earlier as I would have liked to have paid my respects to his family in person. But that was not to be.

Towards the end of February, Ken and I booked into Lough Eske Castle for two nights. It was our Christmas gift from Sam. I must say, it was an amazing experience. There was a spa voucher included with our gift. Ken gave me some more euros so I could have two treatments. Best facial and stone massage I've ever had- magnificent!

Yet another chest infection, this time in March. The second one this year. I was beginning to think something else was going on with me, something more sinister. But the real reason why I was so prone to infections is that I haven't been the same since taking the pneumonia in 2014. That was shortly after learning about the sociopath and what he had been accused of that year. I was coping mentally with all that had happened to me since 2011 but my body couldn't take it. Hence all the sickness. It stands to reason. I didn't end up in the bottle, graveyard or a mental institution, thank God. Learning about that man from my son broke me. I swore I would never let him break me but learning what I did that day did exactly that.

Also in March my daughter had a huge bust up with her boyfriend. Her head was all over the place and still is. They are back together now for who knows how long this time. I see history repeating itself and there's not a thing I can do about it. I tried to encourage her to go for therapy but it fell on deaf ears.

It got to the stage where she stopped telling me they had fallen out because it was only a matter of time before they were back together again. So dysfunctional. God help her and her beautiful wee daughter, my precious granddaughter.

The Cocodamol were absolutely useless so my GP decided to try me on other medication that the doctor at the pain clinic prescribed for me- Tapendol. Same thing, unbearable side effects so I had to quit taking them. I had another appointment with the pain clinic and this time I was prescribed Butec Trandsdermal patch. I began with 5mg, the smallest dose, and now I'm up to 10mg. Thankfully it seems to be agreeing with me. My GP also prescribed 20mg of Duloxetine which helps withmy fibromyalgia and neck pain. At last, after all these years, I'm finally able to move without too much pain. Thank you God.

Mothering Sunday

On Friday, a week before Mothering Sunday, Cathy rang me talking about Mother's Day. She was saying that there was a spiritual event on (The Red Tent, it was called) the following Saturday and that all her spiritual friends would be attending. She went on to say that it would be a great experience for me. I said okay, without really thinking about it. Then on Sunday morning she rang me again to say that she was paying for me to get a haircut before going onto the Red Tent event. She had booked an appointment for herself and said "I will book you in too".

I explained to her that I had got my hair trimmed just the week before and that I didn't need it cut but thanked her just the same. She then said, "Get it dyed then". I said that I wasn't getting my hair dyed any more as I was letting it go grey. I explained further, I needed it done every two and a half weeks and just can't be bothered any more. Cathy then said "Get it dyed grey then. Yeah, that's what you should do".

I had had a drink the night before and couldn't be annoyed trying to explain any more. She wasn't listening to what I was saying anyway. With Cathy it's always about what she thinks I should do or get. As long as it fits in with her plans then she'll be okay. She said that because I was suffering from Fibromyalgia, her friend who she believes to be the best Reiki master, Yoga teacher etc. could really help me. She also believes this young woman can tell you what went on in your past, what is going to happen in your future, and relay messages from our loved ones who have died.

I'm a sceptic when it comes to people who claim they have the power to speak with the dead. I doubt very much if any human being can see into the future. I'm a person who believes in 'Live and let live'. 'Each to their own'. It's just not for me, never was and never will be.

I said no at the start when Cathy said she would pay for me to see her friend. Cathy claimed that her friend had worked on hundreds of people including celebrities. I thought to myself, "If she's that good why hasn't she her own business, why does she need to work for a voluntary agency?"

When Cathy was in India with this friend she told Cathy after looking at my profile picture on Facebook "You would know to look at your mum that she had been abused". I was shocked and absolutely horrified at what she had said. She knows nothing about me apart from what Cathy had told her. I did say to Cathy at the time that I didn't like what she had said at all.

Cathy was like a dog with a bone who just won't let go. She kept going on about how wonderful a healer this young woman is, saying "Honestly mum, she'll make your pain go away". I gave in under the pressure and said "Okay, but I am only going to go if it's just a Reiki treatment. I don't want her asking me questions or talking about my siblings who are no longer here". Cathy seemed fine about it. As I began to brighten up later on in the day I reflected on our conversation. I decided to sleep on it and see how I felt the following day, Monday. I hardly slept on Sunday night. Obviously, our conversation was troubling me. When I got out of bed that Monday morning I reflected some more and decided, "This isn't sitting well with me at all". I truly believed that what Cathy had planned for me for Mothering Sunday (only it wasn't Sunday, it was Saturday) was all about what she wanted. Not what would be nice for me?

I know she probably believed she was trying to do what was good and nice for me. But as I say, on reflection, it seemed to be all about what Cathy wanted. In therapy I was learning to 'self-care'. That means doing what feels right for me. Stop pleasing others at my expense. Being assertive and standing up for myself. Stop being the care-giver like I had been since my early teens.

I decided to speak to her about it. I rang early as I knew she had work to go to. No answer, so I sent her a text which wasn't accusing, blaming, or hostile in any way. I thanked her for her ideas about what to do on Saturday. I continued that, on reflection, I decided I didn't want to go to the Red Tent event on Saturday as it wasn't really my thing. To get one's hair dyed grey is a long process and it can't be done in one visit. I was fine about going to have a treatment with her friend and suggested I book us into a restaurant down near where I live on Mothering Sunday as it was too late to book anywhere else.

She texted me back saying that was fine. She asked if Ken would call up to collect her for the meal on Sunday and bring her back home. I said that Ken would be only too willing to collect her, even though she has her own car. I never heard anything back from her that day, which is unusual. I sent her a text the following day and didn't get anything back. I knew deep down that she wasn't happy about my text message the day before.

I asked my younger daughter Betty if she would like to join us on Sunday. She said no a couple of times, saying she had been invited out for dinner by her cousin Kate and friends. She then changed her mind and said she would come. I suggested she and Kyla stay over at ours so she could enjoy herself on the day and she glady agreed.

Cathy got in touch a couple of days later to say that Sam was coming too with Brianna. Lorcan would be staying with Jackie. She wanted to spend the day with her mum who is quite ill, fearing she may not have the opportunity to next year. I booked a table for seven. Five adults and two children for two o'clock on Mothering Sunday. All was looking good. I then received another text message from Cathy saying that Lorcan would be joining us after all. I was delighted and rang the restaurant right away to book another seat for him. That meant eight were now going. I was so excited and happy to be spending the day with my husband and my entire family.

On Mothering Sunday, Betty called down after one with Kyla. I invited them out the back as it was a lovely sunny day. I had bought two flowering pots, one for Cathy and the other for Betty. Betty got first pick as she was there first. One of the flowerpots was shaped like a bumblebee and the other a frog. Betty choose the bumblebee.

We were just waiting on Sam, Cathy and the two youngsters arriving. I was getting myself ready when my mobile phone rang. I asked Betty to answer it for me and all I could hear was an angry voice at the other end of the phone cursing and swearing. Betty was so calm, just listening and not really saying very much. The conversation ended. I asked Betty what was going on. She said that Sam was on the phone going crazy over Cathy expecting him to call up to her house and bring her down here. I didn't pay much heed and continued getting ready. Betty's phone rang. It was Sam asking to speak with me. Betty handed me the phone and right away Sam began complaining bitterly about Cathy's refusal to get a taxi down to his house. I didn't blame him. Cathy could have easily ordered a taxi to Sam's house. What was stopping her? What I was annoyed about was the way he reacted to it. And why he felt the need to tell me. They are two adults. Why in God's name couldn't they sort it out between themselves without involving me? This was supposed to be my day, after all.

As I was speaking with Sam and trying to calm him down, asking him to just breathe, Cathy rang my phone, crying "Our Sam is a fu*#ing dick. He's not calling for me". At that point I said "I have to go; I'm on the phone to your brother". I went back to speaking to Sam and said, "Just leave it. Stay where you are, it's okay". He replied, "I'm already in the car with the kids and I'm late. I'll see you as soon as I get there".

I went on a complete downer after listening to all that shit. All I could think about was 'What is it about Mother's Day? Cathy messed it up last year too. I detest this bloody day with a passion'. I knew Cathy didn't want to come. She prefers to feel sorry for herself and get drunk with the encouragement of her so-called friends who continue to enable her to stay sick. Only she can't see it. She's so easily influenced by people.

Ken, Betty, Kyla and I drove on to the restaurant. Sam, Brianna and Lorcan were meeting us there whenever they arrived. We didn't want to be late for our two o'clock reservation. When we arrived at the restaurant we decided to wait until Sam and the kids got there before ordering our food. We just sat talking until they arrived. We weren't waiting that long.

In them all came. Sam sat down at our table after seating Lorcan, with Ken opposite me. Betty and Sam were next to each other on the same side as Ken and Brianna sat next to me. Sam handed me a card, still fuming over Cathy. We all ordered our food. I opted for soup first. Sam then handed me a gift bag which I opened and inside was a box with a silver necklace in it. I thanked him for the lovely gift. His phone rang- it was Jackie asking him did I get the necklace or the bracelet? He asked me the same question to which I replied, "It's a necklace". Again, I knew something was wrong. Sam said to Jackie "For fuck's sake can this day get any worse. I can't wait to get out of here and get home and drink my bottle of champagne".

We all realised I had been given the wrong present. It wasn't really that that I minded. It was the language my son was using and knowing that he really didn't want to spend the day with me. I felt that he came down because he felt obliged to. I just wanted to run out of there as quickly as I could. I got up and went to the toilet. It was to stop myself from crying in public and in front of my grandchildren. When I returned to my seat I noticed the present that I had opened had shifted from my side of the table and was now sitting beside Sam. I said to Ken that I needed to get out of there so I got up and left the restaurant, standing by his car and waiting for him to join me. When I realised that he wasn't going to, I went back into the restaurant and took my seat. Sam had moved over to my side of the table. I'm not sure why. Maybe he felt embarrassed and couldn't look me in the face. I honestly don't know. By this stage everyone was eating their food except me. I couldn't bear the thought of eating. I felt sick and a desperate need to get out of there. When Sam and the kids finished their meal they got up to leave. All Sam said to me as he left our table was "It's just a mix-up, nobody's fault". I didn't say anything back to him. He clearly didn't understand how I felt. I said goodbye to Brianna and Lorcan as they were leaving. Normally, Brianna would give me a kiss and hug but not today. It was a terrible day for everyone. I did feel for Brianna as she's at an age where she knows when something's wrong. The atmosphere was as thick as smoke- horrible.

When they left I asked Ken to take me home. The tears were streaming down my face in the car journey back home. Betty never said a word. We arrived at our bungalow and I walked into the living room and sat down. I couldn't stop crying. Kyla was looking at me, the poor child. I said to Betty "Would you take Kyla home as I don't like her seeing me like this". Betty took my right hand and kissed it and then left.

I don't think I've ever felt pain like it in my life. I've been through some pretty painful experiences in my life but what happened that day broke me. Betty and Kyla hadn't long left when I said to Ken that I needed a drink. It was about four o'clock in the afternoon. I had never done that before. I couldn't bear the heartache, the enormity and severity of my feelings. For the first time in my life I wanted to get so drunk that I wouldn't be able to feel anything. I just couldn't handle the reality of that awful black day.

I was still unable to eat anything, which isn't me. Normally, when I'm stressed or feeling hurt I tend to eat my feelings. Ken did persuade me much later on to eat. He was afraid I would end up really sick. I can't remember anything else that happened that day or night.

The next day I just wanted to die. None of my children had been in touch. I became so depressed. My anxiety levels were through the roof. Towards the end of the following week I asked Ken to text Jackie and Betty regarding seeing my grandchildren on Saturday. I thought if they are going to try and stop me from seeing my grandchildren I will declare war. I feared they would try and stop me, I really did.

Ken was a lot more optimistic than me. He felt that they wouldn't try and stop the grandchildren from coming to visit or stay with us. I said to him, "Surely they know what my grandchildren mean to me and vice versa". We didn't get to see Brianna or Lorcan until about three weeks later. I asked Ken "Can you please keep sending texts to Jackie and Betty. Keep sending them. If they don't want me to continue seeing my grandchildren, let them tell me". I had no intention of giving up. They mean the world to me and I know they love spending time with the two of us.

A week after that disastrous day I rang Sam. His phone went onto voicemail. I left a message that said "I know that Sunday was a terrible day for everyone. In future if we want to go out for a meal you and I will decide where and when we go". I ended the message by telling him that I love him. Nothing came back. My psychologist said when I told him that I left Sam a message "Maybe he didn't get your message". I replied, "I thought the same thing myself but he would have known that I rang".

The depression and anxiety grew steadily worse after that day, so much so that I decided this particular day that I would end it all. I was in so much emotional, physical, and mental anguish and thought, "I can't do this anymore". I wrote letters to Ken and my three children. I just felt I couldn't go on. The pain of losing all three of my children felt too much for me to bear. Seeing the grandchildren definitely helped but I was in a very dark place and could see no other way out.

This was the second time I had lost my children. The first time was when they were teenagers and Betty was just a toddler. Now they are all adults and continuing on from where their father left off. That's how I felt. Utterly hopeless. I had enough sleeping tablets and other strong painkillers to kill two people. I gathered up all the tablets I intended taking. The letters I had written were left on my chest of drawers beside my bed. While I was contemplating my suicide, I felt a strange sensation come over me. I felt as if the Holy Spirit spoke to me. I can't remember exactly what was said but I knew I no longer wanted to die.

That was the beginning of acceptance for me that day. I knew God was with me. I wasn't as alone as I thought. The very same day when I believed my life would end was completely turned around. I truly believe that God hasn't finished with me yet. I have always felt very blessed. I am convinced that God chose me out of the five siblings and I don't understand why. I didn't end up an alcoholic or drug addict and I always thanked God for that. I survived my childhood and abusive first marriage.

I found the strength to get through my sister's suicide with God's help. The worst for me at the time was discovering what kind of person I had been married to for fifteen years and the ongoing suffering that he caused me and my children years after my marriage breakup.

By far the worst thing to ever happen to me was losing my three children. The damage was done when they were toddlers. They had been conditioned so young by such a sadistic, manipulative man and they really didn't stand a chance. Me neither, really. I still have moments when I feel angry towards them. I think to myself, "I have three intelligent children, why do they not stop and think that their behaviour towards me, their mother, is wrong?" Then, when the anger in me dissolves and I am thinking rationally about this really sad situation, I know why they continue to behave this way. I have been in therapy for many years. When you don't have a happy stable childhood you either spend years in addiction and die young or go to therapy and try to figure it out. My three children haven't been to therapy since finding out about their father.

I have had to let go and let God when it comes to my children. That doesn't mean that I no longer hurt deep inside, but with God's help I'm taking it one day at a time. I pray for my children every day. I pray that they will change through going to therapy. I don't want them to regret how things turned out between them and me after I'm gone.

I will never stop loving them. I have had to learn to detach with love. Their so-called father will never take away the love I have in my heart for my children, ever. I know I had my part to play in their childhood but I can honestly say that when I knew better, I did better. I have apologised to Cathy for making differences between her and her siblings. I can put my hand on my heart and say with true conviction that I did the very best I could under extremely difficult circumstances for all three of my children. I would challenge anyone, anywhere, that given the same circumstances, would they have done any better?

I am happy to write that my relationship with my three children has improved, thank God. I can honestly state that I am happy with my life. My health still isn't great but I am able to get out and enjoy life. I have finished four oil paintings and I am absolutely loving my art class and tutor. To quote my psychologist, I am living my life as a 'hunter and gatherer'. Meaning, I'm not caught up in in the rat race. I am lucky enough to do the things that nurture my soul.

My reason for writing this book is to speak my truth. I kept my mouth shut for far too long. Its two fingers to all those who judged me in the past and those who still do. Also, I hope that it will help people who are struggling with the many difficult challenges that life can throw at us. My message to you is don't ever give up. That old saying is true. "Whatever doesn't kill us makes us stronger".

www.ingramcontent.com/pod-product-compliance
Lightning Source LLC
Chambersburg PA
CBHW051038250726

48656CB00001B/38